Labor-Management Cooperation
The American Experience

Irving H. Siegel   Edgar Weinberg

1982

The W. E. Upjohn Institute for Employment Research

Library of Congress Cataloging in Publication Data
Siegel, Irving Herbert.
  Labor-management cooperation.

  Bibliography: p.
  1.Industrial relations—United States.   I.   Weinberg, Edgar.
II.   W. E. Upjohn Institute for Employment Research.
III.   Title.
HD8072.5.S57   1982   331.89'0973   82 8487
ISBN 0-911558-99-3   AACR2
ISBN 0-911558-98-5 (pbk.)

THE INSTITUTE, a nonprofit research organization, was established on July 1, 1945. It is an activity of the W. E. Upjohn Unemployment Trustee Corporation, which was formed in 1932 to administer a fund set aside by the late Dr. W. E. Upjohn for the purpose of carrying on "research into the causes and effects of unemployment and measures for the alleviation of unemployment."

ii

iii

Foreword

The traditional adversarial relationship of labor and management in the United States has not precluded ventures in cooperation over the years. Recognition of the mutual interests of both groups in economic goals and objectives has produced a wide variety of efforts at cooperation beyond the normal bargaining-table interactions.

Siegel and Weinberg predict that, due to a number of factors in the economy and in the labor force, the American style of industrial relations will become increasingly hospitable to collaboration. Their examination of the varieties of labor-management cooperation should provide both substance and encouragement to the dialogue of business, labor, government, and civic leaders in exploring the potential contribution to the economic viability of enterprises, industries, communities, and the nation.

Facts and observations presented in this monograph are the sole responsibility of the authors. Their viewpoints do not necessarily represent positions of the W. E. Upjohn Institute for Employment Research.

E. Earl Wright
Director

August 1982

The Authors

Irving H. Siegel has long served as researcher, consultant, teacher, writer, and lecturer in economics, statistics, patent law, and the social implications of science and technology. He has been affiliated with such federal entities as the President's Council of Economic Advisers, the Bureau of Labor Statistics, the Department of Commerce, Retraining and Reemployment Administration, and Veterans Administration; with such nonprofit organizations as the American Chemical Society, the Twentieth Century Fund, and the National Bureau of Economic Research; and with the Johns Hopkins, George Washington, and New York Universities. While on the staff of the W. E. Upjohn Institute for Employment Research (1965-70), he helped to arrange the conference celebrating two decades of the Institute's public service and he also edited and contributed to two commemorative volumes, *Dimensions of Manpower Policy* and *Manpower Tomorrow: Prospects and Priorities.* More recently, he has authored two books published by the Institute: *Fuller Employment with Less Inflation* (1981) and *Company Productivity: Measurement for Improvement* (1980). Dr. Siegel is a fellow of the American Statistical Association, the New York Academy of Sciences, and the American Association for the Advancement of Science.

Edgar Weinberg, a consulting economist, worked for many years in the federal government in the fields of labor economics and industrial relations research. Before entering the civil service, he worked as an editorial assistant for the Amalgamated Clothing Workers of America under J.B.S.

Hardman. His government career has included work as an economist with the Social Security Board, the Veterans Administration, and the Bureau of Labor Statistics. Mr. Weinberg served as deputy assistant commissioner of the BLS Office of Productivity and Technology and was assistant director of the National Center for Productivity and Quality of Working Life where he had responsibility for the Center's program to encourage labor-management cooperation by assisting the formation of joint committees. His last government position was Economic Advisor in the Office of the Assistant Secretary for Policy, Evaluation and Research in the Labor Department. He received the Department of Labor's Meritorious Service Award for his research work on the social implications of automation. In 1978-79, Mr. Weinberg served as President of the Washington Chapter of the Industrial Relations Research Association. He was one of the prize winners of the National Economists Club's 10th Anniversary Essay Contest held in 1979.

Preface

Although labor-management cooperation in the United States is not a novel phenomenon, it has come to wide public attention only in the past decade of persistent economic adversity and increasing political conservatism. A great many joint committees and similar entities were formed in companies, government agencies, and industries—and some also at the community and national levels—to promote the mutual interests of employees and employers.

Such collaborative activity will continue to expand and flourish in the 1980s. Even while this book was being processed for publication, the frontiers of company-level cooperation were being pushed forward into new terrain in accords reached by the United Autoworkers with Ford (February 1982) and General Motors (March 1982). True, these accords were negotiated in a season of economic distress; but the experience of collaboration in bad times may establish and reinforce patterns of behavior that will continue as business conditions improve.

The motivation for this book was supplied not only by a recognition of the timeliness of the subject, but also by certain convictions developed by the authors during their long and varied professional careers. Early, they acquired a respect for the adversarial temper of industrial relations and the role of collective bargaining in a pluralistic and evolutionary society largely guided by law. They also soon recognized, however, that the natural competition and the occasional open hostilities of labor and management do not

vii

foreclose the earnest pursuit of cooperation for mutual benefit, and that the formation of joint committees and the like for special purposes need not be inimical to, and could actually bolster, the normal bargaining process. In addition, they came to the view that communities and the various layers of government are probably making insufficient use of committees as mechanisms for bringing the broader public interest to bear on labor-management decisionmaking.

The authors have had a common core of experience in the manpower field, but also differing degrees of concentration in the area of labor-management cooperation. Siegel's work has ranged widely, but has focued frequently on issues and problems involving or requiring collaboration of the two parties. For example, in the 1940s, he assisted in the stimulation and diffusion of low-cost technological improvements in defense plants; in the promotion of timely planning by communities for jobs and counseling services for returning veterans and displaced war workers; and in the reconciliation of reemployment rights of war veterans and the seniority rights of other workers. In the 1950s, he headed a task force that drafted legislation for upgrading distressed communities, and he began consultation in the design and implementation of programs for measuring and raising productivity, an activity that he continued under auspices of the Department of Commerce in the 1970s.

Weinberg has had more than three decades of continuous service in federal organizations concerned with industrial relations, the economic status of workers, the mitigation of individual hardship incident to the revision of technology and work methods, and the furtherance of labor-management cooperation for enhancing productivity and the quality of working life. Throughout the 1970s, his responsibilities kept him in personal contact with labor and management members of national, industry, community, company, and public agency committees; with officials of university centers set up for aid in the formation and conduct of committees in their geographic areas; and with researchers making studies under contract. These contacts and his duties relating to the development of national seminars and publications on productivity and worklife quality contributed to a wide familiarity with the literature and information sources pertinent to the present study.

The aim of this book is to convey to a broad audience an appreciation of the wide range of opportunities for labor-management cooperations, the attendant problems, and the derivable benefits. Cooperative arrangements are examined at different economic levels, and 65 cases are discussed.

The book has 10 chapters. The first sets up a conceptual framework for the review of American experience in cooperation and for some brief remarks on the outlook. Chapter 2 deals with national committees and commissions set up during and since World War I, with labor, business, and public representatives, to advise the president and the Congress on major policy issues. Chapter 3 relates to joint labor-management committees for five industries—steel, construction, retail food, railroads, and men's clothing. Chapter 4 describes six of the 28 communitywide labor-management committees that were functioning while this study was in progress. The next four chapters concern cooperation in the company. The first of these, Chapter 5, offers an historical perspective. Chapter 6 concentrates on joint programs that aim primarily at improvement of company performance—consultation arrangements, productivity committees, and quality circles. Chapter 7 covers programs oriented primarily toward employee welfare—health and safety, alcoholism, quality of working life, flexible schedules, job assistance, and employee ownership. Chapter 8 considers various incentive programs—Scanlon plans, profit sharing, stock ownership, and pensions.

Chapter 9 acknowledges that government—all levels—is an employer, in addition to serving its other well-known functions, with which labor and management in the private sector must reckon. This chapter examines labor-management cooperation in public agencies.

The tenth chapter looks to the future. It is followed by three appendices, the first of which should be of particular value to specialists in labor relations, students of public policy, and union and company officials. This appendix includes 28 documents relating to labor-management cooperation—excerpts from labor contracts, public laws, executive orders, policy statements, memoranda of agreement, and model provisions and bylaws. Among the highlights are details of the new UAW-Ford agreement and of other documents relating to General Motors, the Bell System, and the steel industry.

Appendices B and C will be helpful to readers who wish to examine more closely the current status of collaboration. Appendix B lists 14 joint committees that were awarded grants for fiscal year 1981 under the Labor-Management Cooperation Act of 1978. Appendix C provides names, addresses, and telephone numbers of 26 major nonprofit organizations offering assistance in the design of cooperative programs.

The authors are grateful to Dr. E. Earl Wright for his encouragement at all stages of the preparation of this book. They also appreciate the deep interest and helpfulness of William L. Batt, Jr., Quality of Work Advisor to the U.S. Department of Labor's Labor-Management Services Administration.

Irving H. Siegel
Edgar Weinberg

Bethesda, MD

Contents

1   Beyond Open Hostilities
    and Collective Bargaining   1

2   The National Scene: Government as
    Third Party   35

3   Industry-Level Collaboration   53

4   Communitywide Collaboration..............   75

5   Company-Level Arrangements:
    A Brief Perspective......................   99

6   Company-Level Arrangements: Consultation,
    Productivity, and Product Quality   119

7   Company-Level Arrangements: Worker
    Satisfaction, Well-Being, and Security   139

8   Company-Level Arrangements: Monetary
    and Quasi-Monetary Supplements   179

9   Public Sector Collaboration..................   201

10   Looking Ahead   227

Appendix A: Documentary Appendix   235

Appendix B: Awards by the Federal Mediation
and Conciliation Service under the
Labor-Management Cooperation Act of 1978,
Fiscal Year 1981.............................   311

Appendix C: Directory of Major Organizations
Assisting Labor-Management Cooperative
Programs   313

1
Beyond Open Hostilities and Collective Bargaining

Prologue

The experience reported in this book reflects favorably on the creativity, versatility, and flexibility of American industrial relations. The deep differences that underlie the traditional adversarial postures of labor and management have not precluded search for, and invention of, opportunities for cooperation to mutual advantage. The interest of both sides in accommodation has intensified in recent years of unrelenting national economic stress, and it promises to persist in a world setting of continuing ferment.

Preoccupation in this book with collaborative schemes should not be misconstrued, of course, as disparagement of other plausible avenues toward needed improvement in our nation's productivity and in the quality and salability of its products. Effective labor-management cooperation can only complement, rather than substitute for, appropriate private decisions concerning, say, the mix and design of products, techniques of production and distribution, the amount and character of physical capital used, wages, and prices. It can only complement, rather than substitute for, appropriate policies and actions regarding, say, the money supply and interest rates, the size and allocation of public expenditures, taxation, regulation, incentives for individual saving and business investment, and support for education and research. Government's manifold involvements, moreover, influence the disposition of labor and management to explore and pursue cooperative undertakings—in addition to affecting the national economic performance in other indicated ways.

Due attention must be paid to intercultural differences and to our own indigenous strengths when the applicability of foreign collaborative arrangements is appraised. At a distance, it is easy to overstate the successes achieved abroad, to misidentify the critical factors, and to misjudge their durability. In any case, literal transplantability is out of the question; and selective adaptation entails costs that have to seem justified by expected benefits.

To concede the obstacles to naturalization of foreign models is not to imply, on the other hand, that domestic imitation or diffusion is easy. A cooperative arrangement that works in one company, industry, or community is not routinely transferable to another. The situation is comparable to that experienced in the propagation of technology: "best practices" are identifiable more readily than they can be copied. Leadership, commitment at the top, acceptance below, good will, knowledge, skill, patience, and proper followup are as essential to domestic diffusion as they are to importation; and labor and management must expect benefits to exceed costs.

These remarks should be kept in mind throughout a reading of this book. They are offered in awareness that news accounts, popular literature, and even the writings of scholarly advocates often exaggerate prospects and mute the caveats. The important large truth that ought to be proclaimed is less exciting: *the adversary style of American industrial relations has permitted, rather than forestalled, ventures in cooperation, both home-grown and adapted, and it remains sufficiently plastic to adjust to new parameters.*[1] The contents of this book should provide encouragement, ideas, and guidance to business, labor, government, and civic leaders wishing to realize more fully the potential contribution of cooperation to the quality of the nation's output and worklife, its productivity, and its competitiveness in world trade.

Scope

As the chapter title suggests, this book is concerned with varieties of cooperation that complement or supplement the normal arrangements of labor and management for adversarial interaction in pursuit of predominantly economic objectives. It features American experience, concentrating, in turn, on each of the principal theaters in which significant cooperation has occurred or is expected to occur. It pays special attention to, but does not focus exclusively on, the workplace, the most obvious site of cooperation and the one that is typically emphasized in the literature. Furthermore, it acknowledges that government has become not only a major employer of labor but also a major presence with which labor and management must, or should, reckon.

More specifically, this book examines cooperative arrangements in five theaters:[2]

1. The national scene, where the federal government usually participates as a third, but indispensable, party—serving, for example, as a catalyst, goad, arbiter, sponsor, intermediary, standard-setter, monitor, guarantor, or cofinancier (chapter 2).

2. The industry level, where the perception of a national interest may again accord a key third-party role to the federal government (chapter 3).

3. The subnational—community, area, or regional—level, where state and local governments may have explicit roles and the federal hand may still be visible (chapter 4).

4. The private firm or plant, where labor and management have to take cognizance of parameters set by government policies but generally arrive at agreements without appeal to, or intrusion by, a third party (chapters 5-8).

5. The public agency or a component thereof, where the federal, state, or local government is itself the employer—i.e., "management" (chapter 9).

In addition to looking beyond the workplace and giving explicit and due recognition to the pervasive government presence, this book has a second distinctive feature: It includes a documentary appendix. This appendix, which should be of practical value as well as have scholarly interest, presents sample agreements between labor and management respecting cooperation and also exhibits pertinent provisions of various legislative proposals, laws, avuncular guides, and policy statements. Two other appendices offer additional information that should appeal to practitioners and students of industrial relations.

Although this book ranges widely, it cannot, and does not, purport to cover the whole eligible domain. The relevant unpublished information is much vaster than the accessible portion reviewed by the authors; and, unsurprisingly, the published information has its gaps and its favorites.[3] No attempt, furthermore, has been made to exploit the available literature exhaustively or to survey certain kinds of cooperation that some readers or other writers might deem pertinent or worthy of treatment in depth.

Among the possible additional subtopics of interest, one does receive some attention in a later chapter and also in this one but is not treated in depth: cooperation at the company level *in extremis,* which involves the sharing of economic burdens or losses to avoid shutdowns or severe reductions of the workforce and which may inspire subsequent cooperation of the kind that this book emphasizes.[4] No detailed consideration is given to employee representation plans, company unions, cooperative associations, or other configurations established (particularly before 1930) by employers eager to maintain an "open shop."[5] Also omitted from this book is the discussion of "sweetheart" bargains between labor and management and other deplored or possibly illegal forms of "racketeering." Only passing reference is made to the supply of technical and related consulting services by union leaders and their designees to management (as distinguished from the active participation of the rank and file of workers) in the interest of reducing unit costs and increasing price competitiveness.[6] Another matter left for other investigators is the engagement of labor and management in joint or parallel activities to protect or advance particular firms, industries, or communities through advertising, political lobbying, possibly illegal collusion against competitors, or litigation.[7] Finally, we do not treat informal, spontaneous collaboration that is so natural to very small enterprises in which workers and employers have frequent personal contact.

Some Definitions[8]

A few of the terms already used have multiple meanings or may, for other reasons, require commentary. Discussion of them extends our remarks on the scope of this book. It may be gratuitous to dwell on the different connotations of words like "labor," "management," "government," and "state," but it should help the reader to know that "cooperation" and "collaboration" are used interchangeably.

It is difficult, but also unnecessary, to draw a precise boundary between "normal arrangements" for adversarial interaction and the extra-normal modes of collaboration that are of primary interest to this book. In a country like ours, the field of industrial relations as a whole is still open, growing, and evolutionary. What may be considered extra-normal at one time or in one place could well appear normal later or elsewhere.

"Open hostilities," a term used in the chapter title, refers to the most dramatic, but fortunately not the most prevalent, of the interactions between labor and management. It includes strikes, strikebreaking, "job actions," "sit-ins," "sick-outs," mass picketing, boycotts, injunctions, lockouts, etc. Such hostilities have sometimes involved serious property damage, armed confrontations, and violent "massacres."[9]

A much more common mode of adversarial interaction is negotiation, best exemplified nowadays by "collective bargaining"—to which the chapter title also refers. Such bargaining has been politely described as "a process of reasoning and persuasion,"[10] and, even more loftily, as the foundation for a system of "industrial jurisprudence."[11] It does not, however, exclude threats of resort to open hostilities and is sometimes reinforced by demonstrations and token work stoppages. Yet, despite its histrionics, bluster, tensions, crises, and frustrations, the bargaining ritual eventuates, as a rule, in temporarily acceptable or tolerable contracts relating to base pay, escalator adjustments, overtime, fringe benefits, hours and conditions of work, criteria for promotion and layoff, pensions and supplementary unemployment benefits, retirement, rights and obligations of employees, and the prerogatives of management. As the Secretary-Treasurer of AFL-CIO remarked at a conference of 1980 on productivity and the quality of worklife, collective bargaining is, indeed, "difficult and untidy at times," but it has also "proven workable and fair on . . . major issues"; and it could, furthermore, serve as "the logical mechanism for increasing the involvement of workers" in cooperative endeavors.[12]

Negotiation also includes requested third-party intervention for arbitration or mediation to settle contract disputes. Collective bargaining agreements often make provision for such intervention—in addition to provision for the establishment and administration of in-house machinery to deal with worker complaints, grievances, and discipline problems. All such arrangements are interpretable as forms of cooperation, but they are also "normal" enough to be regarded as outside the scope of this book. Certain other contractual provisions for cooperation along specific lines do, however, qualify for attention here; they may either concern matters sufficiently different from the ordinary bargaining issues or represent the culmination of experimental ventures that began outside the bargaining process. Some such ventures start as initiatives of management; others originate with dual blessing of labor and management, sanctioned by letters or memoranda of understanding.

The degree of extra-normal cooperation sought by the two (or three) parties varies according to the problem and the circumstances. Cooperation may be limited to discussion or consultation on specific matters of mutual interest (e.g., productivity, product quality, or industrial peace); or it could also involve the adoption of agreeable procedures and action in accord therewith (as in the cases of safety, health, and alcoholism). At first, a need may be perceived for opening and maintaining two-way channels of communication to assure the effective implementation of contracts or arrangements already in force; but, having achieved functional rapport and looking to the future, labor and management may wish to make joint exploration of additional complex or technical issues (e.g., adjustment to technological change) in an atmosphere of calm without the pressure of tight deadlines. The aim of such an endeavor may be the formulation of a timely acceptable program; or it may also envisage installation and administration (as in the cases of pensions and Scanlon plans).

The disposition to collaborate and the choice of appropriate joint undertakings depend not only on the spectrum of visible mutual concerns but also on less evident considerations. These considerations may be "philosophical," strategic, economic, or political. Labor and management both have traditional reservations regarding a semblance of open courtship. They could also have sharply different evaluations of the costs and benefits of particular cooperative programs. They may, furthermore, be subject to unequal influence by such external factors as the business cycle, legislated standards and regulations, and earlier judicial rulings.

Among the vehicles of extra-normal collaboration are boards, commissions, councils, committees, and less formal study groups, work teams, and task forces. As has already been implied, *ad hoc* entities may first be set up experimentally; if they prove constructive and viable, they may acquire permanence and recognition as "normal." Where the nature of the cooperation does not require active rank-and-file participation, no explicit and identifiable joint structure may need to be set up.

Cooperation in the Adversarial Context

Familiar connotations of the adjective "adversarial" tend to obscure the place of cooperation in human affairs in general and in American industrial relations in particular. Since the opening sentence of a preceding section says that "this book is concerned with varieties of cooperation that complement or supplement the normal arrangements of labor and management for adversarial interaction in pursuit of predominantly economic objectives," some discussion of cooperation in an adversarial context is appropriate.

We start with a universal truism that, once stated, appears self-evident: Any protracted relationship among people is bound to exhibit elements of *conflict, competition,* and *cooperation.*[13] The mix of elements varies, of course, from case to case; and, for each case, the mix varies through time also. When we call behavior "adversarial," we really mean that conflict and competition are conspicuously present or even are dominant, rather than that cooperation is completely absent. Thus, whatever opinions labor and management may hold of each other, they agree more often than not to function as "factors of production"—to cooperate sufficiently for the generation of the output and income that both want. When they bargain or otherwise negotiate over income shares and other matters, they tacitly or explicitly agree to follow various rules prescribed by custom, law, or common sense for arrival at mutually (if only temporarily) tolerable results. Even during strikes and other open hostilities, aggression and violence usually are controlled, directed, or sublimated to avoid irreversible harm to the "production function"—to avoid either extreme damage to plant and equipment or the "annihilation" of either party.

Another truism requires statement here, even though it too may seem gratuitous once it has been expressed: The inevitability of some degree of cooperation in any human enterprise does not assure either a full constructive realization of the potential benefits of cooperation or a fair sharing of them. In the absence of complete mutual trust (the usual situation), even a genuine offer of extra-normal cooperation by a stronger adversary may be perceived by the weaker party as coercive, patronizing, or debilitating; and a similar gambit by a weaker adversary could in turn be perceived by the stronger one as a bid for change in the power balance. Again, in the absence of trust, the two parties may resign themselves to a life of barren circumstantial tangency instead of seeking more positive mutual fulfillment. This familiar dismal equilibrium itself inspires many observers to preach the remedy of cooperation.

Historians, political leaders, and elder statesmen of the business world and the labor movement often think of "progress" as a succession of social states dominated by single behavioral elements. Thus, they often see the arrow of human evolution or "civilization" pointing away from a "primitive" stage of conflict toward a more "advanced" stage of competition, and thence toward a "mature," and possibly "ideal," order of cooperation. In the realm of industrial relations, some such motion has actually occurred. The exigencies of two World Wars and the "laboristic"[14] legislation of the New Deal (especially the Norris-LaGuardia Act of 1932, the National Industrial Recovery Act of 1933, and the Wagner Act of 1935) helped to replace an era characterized by labor-management conflict by an era featuring competition. These developments helped to shrink and to bound the vast original domain of "management prerogatives" that had been as sacrosanct as the overlapping domain of property rights; to confer legitimacy and respectability on unionization; to establish collective bargaining as a national norm; and to diminish the violent potential of labor-management disputes.[15]

The "progress" toward competition, however, is hardly complete. The strike weapon, for example, does not yet hang on a wall to rust. It is used with discomfiting frequency by street cleaners, transport workers, teachers, police officers, firefighters, and other local public servants. It is still used occasionally in major industries, such as coal mining, that follow the rule of "no contract, no work"; and "wildcat" walkouts may occur almost anywhere. Especially remarkable was the illegal strike of air traffic controllers, a group of federal employees, as recently as August 1981. "Progress" toward competition, furthermore, has not meant economywide establishment of unionization on a firm foundation of collective bargaining. Witness, for example, the enactment of "right-to-work" laws in many states under the umbrella of Section 14b of the Taft-Hartley Act of 1947; the declining proportion of the workforce enrolled in unions; and the frequency with which government has acted as "first" party, rather than third, to promulgate work-related standards and guidelines.

The time appears right for a more determined exploration than ever of the benefits derivable from labor-management cooperation, even if the 1980 elections portend a contraction of the federal role as third party. Visions of entry into a new era of collaboration, however, should be discounted in view of the preceding paragraph; the potentials of our own era of competition have been only partly realized, and vestiges of the era of conflict have not been exorcised. While welcoming new opportunities for joint action to mutual advantage, labor and management have good reason to cling to the adversary system and to continue circling each other in wary competition. The authenticity of the agreements emerging from their future interaction depends on the preservation of their individualities, which have been shaped by function, history, and memory. Their identities should not now be casually shed; cooperation should not become a synonym of co-option, nor should it become a euphemism for ir-revocable transfer of economic decisionmaking power from the two parties to government in an unequal triple "partner-ship."

The remarks just made probably still represent the major-ity sentiment in business and labor ranks. Even if elder statesmen fail to mention reservations, limits, and cautions in their calls for attenuation of the adversarial spirit, the silent qualifications need to be kept in mind. After all, this spirit has served us well over the years—if the payoff is reckoned in terms of material well-being, leisure, the amenities and the "democracy" of the workplace,[16] and the vigor, diversity, and openness of our society. Under "capitalism" with a human face, American workers have been able to strive successfully for the "more" that Gompers envisaged; they did not have to organize into a permanent "class" party and resign themselves to grim collective strug-gle for problematic personal economic improvement under the banner of Marxism, socialism, or syndicalism.[17] Further-more, workers remain free to seek union representation where it does not exist (e.g., in various "sunbelt" areas and in new Japanese-owned plants); and they also are free to petition and vote for decertification of unions already established. Management, too, is active in its own behalf, legally discouraging unionization and filing complaints, as required, against secondary boycotts and unfair picketing.[18]

Cooperation in Industrial Relations Literature

Students of industrial relations have, of course, recognized the element of cooperation in both the statics and dynamics of the adversarial interaction of labor and management. In one well-regarded book, this interaction is called an "armed truce."[19] Another prominent author has called it "antagonistic cooperation," borrowing a phrase from W. G. Sumner, the pioneer American sociologist; and he spoke of the goal of "mutual survival," rather than victory by annihilation.[20] A leading economist and systems theorist has observed that labor and management are bound together in a workable, though untranquil, marriage of convenience and necessity:

> Industrial conflict is . . . a curiously ambivalent affair, closer to the domestic battle of the sexes than to the clash of armies. Consequently, it is not difficult to build on the positive-sum or cooperative aspects of the game and to develop institutions that express this aspect. This is perhaps why the union, which may have been originally devised to prosecute conflict in many instances becomes an instrument to resolve it in a way . . . that an army never does.[21]

The "positive sum" mentioned in the preceding quotation is a desideratum commended by many thoughtful commentators on industrial relations. In other terminological guises, it is esteemed in the classical writings of such fields as scientific management, industrial psychology, personnel administration, organization theory, and group dynamics.[22] A designer of quality of worklife committees, writing in 1980, was surely thinking of the the difference between a positive-sum game and a zero-sum game when he observed that labor and management must be taught the existence of cooperative modes of interaction having "win-win options" as alternatives to more familiar modes having "win-lose outcomes."[23] A major textbook of the 1960s concluded with the proposal that the two parties should progress from mere "conjunctive bargaining" to "cooperative bargaining," which is "at least a stage higher in the industrial relations evolutionary hierarchy." In the first of these two varieties of bargaining, excessive emphasis is said to be placed on "competition," with possibly adverse spillovers for the general public; the second seeks "fuller exploitation of the special contribution which each party can make to an improved performance," and without collusion at the expense of others.[24] Another book of the same decade contrasted "distributive" bargaining, which focuses on relative shares of the common output, with "integrative" bargaining, which features (as in the Scanlon plan, discussed in chapter 8) cooperative problem solving in the interest of enlarging the common output.[25]

Experience gained on the production front during World War I increased awareness of the potentials of cooperation in the workplace. In 1918, the year in which he was elevated to the Supreme Court, Brandeis lent his legal prestige to the proposition that the participation and "consent" of employees in the formulation of work rules and policies were more conducive to "efficiency" than was the usual management practice of dictation.[26] Elton Mayo was saying similar things at the same time.[27] Mary Parker Follett, an influential business philosopher and consultant of the 1920s—a period in which advanced management adroitly fought the inroads of unionism by more imaginatively addressing the wants of labor—noted that disputes could be settled by three means: domination, compromise, and "integration."She advocated cultivation of the third approach, which requires no fundamental concession by either party yet yields ponderable benefits to both.[28] A business professor seconded the motion, referring to this constructive win-win outcome as the "double plus."[29]

Seasoned labor leaders have also looked forward to peaceable times in which workers, management, and the public could realize the fruits of cooperation. In 1925, William Green, head of AFL, proposed that "the antagonistic and hostile attitude, so characteristic of the old order in industry, must be supplanted by a friendly relationship and a sense of obligation and responsibility." Indeed, through good faith on both sides, he ventured, "the common problems of industry can be solved, efficiency in service promoted, and economies in production introduced."[30] He was surely mindful of the contrast between labor's positive acceptance during World War I and the anti-union reaction of the aftermath. In 1940, when World War II had already engulfed Europe, Philip Murray, the head of CIO, envisaged that true acceptance of collective bargaining would lead to greater cooperation, with the union instrumental "in achieving efficient plant operation." Clinton Golden, an associate of Murray's in organizing the steelworkers, expressed a similar sentiment more strongly in a book published in 1942: "union-management cooperation tends to make management more efficient and unions more cost-conscious, thereby improving the competitive position of a business enterprise and increasing the earnings of both workers and owners."[31] In 1973, I. W. Abel, president of the United Steelworkers, recalled Murray's view of 1940 that labor and management could cooperate to meet threats to their common interests; he was writing in favor of the Experimental Negotiating Agreement (of which more will be said later), a "revolutionary new bargaining procedure" eliminating the possibility of a nationwide strike or lockout and providing for voluntary arbitration of unresolved issues. This new approach was motivated by recognition of the ravages of the 1959 strike and of the encouragement given to stockpiling and to imports by uncertainties as to the outcome of subsequent rounds of contract talks.[32]

In the 1979 address of the president-elect of the Industrial Relations Research Association (IRRA), the "adversary" and "voluntary" principles were hailed as the twin pillars of the "American Ideology." According to this assessment, the two principles have served well historically, the tension between them keeping the tension between labor and management generally within bounds. As a rule, the two parties have proved "practical" and "pragmatic," disposed to seek and accept compromise and incremental change. They have tacitly agreed to "institutionalization" of the "bargaining game," with increasing reliance on "professional" players for attainment of "some equitable combination" of wages and profits. Furthermore, they have probed opportunities for "more direct collaboration," for establishment of "more constructive, integrative, cooperative, problem-solving, and trusting relationships—to use the terms that have been variously applied to the 'higher' stage of industrial relations development."

But, according to the same IRRA observer, something has been happening along the way to "voluntarism"—the principle that requires private parties to try to adjust their opposing interests with "maximum freedom" from outside interference. He sees this principle "subjected to attrition by increased doses of state intervention" as the complementary adversary principle proves unable, or too slow, to meet certain new and important challenges. Among the egregious failures are: the peaceful and fair resolution of wage and other issues in the public sector, the acknowledgment and just disposition of the claims of women and minorities in company agreements, a proper recognition of the social concern to halt inflation, and the satisfaction of many non-monetary needs or wants of workers (such as improvement of worklife quality and of measures for occupational health and safety). Consequently, the IRRA observer sees private decisionmaking, particularly at the level of the firm, being outflanked; the state, as third party, is "moving in to regulate the results as well as the procedure of bargaining." He is discreetly silent on the encouragement of state incursion offered by the private parties themselves—not only through their neglect of changing labor market and socio-demographic realities but also through their active courtship of political power.

The Governmental Presence

The preceding section and the description of the five theaters at the outset attest to the pervasiveness of government's involvement in contemporary economic affairs. The scale and diversity of federal participation have increased enormously under a wide assortment of influences, especially in the past two generations or so—influences, incidentally, that will largely persist even if the 1980 elections are validly interpretable as a "mandate" to halt the proliferation and to reduce the variety and cost of federal programs. Some of the inspired cutbacks will have to be compensated, however tardily and reluctantly, by state and local (as well as new private) expenditures. Besides, some of the reductions will be replaced, or more than replaced by enlarged federal outlays for other purposes (e.g., defense). Accordingly, the share of all government jurisdictions in the gross national product will not decline significantly or at all. The economy, in short, will remain clearly "mixed," rather than become evidently private; and the long term trend toward governmental "monitoring" or regulation of the private sector's interactions is more likely to be redirected and to become more diffuse than to be arrested for long or clearly reversed.

The proliferating federal economic role has been shaped by many social, physical, technological, and psychological factors, and, of course, it has affected many of these in turn.

It represents a response, in part, to the altering size, composition, and geographic distribution of the population, labor force, and industry. It also reflects, in part, the transformation of popular values, attitudes, and life styles. Thus, with the rise of material welfare and leisure, "industry and frugality" have lost their old vitality as personal precepts; and other storied virtues, such as individualism and self-reliance, have likewise lost much of their pristine appeal. Furthermore, voluntary association for the advancement of group interests, so much admired by early foreign observers like de Tocqueville, has increasingly involved the unabashed quest of political favor and even of public financial assistance. But American society is still open, as the 1980 elections remind, so it remains responsive even to nostalgia in its continuing evolution.

Does the 1980 shift in the political spectrum foretoken a diminished federal presence in industrial relations? Probably not, despite some decentralization of power to the states and greater reliance on private decisionmaking. Not only will the traditional concerns that prompted the past growth and diversification of the federal economic role persist, but many new issues and problems will also demand federal address. For such reasons, government may be expected to remain a visible and potent third party in industrial affairs. Furthermore, it may be tempted during the first presidential quadrennium of the 1980s to act like a dominant first party—for example, prescribing new rules of behavior for the other two parties, reversing the relative influence of labor and management in public counsels, and relinquishing established responsibilities or relegating them to the states. Such alterations of the *status quo* could, for a while, encourage retreat from competition to conflict in industrial relations. On the other hand, they could also improve the willingness of labor and management to seek cooperative solutions to the common problems that they face at the company, community, and industry levels. The coexistence of cooperation and adversarial strivings, as we have said so often in preceding pages, is not at all paradoxical.

American and Foreign
Cooperative Styles[33]

At this juncture, we extend our opening remarks on international and intercultural differences affecting cooperative styles. We start with a few observations, some of them restating points already made, about the United States. Then we proceed to comment briefly on other nations with which we trade and compete for markets.

Five points regarding the United States deserve mention:

1. The basic adversarial premise of American labor-management relations historically has proved consistent with a preference for negotiation over open hostilities and, moreover, with a disposition to seek collaboration beyond the pale of prior contract.

2. The large federal presence has exerted a subtle pressure for labor-management cooperation, and this pressure can only increase with the devolution of various federal responsibilities to the states.

3. Cooperation is also favored by the relative informality of interpersonal communications in our country—between workers and their leaders, between workers and their supervisors, between ordinary citizens and government officials.

4. The same may be said about the comparative lack of class rigidity and class consciousness (and the corollary notion that room still exists for upward economic and social mobility).

5. The usual focus of American contract negotiation is the company or plant, even when bargaining is conducted on an industry level. (Thus, attention is given to local, shopfloor issues and to the workers' immediate concerns with pay, leisure, status, and aspects of the quality of working life. Matters left unresolved by contract are more likely to be ad-

dressed cooperatively than to be deferred to tripartite commissions or to national elections.)

Manners of speaking in Western Europe may have contributed to a mistaken view that workers there enjoy a
superior shop environment. In 1969, a Canadian professor
of industrial relations perceptively remarked that
"misleading labeling" tends to convey the impression that
"North American workers have less control over their daily
lives than do their European counterparts." Actually, "the
situation is just the reverse":

> Neither codetermination, nor works councils, nor
> anything else European industrial relations systems
> have thus far produced protects workers as much as
> a local union can in North America, given the more
> sophisticated nature of our collective agreements
> and our grievance and arbitration procedures.[34]

This appraisal still appears valid after a dozen years of
quickening interest on both sides of the Atlantic in measures
to "humanize" work or otherwise to improve the quality of
working life. Three later informed comments follow.

In a comparative survey of industrial relations made in the
late 1970s, American students saw labor and management in
the United States matter-of-factly testing schemes of
cooperation that were euphorically and grandly being identified in West Europe with "industrial democracy" and with
evolution from "economic man" to "social man." Indeed,
some of the European advances would not have been regarded in the United States as evidences of "democracy" at all,
or have been welcomed by workers there any more en-
thusiastically than by managers. The American observers
considered symptomatic the absence, at a major conference
on worklife quality held in the United States in May 1977, of
buzzwords familiar to the European scene: *codetermination,
works councils, self-management, worker influence, rights*

to consultation, financial participation, shopfloor democracy, and so forth. Instead, they heard "words coming from deep inside the American libertarian tradition,"[35] words like *cooperation, dignity, trust, experiment, shared, collective bargaining, involvement,* and *human.* In the European cases that they studied, they discerned little emphasis on worker decisionmaking and voluntary union-management collaboration; they missed the "pragmatic uniquely American sense of evolutionary trial and error growth without legal prescriptions therefor."[36]

A group of American labor and management representatives touring three West German factories in May 1981 found, unsurprisingly, that "the work humanization movement, now about 10 years old, is taking divergent approaches in different countries, depending largely on each nation's culture." In the United States, where "individualism" has long held sway, the emphasis is on rank and file involvement in shopfloor decisionmaking. In West Germany, where "humanization" is supported by government as well as private funds, an elected works council consults with management on productivity issues. At each of the visited plants,

> council members seemed offended when asked if they had an organized method of eliciting work-improvement ideas from ordinary employees, such as quality-of-worklife committees and quality circles so popular now in the U.S. and Japan. "We know what the workers want," they would reply.[37]

A principal official of the United Auto Workers (UAW), writing in 1974, underscored the American difference while conceding European priority in efforts to increase significantly the explicit participation of workers in management.[38] First, he observed that American unions have a daily and persistent responsibility for improvement of worklife quality, as any modern contract should make clear. Second, he stated that American unions would rather join with management in the design of satisfying jobs than stand by passively. Third, he claimed that greater participation of workers in decisionmaking is perceived in the United States as one of the elements of worklife quality. Such participation, he further opined, would, in keeping with the nonideological temper of American industrial relations, develop incrementally and focus on "managing the job" rather than "managing the enterprise."

Before turning to Japan, we note a curious proposal made in the European Economic Community in 1981 that is at great variance with the spirit of diversity that rules, even in the quest of greater cooperation, in the United States. This proposal contemplated compulsion of member countries to adopt a standard form of consultative council or board to serve as the vehicle of worker participation. It looked toward "harmonization" through a choice among four forms already used in Europe, including the German-style works council.[39]

The cultural heritage of Japan has decisively shaped her pattern of industrial cooperation. It has transmuted such "American" ideas as statistical quality control and matrix management as tellingly as it has absorbed and exploited the principles and processes of Western technology. It is a holistic tradition that sets high value on patience, education, industriousness, parsimony, loyalty, mutual obligation, peer approval, respect for age and authority (which tend to be highly correlated), conformity, and consensus. Workers prefer attachment to firms offering lifelong employment; do not mind membership in company unions; identify their own welfare with their employers'; reputedly put forth more effort than their counterparts in the United States or West Germany; often try to learn each other's jobs; accept pay that largely reflects company performance and their own age and seniority; and willingly master elementary statistics for better communication with supervisors and resident engineers on production problems. Management seems to be accessible and paternalistic, and department heads apparently avoid suboptimization in pursuit of company profitability. Particularly impressive to foreign observers is the close integration of productivity and cost objectives with the maintenance and improvement of quality, which is a paramount concern of all employees, all departments, and even of vendors and suppliers.

A few quotations from very recent (1980-81) writings add some detail to these general remarks on the significance of cultural factors in defining labor-management cooperation in Japan:

1. An article in an American business magazine states that the mass of learned studies of the Japanese style leaves "totally ignored" one vital element: "Japanese managers trust not only their workers but also their peers and superiors." This "all-encompassing trust leads to a simplified organizational structure that has helped many Japanese companies become low-cost producers."[40]

2. According to the founder and president of a Japanese company making tapes and electronic parts, "the Japanese way of thinking about the enterprise is based on Buddhism: dedicating oneself to pleasing other people in the company."[41]

3. A survey of Japanese industry made by a leading British weekly finds that "unions are still a cross between collective bargainers and personnel departments; 16 percent of company directors in Japan have once been union officials." In some of the large companies, unions are apparently retained "only as a formality."[42]

4. The manager of the Washington office of the Japan Productivity Center declared in an interview that the worker safety record of his country is far better than ours and that "absenteeism is almost unheard of." He noted that chief executive officers are "usually" 65-70 years old and that pro-

motion on the basis of seniority is still the rule: "If we don't do that, it will disrupt that teamwork concept." A foreman has at least 10 years of prior company experience and is also skilled in a broadly defined craft. Because he is allowed to be a member of the company union, he is a particularly useful two-way channel of communication between labor and management. Furthermore, he is encouraged by management to be close to his workers, ideally to serve as a "parent figure."[43]

5. Statistical quality control has become a national creed and the subject of a coveted annual prize and subsidiary awards. The prize is named for W. Edwards Deming, the American who lectured on the nature and use of the statistical technique in prostrate Japan after World War II. The award ceremonies are broadcast live on television. "Each year the competition grows in intensity as more and more companies volunteer to undergo the close scrutiny required." Winners of the prize and associated awards gain in "profits and prestige." For other companies, "the ceremony is a time for self-reckoning."[44]

6. An American expert on business in Asia notes that "in Japan quality control is a management technique. It is a method of mobilizing, organizing and motivating people, a way of treating them with respect."[45]

7. The managing director of a prominent Japanese firm speaks of the quality control circle as a means of restoring the "joy of production," the pride of craftsmanship, lost in scientific management. Members of the circles have the "pleasure" of hearing evaluations of company products directly from customers and also have the "excitement" of making presentations to their fellows.[46]

8. The director of productivity improvement of an American aircraft company that has adopted the quality circle points to 15 years of Japanese development of the concept before its attainment of worldwide attention. Our own culture, he surmises, may "not yet" provide a "fertile soil" for the concept, being disposed to seek "quick results" and

"panaceas." All quality circles in our country represent, in his view, "pilot projects," none having yet "achieved institutionalization."[47]

Collaboration for Economic Renewal

In the years ahead, American labor and management will have good reason to explore more seriously than ever the potential benefits of cooperation. Foreign competition will prove a more cogent goad than will the claims made for foreign models. But additional threatening circumstances will also compel labor and management to adjust bargaining aims, strategies, and postures with more evident regard to their common interests. Among these circumstances are: a stubborn, revivable inflation; sustained high interest rates and reduced federal expenditures, both of which are intended to check this inflation; a further revolution in energy costs; and a major retreat of the federal government from responsibilities assumed during the past half century. The combined effect of all these pressures is to menace the profitability and viability of many major manufacturing firms and industries, the credibility of unions and of common managerial practices, the stability of once flourishing communities and regions, and the future availability of jobs.

Cooperation will presumably be facilitated by a widespread and sober realism concerning the conditions of, and impediments to, success. Experience cited in later chapters should have taught labor and management that, despite the enthusiasms of many popular and scholarly writings, the path to significant and mutually beneficial collaboration is neither smooth nor unique, the journey is not costless or quick, and the desired end results are not assured or necessarily durable. Experience also underscores the importance of top-level involvement, sustained commitment by the two parties, professional guidance and special training of pertinent personnel, reorientation of attitudes of middle and lower-level management as well as of local union officials, and so forth. The great payoff within a firm, industry, or community can come only with an evolution from isolated and tentative "experiments" in cooperation to more comprehensive and institutionalized practice.

In addition to the voluminous evidence of contemporary experimentation, it is desirable to take note of earlier impressive collaborative responses to perceived industrial challenges. Outstanding in our nation's history was the formation (detailed in chapter 5) of some 5,000 plant committees to help meet the massive production demands of World War II. Similar responses on a much smaller scale have also been called forth in the aftermath of disastrous strikes in various industries—e.g., railroads, steel, and men's clothing.[48]

Indicative of the new inclination to collaborate is the creation of a prestigious Labor-Management Group in March 1981 without government participation. The coordinator of the Group is John T. Dunlop, a former Secretary of Labor who has long been a leader in the field of industrial relations. According to the Group's statement of purpose (see documentary appendix), "the national interest requires a new spirit of mutual trust and cooperation, even though management and organized labor are, and will remain, adversaries on many issues." Among its tasks will be the exploration of "a wide range of issues with particular emphasis on revitalizing the nation's economic base, rebuilding the private and public infrastructures on which our productive capacity as a nation depends, and stimulating safe and efficient means for meeting the nation's energy needs."[49]

Another indication of the ripeness of the time for widespread commitment to collaboration beyond the usual limits of collective bargaining is contained in the 1980 address of the president of IRRA, the same scholar whose 1979 observations have already been summarized. "A questioning mood," he stated in 1980, "is abroad in our land as we grope for explanations of our economic comedown in the world—if we have come down." Indeed, "in industrial relations we are questioning once again the adversarial principle and its institutions." It is evident that, in the public sector, especially at the local government level, the principle too often is applied with great inconvenience to the citizenry. In general, the institution of bargaining operates best in determining financial rewards and the distribution of economic power. But, "come new questions like inflation, quality of worklife, affirmative action, which involve problem-solving rather than distributive processes, and collective bargaining either rejects these sorts of issues or adapts only with great strain." Our time of adversity requires a rethinking of "ancient truths." The afflicted automobile and steel industries provide a "laboratory" for new "experiments" in the "art of collaboration and problem-solving"—experiments concerned with " 'co-determination,' employee ownership, quality of worklife, and quality control."[50]

An article of February 1981 in a major business magazine bears on the change in traditional attitudes already occurring in the beleaguered automobile industry. The UAW leader at Chrysler (where workers had agreed in 1979 to give up some of their negotiated gains in wages in behalf of employment maintenance and future profit sharing) is quoted as saying that his union would show "how to build cars cheaper, or to save on scrap" if such assistance would help keep a high-cost plant open. At Ford and GM, the article noted, management still balked at the suggestion of profit sharing, but "opposition to some forms of decisionmaking with the UAW may not be as adamant as in the past." According to a "management insider,"

> We can't afford to be too adversarial any more.
> The Japanese are taking care of that for us. A differential of $700 a car is pretty persuasive evidence
> for gaining the cooperation of the union.[51]

By the end of 1981, Japanese competition and sluggishness of the American automobile market obliged (1) several UAW locals to accede to cost-saving work-rule concessions and (2) the national union board to allow company-level discretion on the reopening of the contracts before expiration. Commenting on the work-rule concessions, the president of UAW noted that "adversity causes people to change their minds." Other remarks suggest that the new bargaining agenda will include profit sharing and worker representation on company boards of directors—as well as work-rule and wage concessions.[52]

The 1980 contract between steel producers and the United Steelworkers (USA) called for establishment of "labor-management participation teams" as a means for improving productivity and worklife quality. This venture will be discussed in chapter 6. Meanwhile, we note a report on training begun for teams set up at selected plants on a trial basis that states: "The biggest problem, as other industries have discovered in trying the participatory approach, is convincing first-line supervisors that they must change their management style and listen to the suggestions of workers instead of merely barking orders." There are skeptics, of course, in both USA and the companies, but a major movement has started with awareness that, at best, "it will take years for this shopfloor cooperation to spread throughout the industry."[53]

Are the automobile and steel industries unique in their readiness to reconsider the sociology of work? No. In many others, such as aircraft and machinery construction, communication equipment, and food, the enlistment of blue-collar interest in production methods, quality, and performance is on the union-management agenda.[54] "Evidence suggests," according to an article of March 1981, "that the untapped potential may be substantial." The finger is now "pointing to managerial failings as a major cause of the decline in competitiveness"; and one egregious alleged failing is that a "poor job" has been done "of enlisting employees on the side of increasing productivity." The same article cites a poll conducted for the U.S. Chamber of Commerce that indicates a surprising percentage of American workers thinking about ways to enhance company performance. It concludes that "good management" would encourage such thinking by treating employees as "collaborators."[55]

The Secretary-Treasurer of AFL-CIO concurs that workers constitute a "virtually untapped natural resource of ingenuity and enthusiasm." In an article published in 1980, he proposed that management can tap this resource by allowing significant scope for worker participation in decision-making. Within the adversarial framework of collective bargaining, he called for a "limited partnership"—for labor-management cooperation through committees, etc.—to quicken national productivity and raise worklife quality.[56]

We close this chapter with the pertinent authoritative testimony of the retiring chief executive officers of two of the nation's largest corporations. In an interview reported in February 1981, the retiring head of Du Pont attributed the Japanese productivity achievement to the close relationship between workers and management and tartly observed that his own company's efforts to maintain such a relationship since 1802 had often been deplored as "paternalistic."[57] The other retiree, from leadership of General Electric, told the same interviewer in March 1981 that "managerial malaise" is a principal factor in the decline of quality of American manufactures. He counseled a shift in company emphasis from short-run profit to longer term targets. He also saw a need for more direct involvement of workers in quality and productivity improvement: a turnaround is achievable, in his view, "only with tremendous cooperation between labor and management."[58]

NOTES

1. Our position, or at least our language, differs from that of, say, *Business Week,* May 11, 1981, p. 85, where the adversarial approach is declared outmoded and obsolete, a threat to "the competitiveness of many industries"; and where a "march away" is sensed "from the old, crude workplace ethos and the adversarial relationship it spawns." We prefer a different well-established view that the adversary principle is a fundamental feature of the American system of labor-management relations and that it is not incompatible with the quest by both parties of more cooperation to mutual advantage.

2. Shorter wide-ranging treatments of cooperation are available, of course, in many places. See, for example, T. A. Kochan, *Collective Bargaining and Industrial Relations* (Homewood, IL: Irwin, 1980), p. 417 ff., and two articles by Edgar Weinberg: "Labor-Management Cooperation: A Report on Recent Initiatives," *Monthly Labor Review,* April 1976, pp. 13-22, and "Survival Tactics," *Executive,* Fall 1980, pp. 17-21.

3. H. M. Douty, *Labor-Management Productivity Committees in American Industry* (Washington: National Commission on Productivity and Work Quality, May 1975), pp. 49-52 presents and evaluates some of the published statistics on company and plant committees.

4. Cooperation in retreat may well become an outstanding phenomenon of industrial relations in the 1980s as stringent monetary and fiscal policies aggravate the plight of financially troubled firms. See Kochan, *Collective Bargaining,* pp. 439-41, on wage concessions prompted by the near bankruptcies of New York City and Chrysler Corporation; and *Monthly Labor Review,* March 1981, p. 73, for followup adjustments required at Chrysler. The latter publication also tells (p. 74) of labor cost concessions worked out at Firestone by a Joint Labor-Management Survival Committee; and of an indefinite salary freeze for nonunion workers at International Harvester motivated by high interest rates and a contraction of demand for farm and construction equipment. Pan American World Airways, according to *Business Week,* June 15, 1981, p. 37, asked its workers on June 2 to accept an immediate wage freeze and to contribute 10 percent of any pay increase negotiated through the end of 1983. United Airlines has obtained important productivity concessions (especially the use of two pilots instead of three in the cockpits of Boeing 737s) in a new contract negotiated with pilots (*Business Week,* August 17, 1981, pp. 27-28). In return for a profit-sharing plan, Trans World Airlines has asked workers to accept an immediate pay freeze through the end of 1982 (*Washington Post,* July 28, 1981). In July 1981, Chrysler and the United Auto Workers agreed on a profit-sharing plan (beyond employee stock ownership) to help workers regain pay sacrificed in keeping the company alive (*Washington Post,* July 24, 1981). For additional examples and comment, see last section of this chapter; chapters 3, 4, 7, and 8; and Peter Henle, "Reverse Collective Bargaining: A Look at Some Union Concession Situations," *Industrial and Labor Relations Review,* April 1973, pp. 956-968.

5. See, for example, C. R. Daugherty, *Labor Problems in American Industry* (Boston: Houghton Mifflin, 1936), chapter 27; J. T. McKelvey, *AFL Attitudes toward Production: 1900-1932* (Ithaca: Cornell University Press, 1952), pp. 56-60; and Reinhard Bendix, *Work and Authority in Industry* (Berkeley: University of California Press, 1974), chapter 5.

6. This variety of cooperation is discussed by Slichter, Healy, and Livernash, *Impact of Collective Bargaining,* pp. 846-51.

7. Contemporary examples are numerous. In the needle trades, management as well as labor has promoted consciousness of the union label. According to the head of the Interna-

tional Ladies Garment Workers Union, furthermore, "some of the most notorious anti-union manufacturers regularly go to Capitol Hill with us" to petition for protection against the flood of imports (Philip Shabecoff, "Labor and Management Amity," *New York Times,* January 11, 1981). Similar joint petitions have emanated from the textile, automobile, and steel industries. In *Business Week,* April 13, 1981, pp. 45-46, it is reported that a "coalition of unions and corporations is pressing to rewrite the rules under which $7.3 billion worth of usually dutiable imports entered the U.S. free of tariffs last year"—rules established in accord with 1974 legislation intended to assist 140 less developed countries but now, ironically, deemed inimical to the interests of even "the $18 billion high-technology electronic components industry."

For some earlier instances of joint or parallel action, see S. H. Slichter, J. J. Healy, and E. R. Livernash, *The Impact of Collective Bargaining on Management* (Washington: Brookings Institution, 1960) p. 841; and N. W. Chamberlain and J. W. Kuhn, *Collective Bargaining* 2nd ed. (New York: McGraw-Hill, 1965), p. 430.

In 1980, a federal district court found price-fixing and *per se* violation of antitrust law in the 1976 agreement between the National Electrical Contractors Association (NECA) and the International Brotherhood of Electrical Workers. The decision left the two organizations vulnerable to claims for injunctive relief and triple damages (totaling about $100 million) by as many as 7,800 nonmembers of NECA.

8. Our comment on the adversarial approach in footnote 1 should be recalled here.

9. According to Philip Taft and Philip Ross, "American Labor Violence: Its Causes, Character, and Outcome," in *Violence in America: Historical and Comparative Perspectives,* Report to the National Commission on the Causes and Prevention of Violence, Washington, June 1969, Vol. I, pp. 221-301, "the United States has had the bloodiest and most violent labor history of any industrial nation in the world." They note some calming of labor-management relations, however, with the provision of a legislative basis for a national labor policy in the 1930s and subsequent years.

10. D. L. Cole, *The Quest for Industrial Peace* (New York: McGraw-Hill, 1963), pp. 95, 155.

11. S. H. Slichter, *Union Policies and Industrial Management* (Washington: Brookings Institution, 1941), p. 1.

12. T. R. Donahue, "The Human Factor in Productivity," *AFL-CIO American Federationist,* December 1980, p. 13.

13. An illuminating discussion is provided by Lewis Coser, *The Functions of Social Conflict* (New York: Free Press of Glencoe, 1964). Some readers may also find of interest a recent article by Robert Axelrod and W. D. Hamilton, "The Evolution of Cooperation," *Science,* March 27, 1981, pp. 1390-1396. It seeks to account for the development of "cooperation, such as altruism and restraint in competition" and thus to overcome a "difficulty" of Darwinism, which stresses "the struggle for life and the survival of the fittest."

14. This adjective is often attributed to S. H. Slichter.

15. See footnote 9.

16. "Industrial democracy" is a hardy term of the labor lexicon, endowed with different meanings in different contexts and countries and nowadays commonly identified in the United States with greater work autonomy, participation in management, and other aspects of worklife quality. See two articles by Milton Derber in *Labor History:* "The Idea of In-

dustrial Democracy in American: 1898-1915'' (Fall 1966) and ''The Idea of Industrial Democracy in America: 1915-1935'' (Winter 1967); McKelvey, *AFL Attitudes;* C. S. Golden and H. J. Ruttenberg, *The Dynamics of Industrial Democracy* (New York: Harper, 1942); P. D. Greenberg and E. M. Glaser, *Some Issues in Joint Union-Management Quality of Worklife Improvement Efforts* (Kalamazoo: W. E. Upjohn Institute for Employment Research, 1979); and Irving Bluestone, ''Emerging Trends in Collective Bargaining,'' in *Work in America: The Decade Ahead* (New York: Van Nostrand Reinhold, 1979), pp. 231-252.

17. The pragmatic and opportunistic cast of mainstream American unionism was developed only after efforts to organize along ''European'' lines. Gompers, it should be recalled, started as an ''immigrant radical,'' not with the notion of ''business unionism'' that has proved so successful in the American setting. See Daugherty, *Labor Problems,* p. 442.

18. See, for example, H. E. Meyer, ''The Decline of Strikes,'' *Fortune,* November 2, 1981, pp. 66-70; and two articles in *Business Week:* October 12, 1981, pp. 100, 102, and October 19, 1981, pp. 43-44.

19. F. H. Harbison and J. R. Coleman, *Goals and Strategy in Collective Bargaining* (New York: Harper, 1951), pp. 20-21.

20. E. W. Bakke, *Mutual Survival: The Goal of Union and Management,* 2nd ed. (Hampden, CN: Archon Books, 1966).

21. K. E. Boulding, *Conflict and Defense: A General Theory* (New York: Harper Torchbooks, 1963), p. 226.

22. Among the many authors whose names come to mind are: Argyris, Barnard, Bennis, Cooke, Drucker, Gantt, Herzberg, Leavitt, Lewin, Likert, Maslow, Mayo, McClelland, McGregor, Roethlisberger, Shepard, and Trist. (See Bendix, *Work and Authority,* pp. 274-281, for a discussion of F. W. Taylor's views; and pp. 308-319 for a comparison with Mayo's.)

23. D. L. Landen, ''Labor-Management Cooperation in Productivity Improvement,'' in *Dimensions of Productivity Research,* Vol. I (Houston: American Productivity Center, 1980), p. 434.

24. Chamberlain and Kuhn, *Collective Bargaining,* chapter 17.

25. R. E. Walton and R. B. McKersie, *A Behavioral Theory of Labor Negotiations* (New York: McGraw-Hill, 1965).

26. L. D. Brandeis, ''Efficiency and Consent,'' *Industrial Management,* February 1918, pp. 109-110.

27. Bendix, *Work and Authority,* pp. 316-317.

28. M. P. Follett, ''The Psychological Foundations: Constructive Conflict, in H. C. Metcalf, ed., *Scientific Foundations of Business Administration* (Baltimore: Williams and Wilkins, 1926), pp. 114-131.

29. Attributed to C. I. Gragg of Harvard Business School by A. T. Collier, ''Business Leadership and a Creative Society,'' *Harvard Business Review,* January/February 1953, pp. 29-38.

30. Quoted by Daugherty, *Labor Problems,* pp. 578-579.

31. M. L. Cooke and Philip Murray, *Organized Labor and Production* (New York: Harper, 1940), p. 188; and Golden and Ruttenberg, *Industrial Democracy,* p. 263.

32. See remarks by Abel in *Sloan Management Review,* Winter 1974, pp. 90-96.

33. This section has benefited from perusal of many documents in addition to the ones cited—especially B. C. Roberts, Hideaki Okamoto, and G. C. Lodge, *Collective Bargaining and Employee Participation in Western Europe, North America and Japan* (New York: Trilateral Commission, 1979).

34. John Crispo, "Discussion," in *Proceedings of the Twenty-Second Annual Winter Meeting, Industrial Relations Research Association,* December 29-30, 1969, p. 201. Remarks in a similar vein are made by Mitchell Fein in *Sloan Management Review,* Winter 1974, p. 74.

35. *Industrial Democracy in Europe: A 1977 Survey* (Washington: American Center for the Quality of Work Life, 1978), p. 26. This report starts with a useful 12-page glossary—"a rough guide through a multilingual wilderness."

36. *Ibid.,* p. 28.

37. *Business Week,* July 27, 1981, p. 90.

38. Irving Bluestone, "The Union and Improving the Quality of Worklife," *Atlanta Economic Review,* May/June 1974, pp. 32-37.

39. *Economist,* March 28, 1981, p. 37. (For an informed recent statement on "Codetermination in West Germany," see the article of this name by Richard Davy in *Journal of the Institute for Socioeconomic Studies,* Autumn 1980, pp. 18-28.)

40. C. H. Deutsch, "Trust: The New Ingredient in Management," *Business Week,* July 6, 1981, pp. 104-105.

41. "Buddha and the Art of Job Loyalty," *Economist,* August 8, 1981, p. 62.

42. *Ibid.,* July 18, 1981, pp. 20, 25.

43. Interview with Joji Arai, "Quality and Productivity," *Quality,* July 1981, pp. 14-19.

44. *Business Week,* July 20, 1981, p. 20.

45. C. S. Gray, "Quality Control in Japan—Less Inspection, Lower Cost," *Ibid.,* p. 31. (The same periodical, June 29, 1981, p. 30, says that, in American usage, "Quality circle" is just "another name for the participatory approach to solving production problems.")

46. Hajime Karatsu, "Quality Control as a Tool for Management," *Manufacturing Productivity Frontiers,* July 1981, pp. 1-6.

47. Robert Patchin, "Quality Circles, Northrop's Experience," *Manufacturing Productivity Frontiers,* November 1980, pp. 1-7.

48. See works of Cole and Douty, already cited; and Kurt Braun, *Union-Management Cooperation: Experience in the Clothing Industry,* (Washington: Brookings Institution, 1947).

49. Press release, "New Labor Management Group Formed," and accompanying "Statement of Purpose," issued by John Dunlop, coordinator, March 4, 1981. (According to *Business Week,* April 20, 1981, p. 131, Dunlop aims to build mutual trust by working out accords on easier issues like energy conservation and then take on "tougher issues, such as

tax policy, job-training programs, wage rates, and use of nonunion labor in government-financed synthetic fuels projects.")

50. Jack Barbash, "Values in Industrial Relations: The Case of the Adversary Principle," *Proceedings of the Thirty-Third Annual Meeting, Industrial Relations Research Association,* September 5-7, 1980, pp. 1-7.

51. John Hoerr, "Auto Workers Inch toward the Driver's Seat," *Business Week,* February 9, 1981, p. 30. (In February 1982, while this book was being processed, Ford and UAW reached an historic agreement providing for profit sharing as well as a wage freeze and moratorium on plant closings. In March, a comparable contract was negotiated for GM. See documentary appendix.)

52. See "Detroit Gets a Break from UAW," *Business Week,* November 30, 1981, pp. 94, 96; and articles in *Washington Post,* December 9, 1981, and *New York Times,* December 10, 1981.

53. *Ibid.,* June 29, 1981, pp. 132-136.

54. See two articles in *Fortune* by C. G. Burck: "What Happens When Workers Manage Themselves," July 27, 1981, pp. 62-69; and "What's in It for Unions," August 24, 1981, pp. 88-92.

55. William Bowen, "How to Regain Our Competitive Edge," *Fortune,* March 9, 1981, p. 84. An article by N. Q. Herrick and R. P. Quinn, "The Working Conditions Survey as a Source of Social Indicators," *Monthly Labor Review,* April 1971, cites (p. 23) an earlier study of worker motivation conducted by the Survey Research Center of the University of Michigan. This study already showed that a "considerable" orientation "toward productivity or achievement" existed and that the implied potential for cooperation "has gone largely untapped."

56. Donahue, "Human Factor," pp. 14-15.

57. Art Pine, "Du Pont's Irving S. Shapiro: Summing Up a Lifetime in Business," *Washington Post,* February 8, 1981.

58. Art Pine, "In Corporate Leadership, an Era Ends at GE Co.," *ibid.,* March 29, 1981. (The interviewee is Reginald H. Jones.)

2

The National Scene: Government as Third Party

This chapter deals with tripartite ventures initiated by the federal government with labor and management representation. These ventures have been concerned with vital national issues of peacetime as well as wartime. Their increasing number and expanding purview over the years attest less to their success[1] than to their necessity and utility as instruments of statecraft. With the continuing growth and changing needs and structure of the American economy in a world becoming increasingly interdependent, the federal hand has also become larger and more visible.

The first chapter has already said something about the growing federal presence, especially during the past half century or so. In 1929, the federal share in the gross national product, reckoned in 1972 dollars, was a bit over 2 percent; in 1980, the corresponding figure was a bit more than 7 percent. The portions of national product identified with state and local government were comparatively static, increasing during the same period from 10.7 percent to 12.3.

Other statistics are sometimes cited to dramatize the growth of central government. Thus, in current dollars, federal expenditures for "grants-in-aid to state and local governments" and for "transfer payments" to individuals have risen even more rapidly since 1929 than the outlay for "purchases of goods and services," which constitutes the federal component of the gross national product.

By the end of World War II, it already seemed appropriate to call our economy "mixed."[2] This designation is likely to remain suitable despite the lingering and revived rhetoric of "free enterprise" and the apparent revulsion of the public against "big government" in the 1980 elections. The addition of other adjectives to "mixed," like "monitored" or "mediated," will also remain appropriate if cognizance is taken of the objectives of continuing federal intervention in the nation's economic affairs.

Although primary attention in this chapter is directed toward entities set up under federal auspices and with federal representation, the government, in addition, strongly affects labor-management cooperation at the company level through laws and the agency programs that implement them. This federal engagement in "action at a distance" is illustrated in the first section of the documentary appendix—a section devoted to the national scene. Thus, some of the items presented there, emanating from the Congress and the executive branch, have aimed at encouraging and assisting the formation of joint, plantwide, labor-management committees.[3]

Joint Consultation in Wartime

At the outbreak of each World War, the president then in office moved quickly to enlist the cooperation of labor and business leaders in the mobilization of the nation's productive resources. On each occasion, the leaders pledged to avoid disruptive strikes and lockouts. Compliance was generally good, impressively so in the light of the high degree of decentralization of bargaining, the great variation in local conditions, and the prior histories of labor-management conflict.

In February 1918, President Wilson convened 10 union and management representatives in a bid to ease evident strains in industrial relations. Labor leaders agreed to refrain from strikes and major organizing drives, while business leaders agreed to operate under collective bargaining and to suspend anti-union campaigns.[4] In April 1918, as a followup, a tripartite National War Labor Board was established for the settlement of labor disputes.

Even the year before, in 1917, other important steps were being taken to strengthen the homefront. Thus, labor representatives were appointed to key coordinating bodies—the War Industries Board, the Food Administration, the Energy Conservation Board, and various Army, Navy, and shipbuilding entities concerned with the "adjustment" of wages, work standards, and grievances. Inclusion of union officials in these endeavors helped the labor movement to acquire a much needed aura of legitimacy.[5]

Ten days after Pearl Harbor, President Roosevelt, who had had experience in wartime industrial relations as Wilson's Assistant Secretary of the Navy, convened 26 union, business, and public leaders to assure needed cooperation in production. The conferees quickly consented to ban strikes and lockouts for the duration of World War II. They also consented to establishment of a tripartite National War Labor Board for expeditious resolution of disputes over wages, working conditions, and union security. Again, labor leaders were included on equal terms with businessmen in entities dedicated to achievement of a supreme national purpose.

When each World War ended, the willingness to cooperate that had been engendered by a sense of extreme common danger vanished. Presidential efforts to keep alive the transient spirit of unity proved vain. In September 1919, Wilson called a conference on postwar labor-management accord, but no agreement was forthcoming on such major issues as the 8-hour day, child labor, and worker rights to organize and bargain collectively. In 1945, Truman's National Labor-Management Conference similarly failed to achieve consensus on key matters—the scope of management prerogatives, acceptance of collective bargaining, and avoidance of strikes. During the two World Wars, union membership grew; and the implied shifts in the balance of power between labor and management needed testing and clarification in the field before Washington table talk could become productive.

Cooperation during the New Deal[6]

The first two years of the first Roosevelt Administration witnessed remarkable changes in industrial relations and in the magnitude and diversity of federal involvement in economic affairs. The Great Depression inspired numerous schemes for reviving employment, production, and purchasing power. A frequent assumption underlying these proposals was that the economy was "mature" and faced with chronic "stagnation." Unprecedented labor-management cooperation under federal aegis seemed to spell the only possible solution. Some businessmen favored a triple "partnership" modeled on the War Industries Board. Some favored instead the planning of production and the adjustment of prices through stronger trade associations. Labor leaders, especially in such depressed industries as coal and clothing, opted for a 30-hour week and for tripartite stabilization of output and employment. Sentiment built up for even more fundamental changes in the character of our republic—for central planning with industry councils of employers, investors, and workers empowered to make market allocations. Voices were many, and often shrill and confused; and, as the sense of crisis deepened with plant shutdowns, price and wage cuts, and growing unemployment, the pressures for governmental action became irresistible.

Perhaps, the single piece of legislation that is most often identified with the New Deal is the National Industrial Recovery Act of 1933, which looked to a system of "self-government in industry under government supervision." According to Title I, the intent of the Congress was to promote "the organization of industry for the purpose of cooperation among trade groups." An outstanding feature of the Act was the requirement that a National Recovery Administration (NRA) establish industry codes of fair competition. These codes set minimum wages and maximum hours, proscribed child labor, and sought to eliminate certain unfair trade practices and destructive price-cutting. Employers who upheld labor standards were to be protected from loss of business to competitors who undercut wages.

A most controversial aspect of the codes was their accord of new status to labor. To counterbalance the right conferred on business to organize trade associations for price-fixing and market allocation, Section 7(a) of the Act set forth a Magna Carta for labor, encouraging, in particular, the formation of independent (i.e., noncompany) unions:

> Every code of fair competition, agreement, and license approved, prescribed, or issued under this title shall contain the following conditions:
>
> (1) that employees shall have the right to organize and bargain collectively through representatives of their own choosing, and shall be free from the interference, restraint, or coercion of employers of labor, or their agents, in the designation of such representatives or in self-organization or in other concerted activities for the purpose of collective bargaining or other mutual aid or protection;
>
> (2) that no employee and no one seeking employment shall be required as a condition of employment to join any company union or to refrain from

joining, organizing, or assisting a labor organization of his own choosing; and

(3) that employers shall comply with the maximum hours of labor, minimum rates of pay, and other conditions of employment, approved or prescribed by the President.

Within six months, the NRA succeeded in writing codes for almost all industries, major and minor. Its symbol, the Blue Eagle with a cog in its talons, was ubiquitously displayed. Advisory boards were established by the president to assure an opportunity for business, labor, and consumer interests to contribute to policymaking and have a stake in the results.

After an initial outburst of enthusiasm and with the first signs of recovery, the NRA came under heavy criticism. A review board found, for example, that the NRA code authorities for many industries were actually dominated by large corporations, to the presumed disadvantage of small business, labor, and the general public. But, even before indicated reforms could be instituted, the Supreme Court declared the whole program unconstitutional in a decision of May 27, 1935.

Apart from the fleeting sense of "national solidarity" that it conferred on a people in despair, the National Industrial Recovery Act left a deep imprint on future labor-management relations. The support that it provided for labor to organize and bargain collectively was carried into the Wagner National Labor Relations Act of 1935. Business strongly challenged this provision, which has, however, survived court tests. The concept became more firmly established after World War II, but it is still not universally accepted (especially in the public sector).

From Eisenhower to Johnson

Fear of a return to the dismal 1930s after the war prompted a federal resolve in the Employment Act of 1946 to aim for "maximum employment, production, and purchasing power." Every president has since had to contend with the problem of maintaining reasonable price stability, a problem that has many sources, especially the tendency of hourly wages to outrun hourly productivity in a regime of high employment expectations. Decentralized bargaining, on an industry or company level, cannot take account of the macroeconomic interest in keeping unit labor cost in general from exerting an upward pressure on prices in general.

During the Eisenhower Administration, labor and management were exhorted to show restraint in bargaining; the imposition of an incomes policy was as unthinkable as the sterner remedy of mandatory wage and price controls. In contrast, President Truman, as his many new admirers may never have known or have forgotten, taunted the Congress with his "do-nothing" epithet because it failed to enact a 10-point program to contain the post-decontrol upsurge of wages and prices. The *Economic Reports of the President* issued in the Eisenhower years talked of "shared responsibility" between the government and private decision-makers for economic growth and improvement, not federal leadership. Despite the shock of a mild post-Korea inflation that is enviable according to today's standards, the *Reports* were satisfied to lecture on wage-price-productivity connections and to exhort private parties to behave responsibly. The unfortunate and lengthy steel strike of 1959, which first opened our markets to sizable imports from Japan, prompted the final (1961) *Report* to warn labor and management that failure to reach voluntary agreements recognizing a public interest could only lead to "new Government controls and new limitations on their initiative." The 1960 State of the Union address declared an intention "to encourage regular discussions between management and labor outside the bargaining table,'' but the idea was not carried out in the remaining months of Eisenhower's tenure.

The Eisenhower interlude of public relaxation after two decades of depression, large war, small war, and cold war was followed by President Kennedy's call to get the economy "moving again.'' A month after his inauguration, he set up a 21 member Advisory Committee on Labor-Management Policy with equal representation of unions, business, and the public. Two of the seven public members of this high-level forum were actually Cabinet officers, the Secretaries of Labor and Commerce, who alternately served 1-year terms of chairmanship. Underlying the president's action was the view, expressed in his address at Yale University, that the central domestic challenges of our time

> relate not to basic clashes of philosophy or ideology but to ways and means of reaching common goals . . . . What we need is not labels or cliches but more discussions of the sophisticated and technical issues involved in keeping a great economic machinery moving ahead.[7]

Executive Order 10918, which established the Committee, outlined a broad agenda: collective bargaining, industrial peace, wage-price policy, productivity increase, and the advance of living scales. Two topics were marked for special study: the international competitiveness of American products and the positive and negative implications of automation and other technological change. The Committee was often consulted by, and held meetings with, the president.

The Committee's first report, *The Benefits and Problems Incident to Automation and Other Technological Advances,* impressively opposed the media-enhanced apocalyptic views prevalent at the time. It considered the advances to be essential, but not to be made without due regard to human values; and it expressed confidence that a proper balance could be achieved by a combination of public and private actions consonant with the principles of our free society. From the specific recommendations, it is evident that business members recognized a need to cooperate with unions in easing the negative impact of technological change on workers and that union leaders were ready to give up the remedy of a shorter workweek.

Two years later, at the request of President Johnson, the Committee again addressed the real and alleged challenges of automation. This time, it sponsored three regional seminars in cooperation with universities. The meetings afforded opportunities for exchange of information and views on measures recommended in the initial report and on the adjustment of companies and unions to technological change.

The Committee's second report, *Free and Responsible Collective Bargaining and Industrial Peace,* affirmed "that free collective bargaining should constitute the primary procedure by which the essential terms and conditions of employment should be determined." It also insisted, however, that such bargaining should be responsive to the public interest. It suggested specific improvements in Taft-Hartley procedures for dealing with national emergency disputes—an increase in the president's authority and a strengthening of the role of the Emergency Disputes Board in mediation, fact-finding, and recommendation of terms of settlement.

Although the Committee was able to agree on such matters as taxation, public expenditures, and Vietnam financing, it failed to achieve accord on wage-price policy.[8] Perhaps, this failure to accept and attempt to rehabilitate the guidepost program instituted in 1962 evidenced a strong conviction that the traditional adversary principle still had a vital role to play in wage determination.

On the whole, the record of the Committee is considered to have been creditable,[9] about as good as might be expected in a democratic and pluralistic society. George W. Taylor, a distinguished mediator, saw in the Committee (of which he was a public member) an important means by which "representatives of the interdependent interests involved might, through understanding, gradually increase the area of common agreement." Furthermore, "the myriad of micro bargainers in our society" needed the considered judgments of "senior peers at the national level."[10] In its final report, the Cabinet Committee on Price Stability offered an optimistic appraisal of its progress to the president (December 20, 1968):

> The Advisory Committee on Labor-Management Policy has made a good start in launching the dialogue necessary to develop rules of the game that business and labor might be willing to accept jointly in order to promote the vital objectives of prosperity and price stability that we all endorse.

With the change in administration in 1969, the Committee was discontinued.

From Nixon to Carter

Economic troubles of the first half of the 1970s—recession, inflation, the energy crisis, slowdown of productivity growth, etc.—prompted new interest in tripartite problem solving. Three entities formed in the Nixon-Ford era stand out: the National Commission on Productivity (established in 1970), the Pay Board (1972), and the President's Labor-Management Advisory Committee (1974).

The Productivity Commission was created by the president with 24 members drawn from labor, management, academia, and government. According to the Secretary of Labor, the Committee's first chairman, the purpose of the new forum was to generate ideas about appropriate economic policy and ways to quicken productivity, and provide a basis "for better wage and labor-utilization policies."[11] In August 1971, when Phase I inaugurated an unexpected mandatory program of wage and price stabilization, the Commission's membership was expanded to give visible representation to farmers, consumers, and state and local government. Section 4 of the Economic Stabilization Act of 1971 provided a statutory basis for the Commission. Echoing language in the declaration of policy of the Employment Act of 1946, the new law stated the Commission's objective to be the enlistment of "the cooperation of labor and management, and state and local government in a manner calculated to foster and promote increased productivity through free, competitive enterprise." Under this broadened charter, the Commission engaged in informational, educational, and research programs as well as made policy recommendations to the president.

Over the next six years, the Commission went through additional metamorphoses, including name changes, as public uneasiness over accelerating inflation and lagging productivity mounted.[12] In June 1974, the Commission was transformed by P.L. 93-311 into the National Commission on Productivity and Work Quality. For the first time, the Congress cited improvement in "the morale and quality of work of the American worker" as a concern of policy. The new law specifically authorized the Commission "to encourage and assist in the organization and work of labor-management committees, which may also include public members, on a plant, community, regional and industry basis." Vice President Rockefeller was appointed chairman.

When the Commission's term expired in November 1975, P.L. 94-136 provided a replacement called the National Center for Productivity and Quality of Working Life. The Center was to be governed by a board of 27 members representing labor, business, and (federal, state, and local) government. The board members were to be appointed by the president with the advice and consent of the Senate.

The main purpose of the Center was to encourage, under joint labor and business guidance, concerted public and private efforts to improve productive efficiency compatibly with other national goals. "Quality of Working Life," a phrase added to the title of the law following much discussion, was defined to concern "conditions of work relating to the role of the worker in the productive process." It was recognized as relevant, no less than the quality of technology and management, to productivity performance.

Like its predecessors, the Center was required to "encourage, support, and initiate efforts in the public or private sector specifically designed to improve cooperation between labor and management in the achievement of continued productivity growth." Its responsibilities also included policy development, sponsorship of research and demonstration projects, and dissemination of information about "best" practices. Two new concerns were a review of government regulation and the coordination of productivity-enhancing activities of other federal agencies.

During the Carter Administration, the Center was apparently marked early as a candidate for extinction in fulfillment of a pledge to reduce the number of government agencies. While continuation of the Center's authorization after September 1978 was being pondered, the chairmanship was left vacant, and the members of the board were not reappointed. The staff, however, continued to carry out its duties, adding to its sizable legacy of widely used reports.

In May 1978, the Carter Administration decided to allow the Center to expire on September 30, 1978. Nominally, the Center's functions were transferred—for interment, it would appear, rather than performance—to various government agencies. A paper organization, the National Productivity Council, was supposed to coordinate the dispersed functions of the defunct Center. This Council rarely met, and its nonaccomplishment has been duly noted in publications and Congressional testimony of the General Accounting Office.

When the nation embarked on a program of mandatory controls in 1971, the thorny perennial problem of harmonizing micro decisionmaking with respect to wages and the macroeconomic desideratum of reasonable price stability had to be squarely faced. Immediately after the imposition of a 90-day price and wage freeze in August 1971, a tripartite Pay Board was set up to function in tandem with a Cost of Living Council. Its job was to promulgate standards for wage increase and to decide cases. The Board included 15 members representing labor, business, and the public. Several members of the National Commission on Productivity were included in this group. The appointment of a judge with no experience in collective bargaining was an unfortunate one. Labor's participation hardly lasted beyond the vote on the Board's basic rules of operation. Indeed, the labor members withdrew a month after the Board's formation, charging inequity and injustice in its earliest decisions.[13]

The advent in January 1973 of Phase III of the mandatory stabilization program occasioned the formation of the Cost of Living Council. The widely respected John Dunlop was installed as director. Ten business and labor leaders, 9 of whom served on the National Commission on Productivity, were appointed as a Labor-Management Advisory Committee. The purpose was to advise the Cost of Living Council on the consistency of particular wage settlements with national stabilization objectives. The Committee met often between January 1973 and May 1974, concentrating on collective bargaining in such inflation-prone industries as food, health, energy, and construction. For these industries, it helped set up labor-management committees to assist the Cost of Living Council.

In the spring of 1974, the mandatory stabilization program came to an end. The Administration refrained from asking the Congress to renew authorization of controls. The Labor-Management Advisory Committee concurred in this decision.

A new Labor-Management Committee reminiscent of President Kennedy's was appointed by President Ford after

the business-labor-academic "summit conference" on inflation at the end of 1974. Dr. Dunlop again served as Committee head. In 1975, a year of recession, the Committee met
frequently and agreed on proposals for job creation, tax
cuts, incentives for electric utility and multifamily building
construction, and collective bargaining reform in the retail
food, health care, maritime, and construction industries.

In 1976, the Committee took a dramatic step, severing its
connection with the White House when Dunlop resigned as
Secretary of Labor. His resignation was prompted by the
president's veto of previously agreed upon legislation to
reform collective bargaining in construction. The Committee
continued to function unofficially as a labor-management
group, with members exchanging views on many pertinent
issues. It refrained from offering a wage-price stabilization
plan to the Carter Administration, asserting instead its opposition to voluntary guidelines and mandatory controls.

In mid-1978, the Committee's post-official life ended
when the president of the United Auto Workers and other
labor members withdrew. The climate for labor-
management cooperation had deteriorated as union and
business leaders took strongly opposing positions on pending
legislation concerning industrial relations.

Three Carter gambits deserve mention although they proved unavailing as a result of the Democratic defeat in the national elections of 1980. One of these was the formation of
Synthetic Fuels Corporation to encourage production of
domestic alternatives to imported petroleum with price supports and billions of dollars of federal grants and loan
guarantees. Prominent labor and business figures were to
serve as part-time directors of the Corporation. The second
aborted Carter initiative envisaged the provision of financial
assistance for the revival of lagging industrial regions
through a high-level Economic Revitalization Board. The
Board was to include prominent labor, management, and
public representatives.

The last Carter venture was actually the first of the three in point of time. On September 28, 1979, the Administration and leaders of AFL-CIO reached a bilateral "National Accord," which provided for "continued involvement and cooperation" of organized labor in formulating and implementing "voluntary programs of pay and price restraint" and a "disciplined fiscal policy." An immediate result of this Accord (which itself was made possible by the passage of the Humphrey-Hawkins Full Employment and Balanced Growth Act of 1978, a law that drastically rewrote the Employment Act of 1946) was the creation of a tripartite Pay Advisory Committee.[14] This Committee had 18 members representing labor, management, and the public. Unremarkably perhaps, Dunlop again was in charge.

The Pay Advisory Committee's responsibility was to review and revise the basic standards for allowable pay increases established in 1978 by the Council on Wage and Price Stability (COWPS) as part of the Carter program of voluntary action for pay deceleration (initiated in October 1978). The Carter program was devised and launched without labor and business participation and hence encountered skepticism and reluctant compliance from the start. Although it assisted COWPS, the Committee made clear its position that both voluntary and mandatory wage controls impede bargaining and distort pay patterns. It recommended return to free bargaining as soon as possible.

New Initiatives

Even during the young Reagan Administration, we find the indefatigable Dr. Dunlop trying to bring labor and management together, this time without the blessing of government from the start. As noted in the preceding chapter, he announced formation of a new Labor-Management Group in March 1981. Although he expected the two private parties to remain "adversaries on many issues," he also recognized that "the national interest requires a new spirit of mutual trust and cooperation."

Late in 1981, the Administration launched its own joint national productivity committee under the leadership of a former Secretary of the Treasury. Top-level labor leaders declined to participate, largely because of dissatisfaction with Administration social and tax policies and the treatment of striking federal air traffic controllers. The new National Productivity Advisory Committee included 4 minor union figures in its unusually large membership (33); it also included 21 business leaders, 5 academics, and 2 government officials. The Committee's charge was to "conduct a continuing review and assessment of national productivity" and advise the president and other high officials on the federal "role in achieving higher levels of national productivity and economic growth" and on "the potential impact on national productivity of . . . laws and regulations." No funds were provided for the Committee's work, and December 31, 1982 was provisionally set as the termination date.[15]

The skewed composition of the new productivity committee does not encourage high hopes for practical accomplishment. Like the National Accord, the committee's concept suggests an attempt to erect a "social contract" on too narrow a base. By the omission of management, any national arrangement between labor and government diminishes its chances of stabilizing wages and controlling inflation. Similarly, by giving labor only token representation (or by failing to elicit stronger labor participation) and by using government mostly as an ear, a national productivity committee limits its chances of arriving at potent, implementable recommendations for improvement of economic performance. In short, much room remains in our kind of society for wholehearted tripartite cooperation in the address of issues of major national concern.[16]

NOTES

1. Note, for example, the second half of the title of an article that has been used extensively in the preparation of this chapter: W. T. Moye, "Presidential Labor-Management Committees: Productive Failures," *Industrial and Labor Relations Review,* October 1980. All human institutions, of course, are describable as "productive failures," being much less than perfect but often effective enough to help a nation or a group to get satisfactorily from there and then to here and now. One such human invention, the much admired Constitution of the United States, simply aimed in 1787, according to the Preamble, to form a "more perfect union," not a perfect one.

2. Still useful for its discussion of the background and emergence of the present American economy is G. A. Steiner, *Government's Role in Economic Life* (New York: McGraw-Hill, 1953).

3. The first section of the appendix also illustrates that private organizations, as well as government, seek to encourage labor-management cooperation in the firm for particular purposes.

4. Jack Stieber, "The President's Committee on Labor-Management Policy," *Industrial Relations,* February 1966, p. 2. On signing the Adamson Act (1916), which established the 8-hour day sought by the Railroad Brotherhoods, President Wilson made a statement amounting to "an official declaration of the acceptance of trade unionism as an integral part of the American commonwealth." See H. A. Millis and Royal Montgomery, *Organized Labor* (New York: McGraw-Hill, 1945), p. 131.

5. J. T. McKelvey, *AFL Attitudes toward Production: 1900-1932* (Ithaca: Cornell University Press, 1952), pp. 29-35. On later national experience in wartime wage stabilization (including the Korean Conflict) with tripartite pay boards, see D. Q. Mills, *Government, Labor and Inflation* (Chicago: University of Chicago Press, 1975).

6. See, for example, A. M. Schlesinger, Jr., *The Coming of the New Deal* (Boston: Houghton Mifflin, 1959), p. 93; and W. E. Leuchtenburg, *Franklin Roosevelt and the New Deal, 1933-1940* (New York: Harper and Row, 1963). Although unions were intended to have equal representation with business on boards formulating industry codes, few had sufficient economic strength and technical expertise to play a decisive role in NRA. See Murray Edelman, "New Deal Sensitivities to Labor Interests," in Milton Derber and Edwin Young, eds., *Labor in the New Deal* (Madison: University of Wisconsin Press, 1961), pp. 166-169.

7. A. M. Schlesinger, Jr., *A Thousand Days* (Boston: Houghton Mifflin, 1965), p. 646.

8. Stieber, "President's Committee," p. 13.

9. *Ibid.,* p. 17.

10. See W. J. Gershenfeld's paper on "The Elusiveness of Finality" in E. B. Shils *et al.,* eds., *Industrial Peacemaker: George W. Taylor's Contribution to Collective Bargaining* (Philadelphia: University of Pennsylvania Press, 1979), p. 222.

11. G. P. Shultz and Kenneth Dam, *Economic Policy beyond the Headlines* (Stanford: Stanford Alumni Association, 1977), p. 156.

12. The work of the Commission and its successors is chronicled in its annual reports. See documentary appendix for legislative mandate and policy statement.

13. See Moye's article, cited in footnote 1.

14. For two different views of the National Accord, see the 1980 *Economic Report of the President,* pp. 81-82, 101; and R. J. Flanigan, "The National Accord as a Social Document," *Industrial and Labor Relations Review,* October 1980, pp. 35-50. (The latter gives the text of the Accord.) The documentary appendix contains pertinent excerpts from the Humphrey-Hawkins Act and the Joint Economic Committee's report.

15. The Executive Order establishing the National Productivity Advisory Committee is included in our documentary appendix.

16. Flanigan's discussion of the failure of the National Accord (see article cited in footnote 14) recalls some of the points made in chapter 1 regarding international differences in industrial relations and, in particular, the importance of collective bargaining in the United States. These points are pertinent to any serious effort to stimulate productivity advance.

3
Industry-Level
Collaboration

This chapter deals with mechanisms established at the industry level for labor-management cooperation on matters of mutual concern. It focuses on five major industries that have had extensive experience along such lines: construction, retail food, men's clothing, railroads, and steel. Additional cooperative committees have recently been formed—in the coal, health, and trucking industries. As the first chapter has noted, the federal government is often involved to some extent in the organization or operation of industrywide mechanisms; a notable instance, considered later, is the Steel Tripartite Committee, which has been urged as a model for the automobile industry. As might be expected, the format of cooperation and the dominant concerns vary from industry to industry; and, where geographic differences in conditions and issues are great, as in construction, vehicles for industrywide cooperation may be set up on a regional or metropolitan basis as well as a national basis.

Construction Industry

The size of the construction industry (it has over 4 million workers), its complexity, the diversity of its products, its functional fragmentation, and its geographic dispersion have impeded effective labor-management cooperation therein.

The same factors also underlie better publicized problems of the industry, such as instability of employment, a propensity of costs to outrun estimates, lagging productivity (according to statistics that are, however, admittedly inadequate), and slow or uneven absorption of improvements in technology and materials. Returning to the barriers to cooperation, we should be mindful particularly of the necessity to assemble labor, equipment, management, materials, and energy at different sites in a timely manner and to shift or disperse these inputs upon project completion; the multiplicity of contractors and subcontractors typically required for a project; and the variety of participating crafts, each of which may be represented by a different union.

Despite these negative factors, mechanisms for labor-management cooperation have been established—joint councils, commissions, committees, etc.—to deal with a wide range of topics, including apprenticeship, industrial peace, stabilization, productivity and seasonality. Some have been organized on a branch or trade basis; others involve all branches. In some instances, the federal government has participated in tripartite arrangements.

Apprenticeship and Training

Apprenticeship for skilled trades, which include about half the construction workforce, has long been administered by local joint committees (JACs), composed of an equal number of union representatives (usually rank-and-file members or business agents) and management (usually executives from a local contractor's association or individual employers).[1] Local JACs establish specific standards for their apprenticeship programs, following guidelines suggested by the national JAC in the trade. They also select apprentices from qualified applicants and direct the programs. Labor-management cooperation is encouraged by the U.S. Department of Labor's Bureau of Apprenticeship and Training, which sets minimum standards and registers approved programs.

Joint labor-management programs to upgrade the skills of journeymen have also been organized in some sectors of the industry. The International Training Fund of the plumbing and pipefitting industry, one of the most extensive plans, was established in 1956 by the United Association of Plumbers and Pipefitters and the National Constructors' Association to enrich the competence of the workforce and to assist adjustment to changing technology.

In 1981, the Bricklayers Union and the Mason Contractors Association expanded their longstanding joint programs to improve training and to engage in broader cooperative efforts for enhancement of the masonry industry's competitiveness. A new cooperative entity, known as the International Masonry Institute, was set up for technical research and market development, as well as for training. These functions of the Institute are funded by collectively bargained contributions called for in Bricklayer agreements. The Institute also conducts a labor-management relations program.

Industrial Peace

Although construction is generally described as a "strike-prone" industry, some branches of it have developed voluntary, cooperative means for peaceful settlement of disputes. In this regard, the Council on Industrial Relations for the Electrical Contracting Industry (CIR) has been especially successful.[2] Established in 1921, the Council serves as a national joint tribunal of the National Electrical Contractors Association and the International Brotherhood of Electrical Workers. The Council has rendered final and binding decisions in over 4,000 disputes concerning contract terms or grievances.

CIR meets quarterly and operates with panels of six members appointed by the union president and by the association president. A representative from each side serves as co-chairman. No neutrals have ever been used. Disputes are referred to the Council after local labor-management committees have failed to resolve them. Its decisions are by unanimous vote, and they are final and binding on both parties. With rare exceptions, Council decisions have been observed by the local parties. Virtually no strikes or lockouts have occurred in over 60 years, despite tremendous changes in the industry and the economy.

In addition to industrial peace, CIR contributes to stability by taking into account, in its joint decisionmaking, broad criteria related to the industry's economic health as well as the local interests of the parties. In the long run, of course, the success of this combination of arbitration and negotiation depends on the trust that local parties have in their national representatives.

The CIR system has influenced national leaders in several other branches of the construction industry to develop similar voluntary mechanisms for dispute settlement. The Industrial Relations Council of the Plumbing and Pipefitting Industry and the National Joint Adjustment Board for the Sheet Metal Industry are promising examples.

Tripartite Stabilization

As construction costs began to rise sharply in the 1960s and early 1970s, the government became increasingly concerned lest its programs for housing, defense, and economic stabilization be endangered. Several tripartite bodies were established to deal cooperatively with problems of dispute settlement, wage adjustment, skill shortages, regulations, productivity, and other matters of mutual interest.

The President's Missile Sites Labor Commission, which operated from 1961 to 1967, sought the orderly settlement of disputes over terms of collective bargaining agreements at sites around the country. This group, including union, business, and government representatives, also helped to secure labor-management agreement in eliminating uneconomic work practices.[3] Government funding of the projects was certainly a factor in the Commission's effectiveness.

The Construction Industry Collective Bargaining Commission (CICBC), established by Executive Order in September 1969, functioned until 1976.[4] This tripartite body undertook studies of ways to expand the geographic scope of bargaining and thereby reduce the "leapfrogging" that escalates costs. It also developed a joint program to improve vocational education in construction trades, linkage with the apprenticeship system, the quality of work, and the dignity of skilled labor. Among subjects addressed by the Commission were the reduction of employment seasonality, the modernization of building codes, and the measurement of construction productivity. A bill to replace CICBC with a national tripartite board was vetoed by President Ford. The bill sought to promote regional bargaining, but it also would have allowed situs picketing.

The unusually sharp increases in construction wage rates in 1970 compared to manufacturing prompted establishment in March 1971 of a tripartite Construction Industry Stabilization Committee (CISC), five months before adoption of a national wage and price control program.[5] CISC, operating through craft dispute boards, decided whether or not major local agreements met noninflationary wage and salary standards. CISC also experimented with various arrangements for reforming the bargaining structure, such as regional and multicraft bargaining. The reduction in wage and benefit increases in collective bargaining settlements from 15.2 percent in 1970 to 10 percent in 1971 is attributed to the CISC program. Along with statutory controls for the economy, CISC expired in May 1974, and collective bargaining in construction returned to its earlier status.

Productivity and Seasonality

While national tripartite committees and commissions provide needed linkage with policymakers at the federal level, some form of joint industrywide consultation is also appropriate at the local level, where economic decisionmaking actually takes place. During the past decade, the U.S.

Department of Labor has helped organize local tripartite construction coordinating committees in a number of cities—Chicago, San Francisco, Kansas City, Denver, and Boston.[6] These committees seek more efficient use of construction labor and capital and lower costs by streamlining government procurement, training, and regulatory practices. Local officials of unions, contractor associations, and government agencies meet regularly to exchange information about prospective government contracts, training programs, and environmental policies. The committees avoid involvement in jurisdictional and collective bargaining disputes.

Since government construction often comprises a substantial portion of local activity, the coordinating committees concentrate on testing procedures for spreading out government contracts over the year. Each committee compiles a bid calendar, listing planned public construction to facilitate better coordination of government projects. If too many projects are planned for the same period, the bid calendar discloses this uneconomic concentration and helps in rescheduling. A small Labor Department staff conducts research and disseminates findings on local construction industry trends and on counterseasonality techniques. Unfortunately, the program is wholly dependent on federal funds, so its survival in an era of drastic budget cuts is very doubtful.[7]

In addition to these government-sponsored committees, unions and contractors themselves, in several areas, have agreed to cooperate to improve productivity on the job, mainly in defense against competition from nonunion builders. Prominent among these areas are St. Louis, Indianapolis, Boston, Columbus, and the states of Nevada and Colorado. The committees focus on work practices and other possible sources of insufficient productivity and cost-competitiveness.[8]

PRIDE (Productivity and Responsibility Increase Development and Employment), the cooperative program instituted in St. Louis, has been operating with distinction since 1972. It extends beyond contractors and unions to include construction users, architects, builders, and engineers in a continual dialogue. The building trades and the contractors have modified restrictive manning rules, curtailed jurisdictional disputes, and improved communication and morale at the jobsite. Once ranked among the most expensive home-building areas, St. Louis is now considered among those having lowest cost.

Retail Food Industry

This industry employs over 2.2 million people and has annual sales exceeding $200 billion. Collective bargaining is highly decentralized, with contracts differing from city to city. The contracts cover about 650,000 employees and nearly all of the major chains. Two large national unions are involved: the United Food and Commercial Workers (which was formed in 1979 by merger of the Retail Clerks International Division and the Amalgamated Meat Cutters and Butcher Workers) and the International Brotherhood of Teamsters.

An important incentive for some type of formal accommodation between labor and management is the industry's sensitivity to public opinion. Both parties are especially fearful that government control over wages and prices might be sought if the public perceives collective bargaining to be unresponsive to the national need for moderating inflation. As in the case of construction, extreme structural fragmentation of the retail food industry threatens cost escalation through "leapfrogging" and "whipsawing," as each local union tries to achieve ever higher wage increases and each company fears loss of business to competitors if its service is interrupted.

Origin and Work
of JLM Committee

The Joint Labor-Management (JLM) Committee of the Retail Food Industry has been operating, since 1974, as an arrangement for joint consultation among leaders on major problems that affect the industry as a whole.[9] The decision of the parent unions and the major chains to enter voluntarily into a cooperative arrangement was greatly influenced by 1973-74 experience under the wage-price controls program. For 14 months, a tripartite committee of five labor, five management, and five public members, meeting weekly, helped administer the food industry controls program under the Cost of Living Council. This experience created interest in the possibility of dealing with the industry's collective bargaining problems, after mandatory controls were lifted, through new arrangements for consultation at the industry level. The ubiquitous Dr. Dunlop, then director of the Cost of Living Council, initiated discussions among union officials and supermarket executives that led to agreement to form the Joint Labor-Management Committee of the Retail Food Industry. A participant in the controls program has observed that the Committee "could well be the most important legacy that the food wage control program left for the industry.[10]

A working agenda was drawn up by the presidents of the (then) three major unions and the chief executive officers of eight major supermarket chains and announced on March 29, 1974. The Committee would (1) collect and exchange reliable wage and benefit data to help the parties reach constructive decisions; (2) assist in key negotiations by encouraging early discussion and exchange of information; (3) serve as a national forum for discussion of longer-range industry problems "that often surface in local negotiations and which may benefit from national attention," such as technological change, government regulation, and the authority and responsibility of management and unions; and (4) provide an "ongoing forum to broaden the base of communication between labor and management at all levels and on all subjects of mutual concern to labor and management."

To carry out the work of the Joint Committee, Wayne L. Horvitz, an experienced mediator, was appointed chairman with a small staff of industrial relations experts. The Committee is supported entirely by contributions from member supermarket chains and unions. In its few years of existence, the Joint Committee has gradually evolved, chiefly under Horvitz's leadership, from a tentative experiment to an established institution. Its steering committee of corporate vice-presidents of labor relations and union officers, meeting monthly, has dealt with a variety of major issues of mutual interest with differing degrees of success—such as the improvement of collective bargaining procedures, employee health and safety, adjustment to technological change, and cost of health benefit plans.[11] Comments on each of these four issues follow.

Improvement of Collective Bargaining

The JLM Committee has proceeded by stages to try to improve the process of collective bargaining for the promotion of industrial peace and achievement of "fair and equitable, noninflationary settlements." In its first year, the Committee agreed on a list of basic bargaining procedures that are characteristic of successful negotiations and recommended that both sides in the industry follow them to avoid work stoppages. As both parties have gained confidence in the chairman's neutrality, his role in specific local negotiations has been expanded.

With the cooperation of the Federal Mediation and Conciliation Service, the JLM Chairman now follows the progress of the key negotiations in the industry and determines whether he and members of the Committee might assist in a particular dispute, subject to the agreement of the parties. The Committee has also given the chairman authority to convene pre-negotiation conferences, 90 to 120 days in advance of the expiration of contracts deemed critical to the industry. These conferences help the parties to identify issues likely to prove troublesome and to analyze the implications of possible settlements.

Health and Safety

The two parties have preferred to look after the health and safety of employees by themselves instead of risking the imposition of protective measures by the government.[12] In 1976, for example, the JLM Committee undertook a joint study of the proper use of personal protective equipment in meatcutting operations. Its findings and recommendations resulted in a clarification of OSHA standards that has discouraged litigation.

A more extensive joint effort was initiated in the same year to identify work practices that could cause respiratory ailments among department employees who cut and wrap meat in polyvinyl chloride film. "Meat-cutters' asthma" was generally attributed to the decomposition of plastic wrapping film with a hot wire, but the available scientific evidence was skimpy. Accordingly, JLM health and safety experts agreed to commission a comprehensive study of materials and conditions in retail meat departments, selecting the Harvard University School of Public Health to carry out a five-year research program with partial financing from the plastic film manufacturers. Union leaders, under pressure from the rank and file, naturally preferred a shorter period, but agreed that a voluntary independent study yielding authoritative information was better than legislation or protracted litigation. The study, scheduled for completion in 1981, was expected to provide the basis for an industrywide effort to control an important health hazard.

Technological Change

Electronic scanning at supermarket checkout stands has been recognized as a potential bargaining snag as well as a source of productivity advance. In 1975, the JLM Committee agreed on a set of general principles for negotiators that acknowledged management's and labor's interests in the pending change and the desirability of information-sharing and prior consultation.

While subscribing to the general principles, the Retail Clerks were eager, nevertheless, to prevent loss of any jobs through the elimination of manual item-price labeling. Accordingly, in the early 1970s, they joined with consumer groups and succeeded, by 1976, in obtaining legislation in several states requiring item-price labeling. When federal legislation was introduced in 1977, industry members of the JLM Committee proposed a continuation of item pricing while the effects of front-end automation could be studied over a four-year period; in return, the union was to suspend its lobbying for mandatory legislation. The national union agreed to defer a push for federal price labeling, but it did not discourage locals from seeking state and local restrictions. Union and management officials also continue to bargain at the local or enterprise level over the introduction of new technology, regardless of national developments.

Cost of Health Benefit Plans

The rapidly rising costs of health and welfare plans put unusual pressure on both parties in collective bargaining. The JLM Committee accordingly commissioned an extensive study in 1977 to find possible means of reducing the surging costs of the plans without reducing benefits.[13] To give the study's findings and recommendations the widest circulation, the JLM Committee conducted a series of seminars for union and management trustees, administrators, and lawyers on the nearly 100 funds in the retail food industry.

An Assessment

As might be guessed, some of the participants in the JLM Committee's work consider its accomplishments unimpressive, but there is also no disposition to discontinue the initiative. According to one appraisal, both sides are satisfied with actions taken on several fundamental problems.[14] Business leaders, however, had hoped for more moderate wage settlements from an expansion of the geographic basis of bargaining; but this structural breakthrough has yet to be accomplished. Unions, for their part, remain concerned about job loss through technological change and store closings. Predictably, knowledgeable observers counsel the only possible remedy for the two sides: more efforts to solve problems jointly within the framework of collective bargaining.[15]

Men's Clothing Industry

Union-management cooperation in the clothing industry, both men's and women's, has a long history. Since the 1920s, employers and unions have extended the scope of collective bargaining beyond the elementary matters of employment and wages to include their common interests in stabilizing production, reducing costs, and improving efficiency.[16] Because of the industry's fragmented and labor-intensive character, organized labor—the Amalgamated Clothing and Textile Workers and the International Ladies Garment Workers Union—has played a leading, cohesive role. The competitive threat of nonunion employers has made both these unions especially sensitive to production costs. Indeed, these unions have even employed industrial engineers to help endangered small firms to remain competitive. The surge of imports during the past decade and a half, particularly from the Far East and Eastern Europe, has induced labor and management to adopt a still more comprehensive strategy that includes not only the improvement of productive performance but also a quest for government protection in the form of higher tariffs and stringent quotas.

Joint Job Training and Research

In 1977, leaders of the Amalgamated Clothing and Textile Workers and the Clothing Manufacturers Association met, with encouragement from John Dunlop and the National Center for Productivity and Quality of Working Life, to discuss opportunities for working together to improve the competitive position of the men's tailored clothing industry—a branch of the apparel industry employing about 100,000 workers. It was agreed that major benefits could be derived from improvements in the recruitment, training, and retention of labor; better methods of production, management, and innovation; and expanded technological research and development. A nonprofit corporation—Joint Job Training and Research (JTR), Inc.—was established to design and carry out joint programs to meet these objectives. A board of directors—three officers of the union and three officers of the Clothing Manufacturers Association—supervises JTR. A small, full-time staff of professional experts, independent of the union and management, carries out the policies set by the board. In addition to support from the industry, JTR draws on resources provided by existing government programs.

The first JTR program dealt with the industry's need for a more stable and better trained workforce. Many disadvantaged, low-skilled workers are hired, but small firms can afford only a minimum of training. Turnover is considerably above the average for manufacturing. JTR accordingly organized a National On-the-Job Training Program, with funding by the U.S. Department of Labor at $2.5 million a year. A total of 80 plants are providing on-the-job training to over 4,000 employees who had been previously unemployed or receiving public assistance or wages below the poverty level. JTR reimburses employers for half of the starting wage (not less than $3.25 per hour) for the first 490 hours worked by each trainee. Employers must keep records of the trainee's performance.

Along with the training program, JTR has contracted with Harvard Graduate School of Business Administration to analyze the body of data collected on trainees and to evaluate methods of training used in the industry. Recommendations from the study will provide the basis for reform of recruitment, training, and retention methods.

A second JTR program addresses deficiencies in management methods and procedures. The U.S. Department of Commerce has, under the technical assistance provisions of the Trade Adjustment Assistance Program, made grants to JTR for a series of projects to test new ideas of wide applicability at selected firms. Among these ideas are systems for speeding delivery of garments, reducing investment in goods in process, training first-line supervisors, and controlling product quality. To speed application, JTR reimburses firms for 75 percent of the total cost of an experiment if they agree to share the results with others. Advisory boards, composed of union and management experts, work with JTR in selecting and administering projects to assure relevance to industry needs.[17]

Railroad Industry

Recent initiatives in labor-management cooperation in the railroad industry have been taken against a backdrop of long argumentation over productivity—specifically, the reduction of train crew size and the modification of work rules rendered obsolete by dieselization and later technological changes.[18] The rail unions have strenuously resisted adjustments that would spell force reduction in the face of stagnant or only slowly increasing traffic. Economies through collective bargaining have been difficult to achieve despite the financial frailty of many of the carriers.

A Joint Committee that Failed

Cooperative approaches are not unfamiliar to the railroad industry (recall the "B&O Plan," a textbook model introduced in 1923 after a bitter and unsuccessful strike of railway shopmen), but the new initiatives probably come too late to reverse the decline. In any case, in 1968, the presidents of 11 railroads, the industry association, and six railroad unions established the Railroad Labor-Management Committee to consult jointly on matters of mutual interest, such as safety, training, and legislation affecting the industry's financial difficulties.[19] The committee lasted until 1977, when meetings were discontinued because of a breakdown in bargaining negotiations over crew size.

A Task Force that Succeeded

The defunct committee left a valuable legacy—a Task Force on Rail Transportation that set up cooperative useful projects for improving terminal efficiency. Its method was nonadversarial. It considered not only work rules but the validity of managerial, operating, and marketing practices. It explored work rules and other changes experimentally, measuring the consequences and proposing collective bargaining remedies. It contemplated the prospect of maintaining or expanding employment opportunities through cost savings and improved service that brought new business.

The Task Force's first project focused on the terminal of the Missouri Pacific Railroad at St. Louis. A full-time joint labor-management team was assigned "to identify barriers to efficiency, propose changes in management and labor practices and government policies and regulations, and conduct on-line experiments to test the effectiveness of the proposed solutions." Over a three-year period of the 1970s, the project team conducted 24 experiments, half involving terms of collective bargaining agreements and half involving practices of management. The findings led to shortening of the average time spent by a boxcar in a terminal, increased reliability of car movements, and accident reduction.[20]

The success of the St. Louis project led to similar experiments at the Houston Terminal and the Buffalo Terminal. Others were attempted but were discontinued when the parties disagreed over the scope of the program.

The Task Force's cooperative, problem solving approach has been praised by a railroad labor expert as a "necessary institutional change" that "offers the chance to move away from the rigid, conflict-based bargaining process to explore avenues of mutual concern." Its experience also demonstrated that an alteration of ingrained attitudes and long-standing customs is slow and complex[21]—and could come too late for decisive restoration of a moribund industry.

Steel Industry

Collective bargaining in the basic steel industry, as in other major industries, is seen by labor experts as evolving over the past 40 years from a state of mutual distrust to "more accommodative, sophisticated relationships in which the parties understand each other's needs, motives, and problems, and, more often than not, are able to resolve their differences amicably."[22] In the past 20 years, the steel industry has expanded communication at all levels during the life of contracts, has avoided government intervention in settlements, and has introduced several cooperative arrangements. Since 1959, the parties have negotiated eight times without losing a day in a nationwide strike.

One of the most important inducements for greater union-management cooperation was the great surge of steel imports following the 116-day strike of 1959. The interruption of domestic steel production and the buildup of inventories before the next contract expiration date helped foreign producers to enter and become established in the American market. Subsequent declines in employment, intensifying competition from imports and substitute materials, and low profits have further convinced labor and management of the need for industrial peace and collaborative efforts.

Throughout the 1960s and 1970s, labor and management experimented with various types of arrangements to achieve a more harmonious relationship and strengthen the industry's competitive performance. It is generally agreed that labor-management cooperation was facilitated by the establishment in 1959 of a four-member committee to negotiate on behalf of the 12 major companies on all issues. Later cooperative endeavors, discussed below, include the Human Relations Committee, Joint Labor-Management Committees, the Experimental Negotiating Agreement, and the Steel Tripartite Advisory Committee.

Human Relations Committee

The Human Relations Research Committee was established in the 1960 agreement to study mutual problems not easily resolved under the pressures of periodic negotiations. The parties dropped the word "Research" from the title in 1962, when it became clear that the committee's function was not only fact-finding but also to make recommendations and to conduct negotiations. With the chief negotiators for the union and the industry as co-chairmen, the Committee had a broad mandate "to plan and oversee studies and recommend solutions" of such complex problems as guidelines for the determination of equitable wage and benefit adjustments, the job classification system, wage incentives, seniority (especially as it relates to layoff and recall), medical care, and "such other overall problems as the parties, by mutual agreement, may from time to time refer to the Committee."

While the Human Relations Committee found it impossible to reach an agreement on wage guidelines, subcommittees dealing with less controversial subjects on the list, according to one industry expert, were "highly productive."[23] However, the work of staff technicians on the Human Relations Committee in resolving issues even before bargaining began was resented by local and regional union officials who served on negotiating committees. With a turnover in union leadership in 1965, the Human Relations Committee was eliminated, but the principle of cooperative study and joint consultation on matters of mutual interest was established as a part of the industrial relations system.

Joint Labor-Management Committees

Since the mid-1960s, a variety of joint committees were established under collective bargaining contracts and memoranda of agreement. These committees operate at the industry, company, and plant levels. Some continue work begun by the Human Relations Committee—in a problem solving mode, away from the bargaining table. Some develop information for use in negotiations. They may deal with a wide variety of subjects, such as contracting out, civil rights, safety and health, job classification, incentives, grievance and arbitration procedures, apprenticeship, employment security, and plant productivity.

Experimental Negotiating Agreement

The adoption in 1973 (and a renewal in 1974, 1977, and 1980) of the Experimental Negotiating Agreement (ENA) as the industry's bargaining instrument is considered one of the most important steps toward more cooperation between the steel union and management.[24] Under the ENA, the parties agree to avoid strike or lockout at the expiration of the collective bargaining contract and to submit all national issues not resolved through bargaining to a panel of impartial arbitrators for final and binding decision. Thus, the agreement guarantees no interruption of steel production in contract-bargaining years. By giving up the strike threat, the union hoped to dissuade steel users from building up inventories (including imports) before contract expirations and then cutting back orders after agreements are reached. (In 1968 and 1971, cutbacks in orders resulted in drastic reduction in production and employment.) In return for the national no-strike concessions, the industry agreed in 1973 to the right to strike over local issues, gave a bonus of $150, and agreed to a minimum wage increase of 3 percent per year.

The ENA governed negotiations for the 1974, 1977, and 1980 contracts. Production was not interrupted, but this benefit to the economy came not without cost. The wage settlements achieved in the industry's more harmonious setting have been followed by price increases propagated to many other products, such as automobiles, home appliances, machinery, and buildings.

Steel Tripartite Advisory Committee

The federal Interagency Steel Task Force that in December 1977 recommended a "trigger-price" system for limiting imports also recommended "establishment of a tripartite committee of industry, labor, and government representatives as a mechanism to ensure a continuing cooperative approach to the problems and progress of the steel industry."[25] The Steel Tripartite Advisory Committee was established in July 1978 to study problems of the industry and to prepare recommendations to the president for its revitalization. The Committee includes eight labor representatives, eight management representatives, and various high-level government officials. It is chaired by the Secretary of Labor and the Secretary of Commerce.

Shortly after its establishment, the Committee agreed to concentrate on five selected problems that required government policy changes for their resolution: capital formation, trade, environmental and other regulations, worker and community adjustment, and technology. Tripartite working groups were assigned to develop findings and recommendations on each subject. The results were reviewed by the full Committee and a final report was transmitted to the president.[26] The recommended measures became the basis of a legislative and administrative program announced by the president on September 30, 1980.

The report of the Steel Tripartite Advisory Committee represents an historic event in the steel industry. In its preparation, labor participated as an equal partner. Forty years earlier, Philip Murray and Clinton Golden, leaders of the fledgling Steelworkers Union, proposed a joint labor-management industry council to deal with common problems affecting the steel industry's prosperity and the security of worker livelihoods. Adversity and the maturation of union-management relationships appear to have brought about a high degree of the cooperation that they envisaged; but, unfortunately, their harmony also has inflationary macroeconomic implications that they could not have foreseen and that we, as a nation, are not yet able to handle.

NOTES

1. A full discussion of formal training in the building trades is offered by D. Q. Mills, *Industrial Relations and Manpower in Construction* (Cambridge: MIT Press, 1972), pp. 186-189.

2. D. J. White, "The Council on Industrial Relations for the Electrical Contracting Industry," in *Proceedings of the Twenty-Fourth Annual Winter Meeting, Industrial Relations Research Association,* December 27-28, 1971, pp. 16-24.

3. Derek Bok and J. T. Dunlop, *Labor and the American Community* (New York: Simon and Schuster, 1970), p. 249.

4. Michael Moskow, "New Initiatives in Public Policy for the Construction Industry," *Proceedings of the Twenty-Fourth Annual Winter Meeting,* p. 25.

5. D. Q. Mills, "Construction," in G. G. Somers, ed., *Collective Bargaining: Contemporary American Experience* (Madison: Industrial Relations Research Association, 1980), p. 85; also "Construction Wage Stabilization," *Industrial Relations,* October 1972, pp. 350-365.

6. *Annual Construction Industry Report,* Office of Construction Industry Services, U.S. Department of Labor, Washington, 1980, pp. 73-95. On productivity trends in construction, see Edgar Weinberg, "The Productivity Slowdown: A Study of Three Industries," *Looking Ahead,* March 1980, pp. 7-8.

7. The program was terminated in February 1982, while this book was being processed.

8. *Joint Labor-Management Programs in the Construction Industry* (unpublished), National Center for Productivity and Quality of Working Life, Washington, 1978; Lynn Adkins, "A Formula for Labor Peace," *Dun's Review,* October 1978, pp. 80-82; W. F. Maloney, "Productivity Bargaining in Contract Construction," *Labor Law Journal,* August 1977, pp. 532-538; *Business Week,* November 9, 1981, pp. 103-104; and Irwin Ross, "The New Work Spirit in St. Louis," *Fortune,* November 16, 1981, pp. 92-98. See documentary appendix for text of agreement.

9. W. L. Horvitz, "The Joint Labor-Management Committee of the Retail Food Industry," in J. A. Loftus and Beatrice Walfish, eds., *Breakthroughs in Union-Management Cooperation* (Scarsdale: Work in America Institute, 1977), pp. 30-35.

10. W. M. Vaughn, III, "Wage Stabilization in the Food Industry," in J. T. Dunlop and K. J. Fodor, eds., *The Lessons of Wage and Price Controls—The Food Sector* (Boston: Harvard Graduate School of Business Administration, 1977), p. 179. See documentary appendix for text of agreement.

11. Based on JML Committee *Newsletters,* Nos. 1-13, issued by its chairman. On the productivity lag in the retail food industry, see Weinberg, "Productivity Slowdown," pp. 5-6.

12. P. E. Ray, "A Joint Labor/Management Voluntary Approach to Workplace Exposure Research," *Hazardous Materials Management Research,* March/April 1980, pp. 43-47.

13. *Putting a Lid on Health Care Costs in the Retail Food Industry,* summary of a study prepared for the Joint Labor-Management Committee of the Retail Food Industry, Washington, 1980, pp. 1-8.

14. J. W. Driscoll, "Labor-Management Panels: Three Case Studies," *Monthly Labor Review,* June 1980, pp. 41-44.

15. P. E. Ray, "The Labor Relations Impact of Store Closings in the Retail Food Industry," *Proceedings of the 1980 Spring Meeting,* Industrial Relations Research Association, pp. 482-486.

16. Kurt Braun, *Union-Management Cooperation: Experience in the Clothing Industry* (Washington: Brookings Institution, 1947).

17. *Domestic Apparel Program—Technical Review,* proceedings of a conference held at the U.S. Department of Commerce, Washington, 1980.

18. *Improving Railroad Productivity,* final report of a task force on railroad productivity to the National Commission on Productivity and the Council of Economic Advisers, Washington, 1973.

19. Scott Harvey, "Labor-Management Cooperation Program," in A. D. Kerr and A. L. Kornhauser, eds., *Productivity in U.S. Railroads* (New York: Pergamon, 1980), pp. 34-35.

20. *A Program of Experiments Involving Changes in Terminal Operations: 1974 Progress Report,* Task Force on Terminals of the Labor-Management Committee, 1975.

21. Harvey, "Labor-Management Cooperation," p. 37.

22. Jack Stieber, "Steel," in G. G. Somers, ed., *Collective Bargaining,* p. 205.

23. D. E. Feller, "The Steel Experience: Myth and Reality," *Proceedings of the Twenty-First Annual Winter Meeting, Industrial Relations Research Association,* December 29-30, 1968, p. 155.

24. Stieber, "Steel," p. 207.

25. *A Comprehensive Program for the Steel Industry,* report of the Interagency Task Force to President Carter, Washington, December 6, 1977.

26. *Report to the President by the Steel Tripartite Advisory Committee on the United States Steel Industry,* Washington, September 25, 1980. See documentary appendix for excerpt.

4

Communitywide Collaboration

The message of this chapter is that alert leadership and timely action for labor-management (and broader) cooperation can help a community to keep or recover economic viability. The continual flux of competition always tends to threaten some geographic areas while favoring others. Thus, changes in technology, tastes, demographic characteristics, laws and regulations, the size and distribution of private and public expenditures, and the volume and structure of international trade affect the comparative production costs of different communities (and countries) and the demand for their goods and services. When local enterprises fail to perceive or to respond adequately to competitive challenges, their communities can suffer significant damage. Plant closings, bankruptcies, and employment cutbacks can undermine local tax bases, reduce public services and amenities, encourage outmigration of the young and the skilled, and set in motion a downward spiral that is hard to halt or reverse. Recognizing this common threat, business, labor, and other local leaders have on occasion rallied to counteract or limit the erosion of the economic foundations of the areas in which they live and work. While it may appear that not enough communities rise up to the challenge,[1] it is also probable that no other nation can boast so much evidence of local resourcefulness for voluntary self-help.

This chapter starts with a general review of the nation's experience in local collaboration and then concentrates on six cases: Jamestown (N.Y.), Buffalo-Erie (N.Y.), Cumberland (Md.), Muskegon (Mich.), Evansville (Ind.), and Haverhill (Mass.). These six ventures, all started in the 1970s and still operating, illustrate the variety of motivations, explicit aims, feasible structures, and potential accomplishments of their genre.

A Very Short History

Many urban areas, and most or all states, have had some kind of economic development program since the end of World War II. Faced with the demobilization of millions of men and women and with the closing of war plants and military bases, community leaders across the country made plans to ease the transition to peacetime. In addition to the ineffectual efforts of such unremembered federal agencies as Reemployment and Retraining Administration and the work of local civic and veterans organizations, important contributions to postwar planning on the community level were made by the Committee for Economic Development, a business-oriented group. This group has included the improvement of local job opportunities on its research agenda in more recent years.[2]

Typically, the early private initiatives were dominated by public-spirited businessmen,[3] and only token support was enlisted from labor, educational, religious, civic, and government ranks. One good reason for labor's minor or defensive participation was the insecurity of the hard-won concept of seniority; a Selective Training and Service Act of 1940, not designed originally for a lengthy war, contained a Section 8 on reemployment rights that threatened a basic premise of unionism and had to be clarified in the courts. Two exceptional cities, Toledo and Louisville, did establish early tripartite labor-management-citizens committees, in 1945 and 1946 respectively, to mediate local industrial disputes and to create a climate and image of industrial peace. A later example, which includes only the first two parties in its title, dates from 1963 and relates to the community severely affected by the disappearance of Studebaker from the roster of automobile manufacturers: the South Bend Labor-Management Commission, organized to promote good industrial relations through studies and conferences.

In the 1970s, communities became more aware of peacetime needs for economic cooperation. As the nation's economic growth slowed, as foreign producers penetrated or wrested away markets thought to be "ours," and as inflation and uncertain petroleum supplies altered patterns of investment and consumption, many local areas with long-established plants and industries suffered unexpected hardship. Advocates of labor-management cooperation sought to encourage the idea that the attenuation of conflict might influence corporate headquarters to consider modernization of old facilities instead of shutting them down.

The accompanying table shows 28 cities, towns, and counties in which labor-management entities have been established, mostly in the 1970s and in the northeast and midwest. These joint undertakings are found not only in smaller places, like Cumberland, but also in more populous places, like Buffalo (and its environs)—and, most recently, Philadelphia.

Membership and Financing

Prominent local government officials, whose experience has made them cognizant of the link between amicable labor-management relations and sound economic development, have often taken the lead in bringing the two parties (and others) in a constructive joint organization. In other instances, labor, business, and political leaders have acted more spontaneously in concert after a serious strike or prolonged industrial dispute has made the implications of a permanent shutdown more vivid. Sometimes, a key role has been played by commissioners of the Federal Mediation and

Areawide Labor-Management Committees

Area	Date Established
Over 300,000 population	
Toledo, Ohio	1945
Louisville, Kentucky	1946
Pittsburgh, Pennsylvania	1973
Buffalo, New York	1975
St. Louis, Missouri	1977
Philadelphia, Pennsylvania	1980
100,000 - 300,000 population	
South Bend, Indiana	1963
Evansville, Indiana	1975
Riverside-San Bernadino, California*	1977
Under 100,000 population	
Jackson County, Michigan	1958
Green Bay, Wisconsin	1965
Upper Peninsula, Michigan	1970
Fox Cities Area, Wisconsin	1970
Jamestown, New York	1972
Cumberland, Maryland	1975
Chautauqua County, New York	1975
Mahoning Valley, Ohio	1975
Clinton County, Pennsylvania	1975
Elmira, New York	1976
Springfield, Ohio	1976
Muskegon, Michigan	1977
North Central Area, Wisconsin	1977
Scranton, Pennsylvania	1978
Portsmouth, Ohio	1978
Paducah, Kentucky	1979
Haverhill, Massachusetts	1979
Duluth, Minnesota	1979
Sioux City, Iowa	1981

*Discontinued in 1981

Conciliation Service, who preach the merits of cooperation and assist in defusing tensions between the two parties. Usually, these intermediaries withdraw to background advisory roles if they succeed in stimulating the principals to form cooperative committees; the leadership is left in the hands of labor and management co-chairmen.[4]

The area committees are made up of roughly equal numbers of recognized labor and management representatives who usually serve without compensation and leave much of the active planning, scheduling, and general direction to small executive cores or steering groups. In addition, small professional staffs are hired for day-to-day operations and research. Consultants also are used as required. If the staff is large enough to have a director, his neutrality is important for retention of member confidence. Committee meetings may be held monthly or quarterly, and they are informal as a rule.

Funds for committees come from private sources (e.g., the companies and unions with which members are affiliated) and from government, usually state or local. In the past decade, some committees received seed money from such federal agencies as the Economic Development Administration, the Department of Labor, and the Appalachian Regional Commission. Federal sources, however, are best for short-run assistance at the start or for the conduct of specific projects. A committee that relies too heavily on federal money risks limitation of its activities to meetings and occasional conferences when this funding ceases.

Functions and Objectives

It is up to each committee to determine how best to function. Some are more ambitious than others. All are realistic in assessment of community needs and of the roles in which they could constructively serve. At least five roles are discernible. First, they may serve as *forums* for exchange of ideas between labor and management and for communication and dealings with federal, state, and local governments. Second, they may concentrate (as did the Toledo and Louisville committees, which actually operated as offices within their city governments) on *mediation* of industrial disputes. Third, they may function as *information and research* centers to keep labor and management abreast of changing local circumstances that are relevant to bargaining and of pertinent developments elsewhere. Fourth, they may offer *technical assistance* to employers and unions willing to experiment with new ways of organizing work, etc. Fifth, they may act as *catalysts,* encouraging and assisting labor and management at the company level to organize in-plant committees and to improve internal communications.

Through service in these roles, areawide committees could contribute signally to the current performance and the prospects of their localities. As honest brokers trusted by both sides, they could assist in bringing difficult labor-management negotiations to successful conclusions. They may encourage community colleges to offer courses useful to foremen, supervisors, local union officers, and shop stewards. They may sponsor workshops on collective bargaining, absenteeism, output quality, and productivity enhancement. They could help small firms to upgrade managerial and other pertinent skills. They could mobilize public support and negotiate for government funds for improvement of transportation, establishment of industrial parks, attraction of new business, and so forth. They could conduct programs that aim at lifting morale and civic pride and at changing earlier adverse reputations of their localities as places in which to live and work. A more detailed picture of community strategies and objectives emerges from the case studies that follow.

Jamestown Labor-Management Committee[5]

The joint committee established in 1972 in Jamestown has been acclaimed for its dramatic contribution to the community's self-renewal and has become a model for other distressed manufacturing centers. The immediate crisis that culminated in joint action was the shutdown of a metal furniture plant after a four-month strike in 1971. Over 400 jobs were lost when the unemployment rate already stood at 10 percent. Other companies were also experiencing work stoppages at the time, and the specter of bankruptcy loomed.

These troubles came to this community of some 40,000 persons against a background of earlier labor-management strife and decline or loss of once-thriving textile and wood furniture industries. Indeed, the community had acquired a reputation as a low-productivity and high-cost area with a "poor labor climate."

A decisive factor in Jamestown's turnaround was the leadership of Stanley Lundine, a young, energetic, and determined mayor (now a Congressman). With the help of Federal Mediation and Conciliation Service (FMCS) mediators, he took the initiative to bring together the executives of leading manufacturing firms and the labor leaders of the workers therein, winning their agreement to join in a committee for open discussion of industrial relations and economic revival. This Labor-Management Committee includes representatives of large international conglomerates, large locally-owned companies, and small firms. It also includes representatives of the steel, auto, machinist, furniture, and glass and ceramic unions. The executive director of the Manufacturers Association and of the AFL-CIO Central Labor Council also are members. In 1977, representatives of a hospital and the school system were added. With the aid of a professional staff and occasional task forces including outside experts, a 10-member executive board carries on the Committee's actual business.

The first joint meetings considered alternative development strategies. One featured "conversion," accepting the decline of manufacturing and expanding tourism, recreation, research, and other services. A "replacement" strategy contemplated attraction of new factories to compensate for departure of others. A third possibility, "renewal," envisaged joint action to assist existing industries, the encouragement of new industries in novel ways, and the development of people and programs to meet private and public needs. The "renewal" option was deemed most consistent with the common interests of labor and management.

In the spring of 1972, the new Committee announced four principal goals: "the improvement of labor relations, manpower development, assistance to industrial development programs, and productivity gains in existing industries." Despite a traditional distaste for the proclamation of productivity increase as an explicit objective of a cooperative undertaking, labor members went along. The notion was rendered palatable to rank-and-filers who tend to equate "productivity" with job loss and speedup by elucidation of the term to include less threatening objectives, like reduction of absenteeism and of material and energy waste in the manufacturing process.

The Committee quickly compiled an impressive record of accomplishment. Frequent meetings away from the bargaining arena permitted concentration on community objectives of training and industrial development and helped engender a mutual respect conducive to industrial peace. With a record of fewer strikes, earlier settlements, and a reduction of grievances, Jamestown shed its reputation as a "bad" labor town.

Cooperative efforts to develop needed skilled workers have been particularly fruitful. The Committee has been instrumental in the design of industrywide training courses for upgrading workers in 12 local wood furniture plants to replace retiring skilled craftsmen. It has helped metalworking companies and unions to identify skill needs and has participated with the community college in the design of appropriate upgrading programs. It has sponsored courses for training first-line supervisors in leadership, shop stewards in communication, and management and labor officials in contract administration and grievance processing. Employer and county funds have been supplemented by federal Comprehensive Employment and Training Act (CETA) money.

A unique feature of the Jamestown plan is its strong complementary effort to create in-plant labor-management committees, involving workers and supervisors on the shop floor in the improvement of productivity, quality of worklife, and industrial relations in general. Consultants have assisted in experimental projects concerned with sharing the productivity gains, joint redesign of plant layout, and worker participation in bidding for new business. Many of these in-plant projects were temporary, but they collectively gave rise to community "themes" (such as skill development, gain sharing, and layout redesign) that served to stimulate further organizational change, often in unexpected ways.

The positive climate resulting from the Committee's work has improved Jamestown's economic outlook. Local investors have come to the rescue of five failing firms; in one case, the employees were the investors. Several companies announced enlargement and modernization programs in 1975. For the first time in a half century, a major industrial firm, Cummins Engine Company, decided to move into Jamestown, taking over a vacant plant and creating the potential of 1,500 new jobs.

Buffalo-Erie County Labor-Management Council[6]

Like the much smaller Jamestown community, the Buffalo area has had a long history of labor-management strife and a reputation discouraging to new enterprise. Between 1970 and 1975, it lost 30,000 manufacturing jobs, or 30 percent of the total; and, in 1970-1972 and 1975, it ranked among the top three cities in the nation in loss of worktime due to strikes. In addition to these troubles, the city and county have teetered on the brink of bankruptcy.

These dire circumstances prompted the head of the AFL-CIO Council to meet informally with a leading businessman in the area and with various government officials—the mayor, Congressmen, and county executives. It was decided that a joint labor-management venture could interrupt the downward slide. A joint Labor-Management Council was formed in 1976 with 9 members from management and 10 from labor. Political leaders were not included but were expected to be supportive.

The Council employs an executive director with extensive experience as a mediator and a small staff with backgrounds in business and labor relations. In addition, an Advisory Committee has been established with members from the FMCS, the State Mediation Service, the State Industrial Commissioner's office, private industry, universities, and the AFL-CIO Human Resources Development Institute.

In selecting a strategy for its operations, the Council considered two different models: the Jamestown Plan of training and in-plant labor-management committees and the older Toledo Labor-Management Committee. The latter concentrates on mediation or arbitration by tripartite panels when its aid is requested in local negotiations, strikes, and grievances. It is said to be successful largely because of the network of close contacts among committee members and other labor, management, and public leaders; it can function informally to resolve problems both before and after a dispute is submitted to it. The Council concluded that it could not copy completely either of these models but would draw on both experiences in formulating a program appropriate to Buffalo's larger size, political complexity, and diverse industry and union mix.

The Council has, through its staff, concentrated on encouraging formation of joint committees at the plant level and facilitating the bargaining process. By the end of 1979, the Council was working with 42 in-plant committees in firms ranging in size from 100 employees to 3,000. In some firms, more than one committee was established. In conjunction with Cornell University, the Council has set up training sessions for the committees on grievance processing and analysis, contract administration, safety issues, and techniques for improving operations. On request, it reviews and tries to improve grievance processes where these are controverted in bargaining; this step is necessary before an attempt is made to form a plant committee. As the Council's executive director has observed, "the grievance process must have some minimum level of civility and effectiveness if an LMC is to be effective."[7] Also at the request of the parties, the Council may undertake a fact-finding study prior to negotiations and thereby facilitate concord.

A distinctive contribution to economic revitalization of the Buffalo area has been made through the joint committees that the Council has helped to organize on the waterfront. The Port of Buffalo reached its heyday in the 1950s; by 1975, it had declined far below its peak and the prospects for recovery were considered dim. Here is how the Council has helped to improve the outlook:

1. With the assistance of the Council, three companies in the cargo industry and the International Longshoremen's Association established a joint labor-management committee to study the Port's future and found a significant potential for handling shipping containers at the Port if work practices were modernized and made more flexible. Subsequent modification of the contract for warehousing resulted in lower labor cost and business expansion , which more than tripled employment in two years.

2. In the grain-milling industry at the Port, which processes wheat shipped from the midwest, labor was reputed to be resistant to adjustment of practices and crew size in the face of technological change. A joint study, directed by the Council's staff, found that crew sizes, on the whole, were not unreasonable but that, in a few cases, obsolete work rules did restrict productivity. The study led to changes in

work practices and a better understanding between the parties.

3. In 1978, the local longshoremen's union and five companies in the grain-milling industry, together with the cargo and steel industries and their respective unions, established the Buffalo Waterfront Labor-Management Committee, with the Council's assistance, to concentrate on the economic development of the Port. One of this Committee's major projects was a study of the transportation network. The study led to state approval of funds for modernization of the Port's equipment.

The Council has also contributed to the strengthening of the area's manpower base. In 1977, it established a Human Resources Subcommittee to consider the problem of chronic shortages of skilled craftsmen and to help obtain commitments from employers to hire trainees. When a major steel plant reduced its workforce by 3,000, the Human Resources Subcommittee was asked to assist the laid off employees; it established a Transition Center which centralized and expedited all placement, training, and other community services for the displaced workers. Some of these workers were trained in shortage skills—as welders, machinists, tool and die-maker apprentices, maintenance mechanics, precision machine operators, and industrial electricians. According to the Council director's report, "when the Transition Center closed in late 1978, 1,200 of the 1,891 center registrations were in new jobs, training for new jobs, or back to work with Bethlehem. By mid-1979, all the laid-off employees who had registered were successfully transitioned or recalled."

While the Transition Center was considered a success, the Council decided that work on human resources diverted too much time from its basic mission and recommended the establishment of a city-county Private Industry Council (PIC) under the new CETA program. Many members of the Human Resources Subcommittee were appointed to the PIC, and the Council assumed the avuncular role of "*ad hoc* catalyst to energize the PIC staff."

Federal budget stringency now clouds the future of organizations like the Council, regardless of their effectiveness, and the new mood is to have every local tub rest, if possible, on its own bottom. Although the Council gets funds from the city of Buffalo, Erie County, and union and business groups, it has lately depended most heavily on grants from the Economic Development Administration, an agency marked for sharp reduction or demise.

Cumberland Area Labor-Management Committee[8]

The Cumberland Area Labor-Management Committee (CALM) was established in 1975 "to enhance the economic development potential of the Cumberland area—through programs and activities which focus on cooperative action." Located in the foothills of the Appalachians in western Maryland, the Cumberland area has a population of 84,000, slightly larger than the Jamestown area's, and similar problems of job development. Fifty years ago, Cumberland was a major railroad and coal center, but dieselization and other changes have diminished its importance. Today, the area's main industries make tires, textiles, glass, steel, and paper—all heavily unionized and impacted by severe foreign and domestic competition and by slow growth of demand.

Although industrial relations are now stable, a reputation for labor strife gained in the 1930s and 1940s persists as a discouragement to new investment. The 1974-75 recession, the loss of 1,400 jobs because of a shutdown of a major part of a large plant, and the shaky condition of other firms worsened the long term economic outlook. Cumberland has tried to reverse the unfavorable trend through such industrial development schemes as low-interest financing programs, a 10-year tax exemption on real and personal property, and the construction of industrial and office parks. In 1978, business groups and the Allegany county government launched a civic campaign with the slogan "PACE—Positive Attitudes Change Everything."

Over its first five years, CALM has concentrated on the improvement of labor-management relations at individual plants as one of the keys to assuring retention and expansion of area employment. While recognizing that many economic factors go into decisions to close, expand, or build new plants, the CALM Executive Board agreed that "labor-management relations should *never* be the reason behind a plant shutdown or the rationale for losing a prospective new industry."

CALM's principal contribution to improving the collective bargaining process at member firms is its program to assist the formation and operation of in-plant labor-management committees. The only condition that the CALM consultant imposes on a new committee is that it give the concept a six-month trial before deciding to keep or discontinue. All the in-plant committees concentrate on plant operations—procedures, equipment, maintenance, productivity, and job-related complaints. Grievances under the contract are excluded from their purview. By 1980, there were 10 committees in operation, of which two had been in existence before CALM. More than half of the employees in Allegany County's manufacturing and service organizations with union representation are in firms that have committees; they work in the tire, foundry, paper, steel, and cement industries and in local government.

CALM gives high priority to educational programs in labor relations, for both management and union representatives, as a key to "mutual understanding." Over 400 managers, supervisors, union officials and hourly workers have participated in CALM-sponsored programs. Training sessions are held, free of charge, at the plant site, in the union hall, and at the Allegany Community College and Frostburg State College. A unique program sponsored by CALM features "bootstraps" training of union and employer selectees as instructors in industrial relations; they return to design and conduct in-house courses for local union and company officials. Another unusual CALM project involves team-teaching of a high school course in industrial relations that realistically presents union and management views on issues in the world of work.

CALM has also functioned as a forum for joint action on problems of economic development. For example, it helped persuade the Environmental Protection Agency to allow area industries to convert from oil to the kind of coal that is abundant in western Maryland. It worked closely with the construction industry to assure that several significant building projects were completed within competitive budget constraints. It also focused public attention on the need to minimize overlapping services and contain rising health-care costs.

Finally, mention should be made of the close ties established by CALM with cognate entities—the Allegany County Economic Development Company, the Maryland State Department of Economic and Community Development, and the Maryland Center for Productivity and Quality of Working Life. These connections facilitate diffusion of the concept of community-based labor-management cooperation to other parts of the state.

Muskegon Area Labor-Management Committee[9]

Labor-management cooperation in Muskegon County has evolved as a joint effort to expand job opportunities in this relatively distressed area of about 157,000 people on the southeastern shore of Lake Michigan. Machinery and metalworking are now the primary industries of a region in which lumber and automotive firms once dominated. Unionism is strong, with the United Auto Workers and the Electrical Workers much in evidence. A series of strikes in 1971 aroused local labor, business, and community leaders to the weaknesses of Muskegon's economy. Several major companies were planning either to shut down local plants or to move operations elsewhere. Closer cooperation between labor and management seemed vital to survival.

Several models of community-based labor-management consultation were already in operation in Michigan. The Jackson County Labor-Management Board had been meeting monthly since 1958 to share information and ideas about local and state economic conditions and community betterment. The Upper Peninsula Labor-Management Committee was established in 1970; it concentrates on annual communitywide conferences for improving the collective bargaining process.

The labor and business leaders of Muskegon decided in 1972 to establish the Industrial Expansion Board. From its membership dues, an executive director was hired, and several consultants were engaged to develop a work plan, known as "Project Priority," for the Board's operations. Subsequently, a group of 40 business and labor leaders identified three issues of greatest common concern: poor communications and hostility between labor and management, the need for joint support of a community effort to stimulate economic growth and productivity, and an excessively critical attitude of the news media in their portrayal of local economic conditions. Task forces were assigned to deal with each of the issues. Among the proposed solutions were: the award of major new construction projects to local companies, the establishment of in-plant labor-management forums for discussion of mutual concern, and meeting with representatives of the local news media to discuss the quality of coverage in general and to initiate coverage of Project Priority's activities.

In 1977, the Industrial Expansion Board, having received a grant from the federal Economic Development Administration, was transformed into the Muskegon Area Labor-Management Committee (MALM). The Committee appointed a full-time coordinator, created a board of eight directors (four each from management and labor), and introduced Project Priority. Five objectives were approved:

1. To help raise the quality of working life in Muskegon and contribute to productivity improvement.

2. To assist business and labor or any county organization to increase effectiveness through a joint working relationship as a third party.

3. Upon request, to assist in plant and business seminars for bringing the parties together and solving problems on a cooperative basis.

4. To improve the community image, making it attractive for new business to locate in Muskegon.

5. To respond to requests of local business and labor in problem solving.

Neither the coordinator nor a Committee member may serve as a private mediator in any case involving grievances, complaints, or other labor-management differences.

Continuing attention has been devoted by MALM to the organization of in-plant labor-management committees (or "forums," as they are locally called) and to the encouragement of "brainstorming" sessions on such topics as absenteeism, alcoholism, and quality of working life. One example of payoff refers to a plant making bearings: design changes recommended by a machinist enabled the company to obtain a contract for which it had previously bid unsuccessfully. In several plants, work rules have been modified with benefit to productivity. MALM also shares some of the credit for local decisions to modernize equipment and expand facilities.

The Committee has worked to build public support for a variety of economic development projects. New facilities for solid waste disposal have attracted three chemical plants to the area. Among other forward-looking projects are a new industrial park and a new downtown shopping mall.

Evansville Area
Labor-Management Committee

The economic well-being of this area of some 133,000 people in a largely rural corner of Indiana is linked to the fortunes of a few multiplant manufacturing firms. Evansville makes home appliances, automotive parts, and other metal products.

Two efforts have been made in the area since the end of World War II to organize a communitywide vehicle for the advancement of labor-management harmony and cooperation. One occurred in the 1950s and the other in the 1970s.

The first effort began when the curtailment of defense production after Korea meant the shutdown of area plants of several major employers. Business leaders formed a Committee of 100 to advertise the area's assets to potential industrial developers.[10] After this gambit was criticized by a panel of Indiana University experts as too narrow a concept for revitalization of the economic base, a new organization was formed to draw support from the whole community—the Evansville Futures Committee (EFC). This Committee adopted a broader concept of redevelopment that included the upgrading of education and training and the improvement of industrial relations. A firm of plant location specialists recommended a labor-management council to promote industrial peace and cooperation.

In 1958, the Labor-Management Committee of EFC was formed. It sponsored informal luncheon meetings and a series of institutes on industrial relations, and it also functioned as an unofficial mediator of strikes. During the 1960s several major companies built plants in Evansville, and this return to prosperity diminished labor and management interest in the Committee, which became inactive.

Slow economic growth in general, strikes at major firms in the area, and threats of shutdown and relocation prompted the establishment of the Evansville Area Labor-Management Committee in 1975.[11] A federal mediator played a key role in the formation of this second area venture in cooperation. He attributed the high frequency and long duration of work stoppages to inadequate communication between union and business leaders and noted the connection between industrial turmoil and the reluctance of investors. Under his guidance, ten labor and management leaders met voluntarily for several months before the new Committee became a reality.

The Evansville Area Labor-Management Committee was set up as a nonprofit organization to serve as a forum for open communication on threats to industrial harmony. The board of directors at first included representatives of the local teamster, machinist, electrical worker, and construction unions and of local plants engaged in production of aluminum, electrical goods, containers, home appliances, and food. More recently, representation from the public sector has been added. A professional coordinator was hired with CETA funds in September 1976.

The activities of the Committee are thought to have helped reduce strike-proneness and to promote cooperation. The improvement of attitudes on both sides of the bargaining table are thought to have influenced some major corporations to remain in the area and to expand employment. The Committee conducts seminars, conferences, and workshops on industrial relations and has succeeded in establishing in-plant labor-management committees at eight facilities, two of them operated by major appliance producers.[12]

Haverhill Growth Alliance[13]

In 1979, the Haverhill Growth Alliance (HGA) was launched to help restore the economic vitality of an old, historic city of 75,000 people on the Merrimack River. Once a major shoe center, the city had declined for some eight decades. Western Electric Company, with 5,200 workers, is the dominant employer. Old homes and factories, some abandoned, testify visibly to the area's candidacy for renewal.

The impetus to labor-management cooperation came from outside the community—the Massachusetts Labor-Management Center, a tripartite, nonprofit organization established in Boston to encourage joint consultation in the interest of economic and social development. The Center has been influential in making Massachusetts business and labor leaders aware of innovative practices in industrial relations and in assisting them to organize community-based and in-plant labor-management committees. It was enabled to provide needed technical assistance to Haverhill (and other areas) by a grant from the Economic Development Administration.

The idea of setting up a communitywide labor-management committee as a basis for reviving Haverhill was broached to the mayor and other civic leaders in 1978 by the Center's director. The former mayor of Jamestown was present too. The Haverhill mayor undertook to encourage favorable consideration of the proposal by businessmen and the unions.

Although the experience of Jamestown inspired Haverhill's action, HGA has varied the prototype according to its own circumstances. For one thing, it has opened Alliance membership to all residents on payment of dues. Thus, it is not confined to business and labor support. It focuses on the public sector as well as the private. In addition to concern for improving labor-management relations and worklife quality, it deals with issues of urban rehabilitation—of the quality of life of the whole community. It coordinates the activities of neighborhood associations preoccupied with such issues.

It supports efforts to refurbish the downtown shopping area and to instill a sense of civic pride. A task force organized in cooperation with the North Essex Community College is identifying training needs of local workers and promoting vocational adjustment to demands of high-technology industries.

To encourage labor-management cooperation, the Alliance staff has concentrated on opening up communications and promoting better understanding between the city's managers and public employee unions. It has helped the parties reach an "Agreement in Principle," which outlined joint goals to improve the collective bargaining process. In the private sector, it has organized training workshops for union stewards of the Communication Workers local at Western Electric. It has also sought to increase labor and business awareness of the objectives and techniques of in-plant cooperation. Such cooperation, however, is not likely to become an urgent item on the agenda of a community that lost its main industry decades ago, is not currently wracked by serious labor unrest, and is not awaiting an influx of new industry.

Haverhill's experience suggests that a community may beneficially add an herb of common sense to the medicine prescribed by specialists for a disease from which it does not suffer. This lesson could be very important for the large number of localities that have outlived one economic career and seek another which is not assured. For a community to improve its quality of living is really its prime challenge; and this challenge includes, but is not synonymous with, improvement in the quality of worklife, although the latter often merits a high strategic priority.

NOTES

1. Organizations such as the Appalachian Governors' Conference and the National Council for Urban Economic Development have endorsed the establishment of areawide committees. In 1979, the National Association of Area Labor-Management Committees was formed by 13 such entities to share information and to lobby for federal appropriations for implementing the Labor-Management Cooperation Act of 1978, which would provide grants to cooperative committees at the area, industry, and plant levels. An appropriation of $1 million was finally approved for fiscal year 1981, to be administered by the Federal Mediation and Conciliation Service. See Appendix B for list of 14 grantees.

2. See, for example, a publication prepared by the Area Development Committee of the Committee for Economic Development—*Community Economic Development Efforts: Five Case Studies* (New York: Praeger, 1966).

3. It should be recalled here that the original title (1945) of the sponsor of this volume was The W. E. Upjohn Institute for Community Research.

4. On the nature of community-based committees, see, for example, *Establishing a Community-Wide Labor-Management Committee,* National Center for Productivity and Quality of Working Life, Washington, 1978; *Area Labor Management Committees,* Bulletin No. 12, National Council for Urban Economic Development, Washington, 1977; and J. J. Popular, "Solution—A Community Labor-Management Committee," *Labor-Management Relations Service Newsletter,* November 1979, pp. 2-3. An unpublished study that deserves mention is F. F. Foltman, *Labor-Management Cooperation at the Community Level;* it was prepared for the National Center for Productivity and Quality of Working Life and is available from the author at the School of Industrial and Labor Relations, Cornell University.

5. Detailed accounts are given in reports of the Jamestown Area Labor-Management Committee: *Three Productive Years: The Three-Year Report of the Labor-Management Committee* (1975) and *Commitment at Work: The Five-Year Report* (1977), which is excerpted in the documentary appendix. Also of interest is "How Jamestown Averted Disaster," *Business Week,* July 21, 1975, pp. 66-68; a paper by R. W. Keidel, "The Jamestown Area Labor-Management Committee: An Overlapping of Community and Organizational Cooperation," presented at the Second Annual United States-Polish Conference on the Management of Large-Scale Organizations, Tarrytown, N.Y., June 11-17, 1978; and "Theme Appreciation as a Construct for Organizational Change," *Management Science,* November 1981.

6. The story of The Buffalo-Erie County Labor-Management Council is recounted in a report by its executive director, R. W. Ahearn, *The Area-Wide Labor-Management Committee: The Buffalo Experience,* November 1979; and in a statement by G. L. Wessel, its co-chairman, and I. C. Francis at a Hearing before the Subcommittee on Employment, Poverty, and Migratory Labor of the Committee on Human Resources, U.S. Senate, on *Human Resources Development Act of 1977,* September 27, 1977, pp. 103-161.

7. Ahearn, *Labor-Management Committee,* p. 10.

8. See Popular's article, cited in footnote 4, and a brochure published by Allegany County Economic Development Co., *Cumberland Area Labor-Management Committee,* 1980.

9. On Muskegon's organization, see report cited in footnote 4, *Establishing a Community-Wide Labor-Management Committee,* pp. 22-24.

10. On Evansville's first committee, see the report cited in footnote 2.

11. See article by U. C. Lehner, "Committees of Labor and Management Enjoying Resurgence in Communities," *Wall Street Journal*, August 8, 1979.

12. See the final report submitted to the Economic Development Administration, *Evansville Area Labor-Management Committee*, March 1980.

13. An account of the Haverhill Growth Alliance appears in the April 1980 *Newsletter* of the Massachusetts Labor-Management Center, Boston.

5
Company-Level Arrangements: A Brief Perspective

This chapter and the next three relate to labor-management cooperation at the company (or intracompany) level beyond the minimum requirements of the productive process. Cooperation is usually, but not necessarily, effected through joint committees and other *ad hoc* entities. Through such media, the two parties may consult on "extra-normal" matters of mutual concern or engage in joint exploration and solution of problems without prejudice to their standard adversarial commitments. Where employees are represented by independent (i.e., noncompany) unions, the negotiation of agreements on these additional matters extends the "normal" (wage-hour and noneconomic) scope of collective bargaining, keeping it the all-purpose basic instrument of the American version of "industrial democracy."[1]

General Observations

Circumstances, perceived needs, and the climate of industrial relations critically affect the decision of labor and management to collaborate—or not—beyond the normal bounds of bargaining. These factors also largely determine the topics, modes, and vehicles of collaboration.

A decision to collaborate does not at all assure that a venture will prove successful—will survive and yield the promised bilateral net benefits. Adverse business conditions, cyclical as well as longer term, are inimical to the viability of extra-normal cooperative arrangements once these have been adopted. In the early stages of a venture, strong bilateral leadership at the top, patience, and good will are essential; and so is skill, or knowledge of what to do and how to go about doing it. In later stages, commitment at the top remains indispensable as the original protagonists leave the scene. In particular, as the opening chapter insists, it is futile to try to copy in any literal sense what some other firm is doing in the same or in another industry or in some foreign country. The garment of cooperation has to be tailored; it cannot just be taken off a rack. Finally, company-level arrangements cannot survive in a larger competitive environment unless the two parties retain their adversarial identities. The trick is not to eliminate or suppress the tensions that are so vital to cost control in a plant or shop but to rechannel and release them for constructive advantage to both sides.

Not only are collaborative arrangements slow in developing but they also have a disappointing survival rate. Mortality, however, should not be deplored altogether. If a venture does not serve as intended or desired, there is little point in prolonging its token existence. As with other ventures, benefits should preferably exceed costs, and the reckoning here should include coin other than money in a strict accounting sense. What is regrettable, however, is the too common experience that the cooperative impulse cannot withstand hard times or lack of cost discipline.

Three Categories

The many varieties of collaborative ventures in which company-level management and labor join may be subsumed under three heads. The first of the three main categories includes general purpose committees and other entities that are concerned primarily with *company* functionality and performance. Examples are consultative committees intended to assure reasonably peaceable conditions of operation by dealing with problems as they arise, production and productivity committees, and quality or quality-control circles. In the second category are entities that aim explicitly at contributing to *worker* satisfaction, well-being, and security. Among these are committees concerned with worklife quality, flexitime, health and safety, and alcohol and drug abuse. The third category embraces incentive arrangements that focus on monetary and quasi-monetary *rewards*—the Scanlon plan, profit sharing, and employee stock ownership.

The next three chapters deal with these three categories in turn. More than one variety of arrangement may be encountered in some companies. The reader is reminded that the documentary appendix to this book contains materials relating to the structure, mission and operation of specific cooperative entities. These materials may contain useful hints for the design of additional ventures.

Looking Backward

Contrary to a common contemporary impression, labor-management cooperation at the enterprise or plant level is not a novel idea in the United States. Without difficulty, it may be traced back to the 1920s and World War I. A determined search would even disclose some 19th century anticipations—for example, the Procter and Gamble profit-sharing plan introduced in 1887 and the utopian schemes of the pre-Civil War era, such as Robert Owen's community at New Harmony, Indiana, established in 1825. The rest of this chapter examines some of the cooperative highlights of the decades since the 1920s, when employers subtly fought the unions for the souls of workers and labor leaders offered cooperation in return for a share in gains from higher productivity.[2]

B&O Plan[3]

One of the most publicized ventures in cooperation of the decade after World War I was the program introduced in 1923 at the Glenwood shop of the Baltimore and Ohio

Railroad following the unsuccessful strike of craftsmen in 1922. This shop was regarded as highly inefficient, and the relationship between labor and management there was poor. A background fact of some relevance is that the railway brotherhoods, the usually conservative "aristocrats" of American unionism, endorsed the postwar Plumb Plan, which called for government ownership and operation of railroads with worker participation in their management. The B&O Plan for raising productivity and improving morale at Glenwood began uncertainly but soon seemed successful enough to be adopted in all 45 of the company's shops in 1924. B&O's favorable experience led to imitation in the mechanical or shop departments of other American and Canadian systems in ensuing years.

Joint committees were set up at the various B&O facilities with members chosen from the ranks of the appropriate craft unions and from management. The committees met at least once a month to consider ways to improve performance and working conditions. A higher-level review committee was also established to deal with systemwide issues and to examine proposals referred to it.

In the first 15 years of operation, workers contributed almost 31,000 suggestions for efficiency, safety, training, quality of work, conservation of tools and materials, and so forth. Of the more than 18,000 contributed in the first five years, 83 percent were considered of sufficient merit for approval and application. When cutbacks in employment during the great depression discouraged a flow of labor-saving suggestions, the emphasis shifted toward union-management relations and communications. The B&O Plan became inactive during the 1940s.

The benefits of the program were numerous and bilateral. According to Otto S. Beyer, the consulting engineer who installed and directed it, the public attitude toward the railroad improved, and so did worker morale. Shop discipline and workmanship were better, grievances were fewer, turnover was lower, employment was more regular, and pay was somewhat higher. Goodwill and common understanding provided the basis for practical gains to the two parties.

For trade unions, the B&O Plan represented a fundamental break with past policies. They did not passively acquiesce, but instead actively pursued the improvement of shop methods. In return, they got a company commitment to steady employment and gain-sharing.

Naumkeag Steam Cotton Company[4]

Unfortunately, another experience of the 1920s shows that goodwill and common understanding may not be able to withstand prolonged economic strain. It involves the Naumkeag Steam Cotton Company and the United Textile Workers in Salem, Massachusetts.

In the late 1920s, when labor cost got seriously out of line, the local union proposed cooperation for reduction of waste and inefficiency. In 1928, as the situation worsened, management proposed new work assignments entailing some dismissals and demotions. While the workers were unenthusiastic, the union leadership recognized the need to cut costs for survival.

With management's consent, the union leadership hired a prominent engineer to study plant operations. His recommendations for improving labor utilization led to a union proposal for a joint Waste Elimination Committee to determine new work assignments. A technician who had been associated with union-management cooperation in the garment industry carried out a required joint research program and reported his findings and a plan to the Committee. The result was a stretchout of workloads with more dismissals and demotions, but workers with greater workloads also received pay increases.

Although the company's competitive position improved, the strengthening was only temporary. As the depression deepened in 1931, the company was obliged to propose wage cuts. The workers demurred; they would go along only if the stretchout was discontinued. This counterproposal was refused, and additional wage cuts were made. The strikes that followed sealed the fate of cooperation and of the company.

Labor-Management Committees in World War II[5]

The drive to become the "arsenal of democracy" during World War II provided a unique focus for civilian American energies. Cooperation of labor and management was spontaneous and voluntary, and government had merely to steer it.

Three months after Pearl Harbor, the chairman of the War Production Board (WPB) appealed to employers and unions to organize joint labor-management committees in plants, mines, and shipyards to speed production of needed material. The heads of national unions and employee associations encouraged full participation, having already agreed to the president's proposal for maintenance of industrial peace during the war. The government set guidelines for the committees, offered technical assistance, and monitored progress, leaving the development of the in-house programs to the parties themselves.

About 20,000 defense plants had been urged by mail to set up labor-management production committees, and about 5,000 did so during 1942-45, with about 3,000 the maximum functioning at one time. The 5,000 plants employed 7 million workers, about 40 percent of the target workforce registered with WPB. Although the response may appear small, these considerations should suggest otherwise: the government's low priority on the program and minor investment in it, the immaturity of collective bargaining at the time, the historic distrust of government initiatives that may include reporting, the voluntariness of participation, and the intense antigovernment sentiment that pervaded the business community in particular during the New Deal "revolution" preceding the war.

It is easy to imagine that management in plants experiencing unstable relations with labor just before the outbreak of war might have construed the WPB guidelines as biased. The committees, according to WPB, were to deal with interferences to production, not with issues normally within the purview of collective bargaining and established grievance procedures. On the other hand, recognized bargaining agents were to choose committee members on the labor side. Active unions—the Steelworkers, Machinists, Auto Workers, and Electrical Workers—were especially well represented on committees, but the plants with these committees comprised only a small portion of the total number under contract with these unions.

Perhaps, only 1,000 of the 5,000 committees really dealt with productivity improvement and the conservation of scarce materials and energy. The others were primarily concerned with the boosting of general morale, practical matters like carpooling, or a show of patriotic fervor without functioning at all. On the other hand, even in this dominant category, issues that had an ancillary bearing on production were not entirely neglected—issues such as absenteeism, safety, and provision for, and utilization of, employee suggestions. The committees that did operate effectively also included indirect supports to production (e.g., the health and training of workers) within the scope of their concerns while they centered attention on: efficient use of raw materials, the reworking of damaged products, the salvage of waste materials, redesign of tools and products to facilitate manufacture, fuller use of available capacity, better maintenance and repair of equipment, improvement of product quality through analysis of defects and change in inspection methods, change in methods of work assignment, and so forth.

For believers in cooperation as a social end rather than as an instrument to be chosen or ignored, the denouement is disappointing. When World War II ended, it was as though

Cinderella had reached midnight; most of the committees simply vanished. With wage and price controls lifted, a wave of strikes swept the country in 1946 and 1947. Few tears were shed over the end of an interlude of cooperation reminiscent of, and more enthusiastic than, the collaborative effort of World War I. Labor and management returned to their basic adversarial postures in quest of a new *modus vivendi* appropriate to peacetime and to the unsettled state of industrial relations obscured by the war.

The 1950s: Consolidation and Reflection

In a review of industrial relations in the 1950s, two themes stand out. These themes are also discernible in the subsequent decades; and their importance is underscored, rather than gainsaid, by such adverse developments as the flurry of "wage inflation" in the middle 1950s and the crippling steel strike of 1959.

One of these two themes was the elaboration of collective bargaining between management and unions beyond the nascent state of the 1930s. The directions of elaboration were determined, in part, by the wartime opportunities of union and business leaders to work at closer range. They were also influenced by a public wish for release from sustained tension, a wish expressed in the election of a presidential candidate who vowed to end the stalemate in Korea.

The second theme was the increasing concern of thoughtful students of the economic scene to discover and prescribe formulas for "civilizing" the interaction of labor and management. The costs of disruption to the two parties and to society at large were recognized as excessive; and even a mild inflation, associated with a propensity for peaceable wage settlements to outrun productivity advance, was perceived as dangerous to personal well-being and to economic and social stability if allowed to become virulent through mindless neglect.

With respect to the first theme, some tendencies in bargaining deserve mention. Contracts were extended to subjects not previously covered. Contract periods were increased, and provision was made for arbitration, mediation, and conciliation in the expectation that work stoppages would be reduced thereby in frequency and severity. Similar benefits were imagined from the more general linkage of wage adjustments to the past long term annual advance in the national productivity trend, whether or not the trend was matched by new annual changes in output per hour.[6]

Although many of the contracts of the decade were prefixed by pledges of cooperation on behalf of efficiency, rarely was machinery introduced for enlisting the active participation of workers or their unions. The Korean conflict, incidentally, did not sufficiently burden the economy to require a call for organization of labor-management committees as part of a national scheme of industrial mobilization. True, some participatory programs were installed in the 1950s, such as Scanlon Plans in various companies and Tennessee Valley Authority's system of cooperative committees, but these did not inspire the founding of a fashion.

Labor economists and specialists in labor-management affairs did, however, recognize and articulate the desirability of a heavier accent on cooperation, the next "higher" step in a perceived progression beyond the conflict and competition of the parties. They appreciated the potential of workers and unions to contribute to the upgrading of company performance.[7]

Management, however, was inhibited. One of its reservations was that union and worker participation would strengthen labor in bargaining. Another was fear of dilution of prestige and authority. Still another was doubt that workers and unions could actually contribute much of value. In newly decentralized corporations, plant managers were unsure that they could initiate change without approval of headquarters. Furthermore, corporate officials still harbored the desire to communicate directly with employees over the heads of unions. Finally, where bargaining was accepted with some reluctance in the first place, there was no disposition to enlarge the scope of negotiations.[8]

Labor leaders, especially those of impermanent tenure, also had reservations about formal cooperative arrangements. Among their attributes is memory of labor history—for example, of the futility of extending an open hand to employers bent on "unionbusting" in the 1920s. They have traditionally been wary of seeming to be "too cozy" with management, too disposed to "class collaboration" with the "enemy." Accordingly, union leaders were often content, in the 1950s as in other times, to concede the burdens of production to management and to fight for "more" at the bargaining table—a fight that itself has been rationalized as contributing to technological improvement and to the upgrading of worker qualifications.

The 1960s: Technological Threat

The "automation" scare, real and exaggerated by journalistic hyperbole, prompted a few vulnerable industries to establish joint study groups and other cooperative mechanisms in the 1960s to help them cope with large-scale displacement. These *ad hoc* entities seemed necessary as supplements to "normal" collective bargaining.

As a rule, problems of labor displacement are addressed through contract clauses relating to seniority in layoff and transfer and to severance pay. But the changes contemplated in the meatpacking, longshoring, steel, railroad, and printing industries in the 1960s were so extensive that they required special preparation for easing human hardship. Accordingly, joint study groups were set up to consider advance notice to employees, retraining, interplant transfer, early retirement, attrition, relocation, and so forth, as elements of a mitigative program.[9] In 1963, the Secretary of Labor observed that the complex issues could be addressed "only by a process of accommodation and arrangement which is almost impossible in the countdown atmosphere of the 30 days before strike deadline."[10]

Armour Study Committee[11]

To assist 5,000 workers released by the closing of six obsolete plants and the opening of modern plants elsewhere, Armour and Company set up a joint study committee and a special fund in 1960. Many of these workers were unskilled, poorly educated, and elderly—as in so many other cases of required adjustment to the combined pressures of competition and technological opportunity.

The committee had nine members. Two represented the union of meatcutters and butchers; two represented the packinghouse workers; four were company employees; and the ninth member was a distinguished neutral from academia (Clark Kerr at first, later George P. Shultz).

The committee was given responsibility for designing, initiating, and administering programs for training and interplant transfer, and it also could originate additional corrective measures. A fund of $500,000 was provided.

Over a five-year period, a tailored program was developed for each of the closed plants. The aim in each case was to retrain displaced workers for greater employability. Consideration was also given to relocation and placement in the light of labor market opportunities and the workers' characteristics. Experience gained in one locality was used in the design of programs for others.

The committee's work helped the company to take additional steps that could not be foreseen as useful or necessary. Thus, "flowback" rights were granted in the bargaining contract to disappointed workers who had relocated. Liberalized early retirement benefits were provided for older workers who could not compete in productiveness. What Armour learned also proved valuable in the design of government's own active manpower policy. The committee was disbanded in 1966; the cycle of closings had been completed.

Kaiser Steel Long-Range Committee[12]

Another social invention of the 1960s was the Long-Range Committee established by Kaiser Steel Corporation and the United Steelworkers as part of their separate agreement to end the 1959 strike. The prime purpose was to find a way to avoid future strikes, but the Committee also served to facilitate the modernization of company plants and the reduction of costs to meet foreign competition. The responsibility actually assigned to the Committee was to devise "a long-range plan for the equitable sharing of the company's progress between the stockholders, the employees, and the public." A unique feature of the Committee was the inclusion of three public members in its total of nine. The three were distinguished mediators and arbitrators.

After more than two years of deliberation, the Committee in 1963 presented a plan that was overwhelmingly endorsed by the employees. It was a four-year program providing for virtual guarantee of job security through transfer with maintenance of wage rates; workforce reduction through attrition; and a new group incentive system giving participating employees 32.5 percent of any reduction in the unit cost of production. The group incentive was intended to supplant gradually an older scheme that had developed disparities in pay between skilled and unskilled workers.

At first, the program gave gratifying results, but the new incentive was unable to pay adequate bonuses, so some workers were allowed to return to the older individual basis. The program lasted for two four-year terms. During its lifetime, it lessened resistance to modernization, allowed reduction of crew size on existing equipment, and relieved the parties of crisis bargaining.

The 1970s: Breakdowns
and Breakthrough

An upsurge of labor-management and popular interest occurred in the 1970s in various styles of cooperation at the workplace. This upsurge was manifested in a veritable flood of professional and anecdotal literature,[13] produced under both governmental and private auspices, on programs and experiments[14] relating to worklife quality, the "humanization" of work, participatory management, "shopfloor democracy" and so forth. These topics were also treated in Congressional hearings and at numberless conferences, seminars, workshops, and panels. Newspapers, magazines, radio, and television played dual roles, as in the case of the "automation" scare of the 1960s: they not only provided news but also competitively "educated" the public with human interest feature stories and in-depth interviews. Among the mass media, television was particularly influential in dramatizing cooperative schemes.

Apart from attributing some of the new interest in cooperation in the 1970s to the volume and character of public information, we should take cognizance of three additional (but not independent) influences:

1. A striking change in the tenor of our economy and society, discouraging to the automatic optimism that long inspired a sense of uniqueness among nations.

2. An apparent alteration of attitudes toward work: a disposition to reexamine its nature, purposes, and rewards in the larger context of human values and possible life styles.[15]

3. The proliferation of organizations—governmental, private nonprofit, and academic—available not only for research and information but also for assistance in the design, establishment, and conduct of cooperative labor-management committees. The rest of this section (and chapter) elucidates these three statements in turn.

Among the blows and disappointment suffered by the American economy during the 1970s were several that had a bearing on the need for cooperation:

1. A rising rate of price inflation that at first was expected to be a temporary nuisance but finally had to be acknowledged as a problem of first magnitude.
2. The coexistence of high unemployment rates with high inflation.
3. A revolution in the price of petroleum (and other fuel), with growing uncertainty over its availability.
4. The failure of wage settlements to be keyed to productivity, which advanced less rapidly than in the 1960s and even showed occasional reverses.
5. The loss to foreign competitors of sizable shares of markets, at home and abroad, that used to be dominated by goods of American origin.
6. The difficulty of raising funds for new equipment in inflation-wracked equity and bond markets.

Confidence in the American future and its leadership was also shaken by political scandal, adverse international developments, and disturbing social trends. In the new environment of instability and turmoil that marked the 1960s and 1970s, it no longer seemed unnatural to question long-accepted modes of work and long-established workplace practices. The constants that guided in the past came to be seen as tentative and fluid, subject to reappraisal and revision. In particular, the hard economic facts themselves argued the desirability of trying to improve output per hour and the quality of products, at low cost and with limited new capital outlays, by resort to "soft technologies"—for example, by alteration of individual work schedules, reward systems, job content, worker skills, plant layout, and work flows. The same economic considerations led management in some cases to allow more latitude in decisionmaking and to test cooperative ventures that hitherto had seemed impractical or philosophically offensive.

Many sociologists have attached considerable weight to evidence of a rising "new breed" of self-indulgent labor force participants uncommitted to the "work ethic," skeptical of "material" culture, scornful of "bourgeois" institutions, sensitive to "dehumanization" of work, and desirous of more autonomy in the workplace. They made much in the 1970s of "blue-collar blues" and "white-collar woes," worker "alienation," and signs of dissatisfaction with the tyranny of the assembly line (as in the Lordstown, Ohio strike of 1972). Whether disaffection with work itself had increased in comparison with earlier years, however, was not clear. Again, we must refer to television—this time to the impact of addictive viewing of disparities in wealth and well-being on standards of reference and on modes of expression.

Studies conducted for the U.S. Department of Labor in 1977-78 by the University of Michigan's Survey Research Center did not disclose any crisis of job dissatisfaction. Only about 12 percent of the respondents reported being "not too satisfied" or "very dissatisfied" with their jobs. Furthermore, comprehensive measures of the actual behavior of workers—labor force participation rates, quit rates, absenteeism, and strikes—showed no symptomatic departure from trend in the 1970s.[16]

The Michigan survey did, however, report a substantial proportion of workers dissatisfied with particular noneconomic aspects of their jobs. About a third to a half of the workers cited lack of control over days that they work and their job assignments; rules and regulations inhibiting speech and behavior; underutilization of skills; and lack of feedback on quality of job performance. These discontents are potential sources of "avoidance" behavior (absenteeism, tardiness, grievances, sabotage, low morale, poor workmanship, and indifference to customers) detrimental to organizational efficiency.

As the first section of the documentary appendix shows, the federal government had a visible hand in encouraging employers and unions to consider collaboration to mutual advantage. One of the relevant agencies, the National Center for Productivity and Quality of Working Life, helped (before its demise in 1978) to increase awareness of the potential of joint plant committees. In addition to endorsing the committee concept, providing information on pros and cons, compiling directories of existing committees, holding conferences, and contributing to demonstration projects, the Center stimulated the establishment of several counterpart agencies on the regional and state levels.[17]

The Federal Mediation and Conciliation Service (FMCS), working out of field offices around the country, offered assistance, through its mediators, in setting up plant-level committees. Its functions were expanded by the Labor-Management Cooperation Act of 1978 (Section 6(a) of the Comprehensive Employment and Training Act Amendments of 1978). It was empowered to make grants for the start and support of committees, but no funds were available for the purpose until fiscal year 1981, when $1 million was appropriated and grants were made to 14 projects (see Appendix B).

Other federal agencies were also involved in the 1970s in the support of pertinent research and demonstration projects. Among these were the Economic Development Administration and the Appalachian Regional Commission of the Department of Commerce, the Department of Labor, and the National Institutes of Health.

Nonprofit, impartial organizations were also active in promoting labor-management cooperation. Among these were the Institute of Social Research at the University of Michigan, the American Quality of Work Life Center, Work in America Institute, the American Productivity Center, and the Harvard Project on Technology, Work and Character. These organizations received grants from the federal government, private industry, and foundations. They also obtained fees from companies and unions for consulting services, conferences, publications, and research.

Finally, centers were established in various parts of the country to offer services for facilitating cooperation in their geographic areas. Some of the centers were associated with schools of business administration at state universities, as in Maryland, Arizona, Texas, Pennsylvania, and Utah; some were located at schools of industrial relations, as in California, Illinois, Ohio, and New York. The Massachusetts and Michigan centers were set up as nonprofit organizations separate from universities. The boards of directors of the centers usually include members representing business, unions, and the public. As for financing, the federal government provided start-up funds for some centers, while state agencies, unions, private industry, and foundations made additional contributions or paid fees.[18]

NOTES

1. In addition to works by Milton Derber cited in chapter 1, see his "Collective Bargaining: The American Approach to Industrial Democracy," *Annals of the American Academy of Political and Social Science,* May 1977, pp. 83-84. Also pertinent are Milton Derber, W. E. Chalmers, and M. T. Edelman, *Plant Union-Management Relations: From Practice to Theory* (Urbana: University of Illinois Institute of Labor and Industrial Relations, 1965); and William Gomberg, "Special Study Committees," in J. T. Dunlop and N. W. Chamberlain, eds., *Frontiers of Collective Bargaining* (New York: Harper and Row, 1967), pp. 235-251. For items recently covered in negotiated contracts, see *Characteristics of Major Bargaining Agreements, January 1, 1978,* B.L.S. Bulletin 2065, U.S. Department of Labor, April 1980.

2. H. A. Millis and R. E. Montgomery, *Organized Labor* (New York: McGraw-Hill, 1945), p. 465.

3. See S. H. Slichter, *Union Policies and Industrial Management* (Washington: Brookings Institution, 1941), pp. 437-503; L. A. Wood, *Union-Management Cooperation on the Railroads* (New Haven: Yale University Press, 1934); and C. R. Daugherty, *Labor Problems in American Industry* (Boston: Houghton Mifflin, 1936), pp. 580-582.

4. R. C. Nyman and E. D. Smith, *Union-Management Cooperation in the Stretch-Out* (New Haven: Yale University Press, 1934).

5. Dorothea de Schweinitz, *Labor and Management in a Common Enterprise* (Cambridge: Harvard University Press, 1949).

6. H. M. Douty, *The Wage Bargain and the Labor Market* (Baltimore: Johns Hopkins University Press, 1980), pp. 95-96.

7. In addition to sources cited in chapter 1, see G. P. Shultz, "Worker Participation on Production Problems," *Personnel,* November 1951, p. 6.

8. S. H. Slichter, E. R. Livernash, and J. J. Healy, *The Impact of Collective Bargaining on Management* (Washington: Brookings Institution, 1960), p. 82; and R. W. Ahearn, *Positive Labor Relations: Plant Labor-Management Committees and the Collective Bargaining Process,* Buffalo-Erie County Labor-Management Council, April 1978, p. 2.

9. See J. P. Goldberg, "Bargaining and Productivity in the Private Sector," in *Collective Bargaining and Productivity* (Madison: Industrial Relations Research Association, 1975), pp. 15-42; J. J. Healy, ed., *Creative Collective Bargaining: Meeting Today's Challenges to Labor-Management Relations* (Englewood Cliffs: Prentice-Hall, 1965), pp. 137-165; and W. L. Horvitz, "ILWA-PMA Mechanization and Modernization Agreement," in *Proceedings of the Twenty-First Annual Winter Meeting of the Industrial Relations Research Association,* 1968, pp. 144-151.

10. Willard Wirtz, "The Challenge of Free Collective Bargaining," in M. L. Kahn, ed., *Labor Arbitration and Industrial Change* (Washington: Bureau of National Affairs, 1963), p. 300.

11. In addition to works by Goldberg and Healy cited in footnote 9, see G. P. Shultz and A. R. Weber, *Strategies for Displaced Workers* (New York: Harper and Row, 1966); and H. E. Brooks, "The Armour Automation Committee Experience," in *Proceedings of the Twenty-First Annual Winter Meeting of the Industrial Relations Research Association,* 1968, pp. 137-143.

12. See Healy, ed., *Creative Collective Bargaining,* pp. 244-281.

13. Illustrative of the numerous publications of the 1970s are L. E. Davis and A. B. Cherns, eds., *The Quality of Working Life* (New York: The Free Press, 1975); *Worker Alienation,* Hearings before the Subcommittee on Employment, Manpower, and Poverty of the Committee on Labor and Public Welfare, U.S. Senate, July 25-26, 1972; *Alternatives in the World of Work,* National Center for Productivity and Quality of Working Life, Washington, 1976; and C. R. Price, *New Directions in the World of Work: A Conference Report* (Kalamazoo: W. E. Upjohn Institute for Employment Research, 1972).

14. See R. A. Katzell, P. Bienstock, and P. H. Faerstein, *A Guide to Worker Productivity Experiments in the United States, 1971-75* (New York: New York University Press, 1977). This book summarizes 103 projects, most of which are judged to have had a productivity payoff.

15. Illustrative of the literature on work attitudes are Daniel Yankelovich, "Work, Values, and the New Breed," in Clark Kerr and J. M. Rosow, eds., *Work in America: The Decade Ahead* (New York: Van Nostrand Reinhold, 1979), pp. 3-26; idem, "The Meaning of Work," in J. M. Rosow, ed., *The Worker and the Job: Coping with Changes* (Englewood Cliffs: Prentice-Hall, 1974), pp. 19-43; R. A. Katzell, "Changing Attitudes toward Work," in *Work in America: The Decade Ahead,* pp. 35-57; *Work in America: Report of a Special Task Force to the Secretary of Health, Education, and Welfare* (Cambridge: MIT Press, 1973); H. L. Sheppard and N. Q. Herrick, *Where Have All the Robots Gone? Worker Dissatisfaction in the 70s* (New York: Free Press, 1972); George Strauss, "Job Satisfaction, Motivation, and Job Redesign," in *Organizational Behavior: Research and Issues* (Madison: Industrial Relations Research Association, 1974), pp. 19-50.

16. R. P. Quinn and G. L. Staines, *The 1977 Quality of Employment Survey* (Ann Arbor: University of Michigan Institute for Social Research, 1978), p. 210; idem, "American Workers Evaluate the Quality of Their Jobs," *Monthly Labor Review,* January 1979, pp. 3-12; Peter Henle, "Economic Effects: Reviewing the Evidence," in *The Worker and the Job; Coping with Changes,* pp. 119-144; S. A. Levitan and W. B. Johnson, *Work Is Here to Stay, Alas* (Salt Lake City: Olympus, 1973); R. A. Katzell and Daniel Yankelovich, *Work, Productivity and Job Satisfaction* (New York: Psychological Corporation, 1975), p. 13; and Jack Barbash, "Humanizing Work—A New Ideology," *AFL-CIO American Federationist,* July 1977, pp. 8-15.

17. See, for example, *A National Policy for Productivity Improvement,* National Commission on Productivity and Work Quality, Washington, October 1975; and *Directory of Labor Management Committees, 2nd ed.,* National Center for Productivity and Quality of Working Life, Washington, 1978. This widely used *Directory* provides the names, addresses, and phone numbers of over 200 joint committees; such information permits easy communication and exchange by labor and management representatives with their counterparts in other locations. Another of the Center's publications, *Starting a Labor-Management Committee in Your Own Organization: Some Pointers for Action,* Spring 1975, has also been used extensively. The Center and its antecedent Commissions also supported research by William G. Ouchi and others on Japanese managerial practices—research reflected in his recent book, *Theory Z: How American Business Can Meet the Japanese Challenge* (Reading, MA: Addison-Wesley, 1981).

18. For names, addresses, objectives, programs, and publications of major centers, see *Directory of Productivity and Quality of Working Life Centers, 1978,* published by the National Center for Productivity and Quality of Working Life, Washington. A more comprehensive updated list is provided in Appendix C.

6
Company-Level Arrangements: Consultation, Productivity, and Product Quality

As the preceding "swing" chapter anticipated, this one is devoted to labor-management initiatives that are intended primarily to help companies keep or improve their economic vitality. It is concerned with arrangements that aim at continuity of production, higher productivity, or better product quality. In addition to providing general descriptions of such arrangements, it offers a few examples. Material included in the documentary appendix amplifies the discussion.

Joint Consultation

Entities that are formed to facilitate two-way communication in a company or plant are called by various names—e.g., joint consultation committees, joint study committees, plant coordinating councils, or simply labor-management committees. They provide channels for dialogue on matters of mutual interest. Some of these matters require early address; they cannot be disposed of by benign neglect. Timely sharing of opinions or information, informally and at will, can help maintain uninterrupted production.

As entities designed to deal with a wide range of topics acquire experience, they may sharpen their focus and specialize. Thus, they may concentrate, in response to circumstances or emergencies, on such areas as productivity, worklife quality, or health and safety. In such cases, they become indistinguishable from some other committees discussed later in this chapter and in the next one. Another evolutionary variant, to which further reference is made later, is the entrepreneurial team, in which workers share a high-level decisionmaking responsibility with management.

Where Unions Exist

Joint committees can be especially useful in union settings. The opportunity to discuss problems as they arise permits the defusing of potentially explosive situations. Serious grievance and breach-of-contract cases can be diminished in number or avoided during the life of a negotiated agreement. The experience of dialogue, furthermore, may incline both sides to accommodate or compromise more readily the next time they come to the bargaining table.

In a unionized company, a joint consultation committee may be negotiated into existence or be given formal bilateral recognition through a contract clause or through a special letter or memorandum of understanding. Such a legalistic formulation has the added purpose of precluding committee interference in the bargaining process or in the operation of regular grievance machinery. Advocates of cooperation, especially on the union side, are sensitive to the danger that a committee might appear as an alternative to bargaining, rather than as a complement to it.[1]

Nevertheless, the potential effectiveness of a joint consultation committee as an instrument of "prebargaining" or "continuous bargaining" is recognized and welcomed. A committee may contribute to industrial peace by studying complex issues outside the context of deadline bargaining.

These issues may already be included within the purview of bargaining, or they may be expected to become candidates for inclusion. An analysis of 1,536 major bargaining agreements (i.e., covering 1,000 or more workers) by the U.S. Bureau of Labor Statistics in January 1978 found that 62, covering some 340,000 workers altogether, provided for labor-management committees dealing with "industrial relations issues."[2] Among these issues are job classification, contracting-out, fringe benefits, pensions, and equal employment opportunities.

A Federal Contribution

The Federal Mediation and Conciliation Service (FMCS), as noted earlier, has long encouraged joint consultation as a means of reducing the emotional content of labor-management relations. In fiscal year 1979, mediators were involved in establishment or administration of 375 labor-management committees, 36 more than in the preceding fiscal year.[3] This role of "preventive mediation," authorized by the Taft-Hartley Act of 1947, has received high ratings from students of industrial relations.[4]

"Relations by Objective" (RBO), a technique used by FMCS to promote cooperation,[5] involves a step-by-step approach to identification and solution of in-plant problems:

1. The process starts with a mediator's help to each side in proposing what the other side should do to improve relations and in determining what each side could do itself.

2. After such a separate session, a joint meeting is held to discuss opposing views and to develop a mutually agreeable objective. The meeting is attended by all relevant management officials, from top executives down to line supervisors, an., all relevant union officials, down to shop stewards.

3. Separate discussions of the list of agreed-upon objectives then lead to a joint session on "action steps" for

achieving each objective, assignments of responsibility, and a time schedule for achievement.

4. The process culminates in establishment of a consultation committee to continue and extend cooperation.

The consultation committees vary in composition and mode of operation. FMCS recommends that each side have five members of high rank; it also calls for regular monthly meetings, rotation of chairmanship, an advance agenda, and discussion of the agenda, item by item. In practice, some committees are much larger, having as many as 16 members.

Although committee recommendations are only advisory, the inclusion of the plant manager as a member often helps to secure company implementation. Supervisors and rank and file workers usually do not attend committee meetings, but relevant departmental representatives may be invited to particular sessions.

Example: A Minneapolis Newspaper[6]

A provision in the 1972 contract between the Minneapolis Star and Tribune Company and Local 2 of the American Newspaper Guild established a joint Guild-management committee for monthly consultation during company time on working conditions not otherwise covered by contract and grievance machinery. This committee has been used as a forum for discussing subjects ranging from such routine office matters as a shortage of telephones, office temperature, quality of cafeteria food, and eyestrain due to poor lighting to such policy issues as the quality of reporting and the confidentiality of sources. The committee is also consulted on the selection of supervisors below the city editor level.

The 1976 contract expanded the committee's function to include discussion of "matters relative to the introduction and operation of new automated equipment and the effects of such equipment on the job duties of employees who operate such equipment." These matters have subsequently been addressed in collective bargaining negotiations.

A Wisconsin Paper Mill [7]

The establishment of a labor-management committee in 1970 at a paperboard plant employing 80 in Marinette, Wisconsin followed a period of unrest and discontent over the terms of the collective bargaining contract between the company and its Teamsters union local. With the help of an FMCS mediator, a labor-management committee of three management and three union representatives was established to seek solutions to mutual problems before they became formal grievances. Committee discussions have covered such shopfloor problems as early leaving of work stations by employees, scheduling of shift work, and allowance of days off during the deer hunting season. Contract negotiations reportedly have become smoother, with quicker resolution of recognized issues.

A Paper Mill in Michigan [8]

After a six-months strike in 1976 involving 800 hourly employees at its Escanaba, Michigan plant, the Mead Corporation decided to hire a consultant to initiate a "conflict reduction" program. A problem action committee, comprised of about 40 members from management and four union locals was formed. It now meets monthly to discuss and resolve millwide problems, while five departmental subcommittees meet regularly on their own concerns. Consultants have conducted "organizational development" training seminars for committee members. After a year, several concrete results were reported, including revisions of the employee parking system and of grievance procedures, and establishment of a multicraft maintenance trades program. Opinion surveys are conducted; findings are fed back, and the labor relations climate has been greatly improved.

Evaluations

In general, members of joint committees consider their efforts to be productive. They particularly cite a reduction of grievances and the contribution of easier two-way communication to a lessening of frictions and of demoralizing rumor propagation. The fragility of committees, however, is candidly recognized too.

One of the favorable evaluations refers to five cases in which the RBO technique of conflict management was used. The parties achieved progress toward specific goals they had jointly selected.[9] Another survey, addressed to union and management representatives on 26 joint committees in Illinois, found all but four respondents satisfied; they deemed their committees either moderately or very successful, sufficiently so to warrant continuation.[10]

On the other hand, joint consultation committees are admittedly vulnerable to both apathy and continuing conflict over fundamental issues of economics and power. One investigator, who had studied 38 committees, found frequent complaint regarding absence of commitment to common goals and only perfunctory attendance at meetings. He also noted a "spillover" of attitudes and issues of the bargaining table. Effectiveness, according to participants in the 38 committees, depended not only on the degree of problem solving behavior of the numbers but also on the strength of outside pressures, the relative strengths of union and management in bargaining power, support from the top, the educational level of the workforce, and length of experience in collective bargaining.[11]

From the foregoing, it is not difficult to conclude that prolonged and sharp disagreements between the two parties on wages, fringes, and layoffs could provide occasion for terminating a committee as well as for establishing one. Not everywhere or at every time are the parties ready to adjust their adversarial imperatives to the constructive potentials of joint problem solving. The necessary "attitude restructuring" could be induced by overriding economic necessity. It would help, perhaps, if schooling in group dynamics and organization development were part of the background of persons already skilled in the arts of negotiation and bargaining.[12]

Bilateral recognition of the need for attitudinal change is only the first step toward accomplishing such change. When the two sides have undergone such change, they are readier to form an effective committee. In 1978, the National Center for Productivity and Quality of Working Life distilled 10 points for guiding the formation of effective committees on the basis of discussions with participants. The first point says:

> The parties have a mature, open relationship. Each is willing to listen to the other side. Both agree to concentrate on finding answers to problems at hand and discovering opportunities for collaboration.[13]

The other nine points are shown in the documentary appendix.

Joint Productivity Committees

Like consultation committees that start or remain concerned with general purposes, production or productivity committees aim at maintaining or improving a company's competitiveness—its survivability and profitability. While engineers have traditionally shouldered the explicit responsibility to look after production and productivity, it has also been evident over the years that workers have relevant "know-how," acquired by experience, for reducing waste and otherwise cutting costs. Ample testimony has been recorded on this point. Here is an illustrative statement on the hidden reserves to be tapped in appropriate circumstances, a statement by a graduate of Yale Law School who spent five months working in a Western Electric factory:

> I am certain that workers could increase production if they wanted to. Workers are ingenious at finding short cuts to beat rates set by production engineers. Factory workers, not surprisingly, know a great deal about their own jobs. They have a reservoir of knowledge that is underutilized, since little in the current work structure encourages workers to share their knowledge. There is some sharing among workers but the knowledge is usually withheld from management. Management is aware of this and hopes that instituting changes in the environment and jobs will make workers more receptive to sharing what they know.[14]

Through joint productivity committees, management could benefit from employee knowledge of virtually costless ways to improve company performance. Such a prospect ought to be especially attractive in an inflation-ravaged economy of high interest rates and uncertainty about the near term and longer term business outlook. Furthermore, labor-management cooperation is good, whenever and on whatever topic it can be achieved, in the interest of continuity of operations with less turnover and less emotional stress.

Unlike management, workers and unions are troubled by mention of the work "productivity" in connection with joint undertakings. The word still commonly stirs up images of speedup, skill erosion, and labor displacement. A Gallup poll of 800 working adults in 1980 revealed that most expected relatively little benefit to people like themselves from "improved performance and productivity."[15] A 1974 Yankelovich survey of union officials showed a preference for redefining "productivity" incorrectly—to shift emphasis from output-input ratios to productivity-related ideas deemed less threatening to workers, i.e., to higher output quality and to the reduction of waste, absenteeism, and turnover.[16] Nevertheless, they largely agreed that "it is possible for the union and management to cooperate on specific programs which will improve productivity."

The numerical evidence available, referring to firms that have unions and employ 1,000 or more workers, does not reflect any strong movement there to establish formal programs. The 1978 Bureau of Labor Statistics analysis cited earlier disclosed that only 83 out of a total of 1,536 major collective bargaining agreements provided for labor-management committees on productivity—committees that "meet periodically to discuss in-plant production problems and to work out methods of improving the quantity and quality of production." The 83 agreements covered about 1.3 million workers, more than half of whom were concentrated in the automobile and steel industries.[17] Furthermore, they accounted for many, many more than 83 committees, as the following remarks, confined to steel, will indicate.

Steel Productivity Committees

The declining fortunes of the steel industry and its bleak prospects of recovery led in 1971, and again in 1974, 1977, and 1980, to provisions for collaboration in the bargaining agreements. In 1971, plant committees were formed to advise management on ways to raise efficiency and to promote the use of domestic steel. In 1974, the entities were called "employment security and plant productivity committees." An overarching industrywide joint committee was also established.[18]

About 230 joint productivity committees were said to be in operation in 1974, but many apparently existed only on paper. From the very start, the efficacy of the approach was doubtful because of poor preparation, uneven and insufficient commitment at the plant level, and suspicions felt by each party that the committee format was being used for purposes incompatible with the negotiated contract.[19] Another adverse factor was the resistance of workers in the Chicago region to the program, in defiance of the national leadership. The Chicago faction lost its fight against the Experimental Negotiating Agreement and other national policies of accommodation in the decisive 1977 election.

In the 1980 contract, the employment security and productivity committees were replaced by a system of labor-management participation committees and teams.[20] These would operate at plant and mill floor levels and deal with a wide range of job-related issues. They are intended to assure the teamwork essential to the smooth flow of goods in process from one stage of production to the next. An important departure from the earlier initiative is that the local union and the plant manager are free to participate in the program or stay out. They are not obliged by a central office to become involved. In addition, the program is conceived as experimental, to be continued or discontinued after a three-year trial.

The 1980 plan envisaged two tiers of organization. At the department level or below, "participation teams" would function; on the plant level, a "participation committee" would provide coordination. The teams are authorized to "discuss, consider, and decide" issues relating to the use of equipment, the quality of output and of the work environment, safety and health, scheduling and reporting, absenteeism and overtime, incentives, job alignments, contracting out, energy conservation, and transportation pools.

Both supervisory and production worker members of the teams must agree on all decisions. In the event of disagreement, trade-off bargaining is contemplated—a nice acknowledgment of the complementarity of the cooperative and adversary principles. The teams are authorized to make proposals concerning bonus payments and changes in the incentive scale. They cannot, however, alter terms of the basic contract or interfere with the grievance machinery.

Although company and union headquarters may designate plants to be considered for the experimental program, the final decision is local. A joint review commission will, upon request, provide assistance to plant committees or teams. The international union representative will provide for exchange of information among locals and evaluate the plan's performance. As was noted in the opening chapter, training has begun for teams set up at selected plants on a trial basis; and, as has so often been reported, "the biggest problem" is to teach first line supervisors to "listen to the suggestions of workers instead of merely barking orders."

Examples of "Entrepreneurial Participation"

A variant of the joint production or productivity committee features the involvement of workers in organizational decisionmaking—i.e., above the job or bench level. In the interest of job security, they may cooperate in matters relating to plant layout, product design, or marketing. So-called "entrepreneurial teams" include these workers with managers in task forces aiming at specific objectives.[21]

In Jamestown, one such in-plant team has contributed to the area's job development program by helping its own sponsor. A small shop making hospital equipment was the site of a deal between labor and management to cooperate in a quest for new products needed to keep the staff of 200 workers or, still better, to increase their number. Management agreed to avoid short term layoffs, and the union, a local of the International Association of Machinists, agreed to help improve productivity and product quality. When an opportunity arose to bid on a new product, the management proposed to the joint committee that an *ad hoc* task force of experienced workers and the industrial engineers should take responsibility for preparing a bid. The resulting bid was significantly below those of competitors, and a contract was won for a new product representing about 30 jobs.[22] Unfortunately, this cooperative arrangement has not survived a change in company leadership.

A second example of "entrepreneurial participation" refers to a plant of the Carborundum Corporation that had about 400 employees making cast refractories for the glass industry. The plant manager called on the 12-member labor-management committee, which normally meets bimonthly to consider production problems, quality control, and safety, to work with an engineering consulting firm on the revision of plant layout. The committee solicited employee opinions through small group meetings on company time in each department and shift. The information thus obtained was used in recommendations on machinery placement, materials flow, etc. in redesign and expansion of the facility.[23]

Effectiveness: Yes, But —

As in the case of joint consultation, members of productivity committees generally testify favorably on their experience, but it is obvious that the realization of significant productivity benefits requires strong commitment of both parties. Directly traceable benefits are often difficult to assay, and they could easily be outweighed by the indirect contributions of cooperation through improved communications and labor-management relations. A study of the records of 262 meetings of employees and managers in a unionized foundry over the period 1969-1975 concluded that the productivity impact of a worker participation program was positively associated with the degree of active involvement on both sides and was probably greater than that derivable from a group bonus plan linked to productivity.[24]

Although rare in the literature, case studies of failed productivity committees would also be instructive; they would underscore the fragility of the cooperative process and the strains that often destroy it, such as the rejection of new ideas by management, union indifference to a plant's competitive position, and the chilling spillover effect of conflict over contract issues. The experience of the steel industry with the committees established under the 1974 agreement should not be ignored.

Quality Control

Japanese successes in productivity and marketing in such important export industries as automobiles, steel, and electronic products created a surge of interest in the 1970s in the structure and operation of quality control circles. The creative and prolific use of statistical quality control—a system developed in the United States and brought to Japan by American consultants after World War II—was widely credited with a major share of the responsibility for transforming a nation once identified with low-quality goods into a formidable competitor, even on our own turf.

Because the statistical technique has American roots and because of the demonstrated ability of the Japanese to integrate it so effectively into their own system of production, the superficial conclusion has often been drawn that the Japanese quality control circle is really acultural and is readily duplicable elsewhere. Sight should not be lost, however, of continuing high esteem in Japanese society for pre-industrial institutions and values, such as the stable family, respect for authority, conformity, loyalty, and reciprocity. In the business world, these values translate into a preference for lifetime employment with a major firm, managerial paternalism and worker conscientiousness, progression by age, low absenteeism, and so forth. In the United States, where status has largely been displaced by contract, it is hard to imagine literal adoption of the Japanese quality circle, as distinguished from adaptation without significant reshaping by the adversary principle, independent unionism, and collective bargaining. If transplantation were easy, competitive imitation would surely have led to adoption and adaptation on a much grander scale than we have yet seen.

Quality control circles were actually first introduced in 1962, and a national movement to propagate them throughout the productive system was spearheaded by the Japanese Union of Scientists and Engineers (JUSE). Much preparatory work had been done in the preceding decade, beginning with the missionary work of W. E. Deming and Joseph Juran, who helped train thousands of company directors, managers, and supervisors in the concept and application of quality control.[25] They also helped to establish the principle of total quality control, requiring all employees, not only engineers, to assume responsibility for quality and to take training , accordingly, in statistical quality control. By 1980, about 600,000 quality control circles were in operation in Japan; over 6 million employees, or about 12 percent of the labor force, were members.[26] A reader who is impatient with the American "lag" in following the Japanese example should ponder this paragraph and reflect on the dominant characteristics of our people, industry, and society and on the long interval between the Deming lectures and action, even in Japan.

American Programs

Even before the Japanese phenomenon gripped popular fancy in the United States, some smaller firms here were experimenting with participative shopfloor "circles" intended to raise quality of output while also improving job satisfaction and productivity. Critical emphasis was not placed, however, on a particular statistical approach. The impetus was provided by the same indigenous managerial philosophies that have animated other joint programs described in this book: the worker is a person, not just a source of "labor power," and the more fully his capabilities are enlisted in the workplace and the more fully his aspirations are served there, the better will be his performance.

In 1972, directly inspired by the Japanese example, the Lockheed Missile and Space Company started a quality circle program that attracted wide attention in American industry. Lockheed's experience stimulated other aerospace companies to follow suit. The diffusion was aided by the availability of managers who had organized the Lockheed program as consultants to other firms. It has been estimated that, by 1981, 2,000 to 3,000 quality control circles were operating in the United States[27]—a trivial number compared to Japan's total, and also frequently different in character.

Quality control circles commonly have about 10 volunteers from the same work group who meet weekly, biweekly, or monthly for one hour on company time.[28] Headed by a supervisor or a senior employee, the participants identify, and discuss remedies for, problems of product or service quality. These problems may involve, say, rejects or customer complaints. Proposed remedies are implementable by management upon approval.

A distinctive feature of a real quality control circle is that the participants, as in Japan, are explicitly trained in the theory and practice of problem analysis and solution (including the use of Pareto diagrams, histograms, and other devices familiar to the industrial engineer). The group leaders also receive instruction in leadership, communication, and adult training methods. A company "facilitator" plays a vital role in organizing the circles and providing initial orientation.

While many employees prize highly the opportunity to use their talents more fully and to make presentations to company officers, monetary rewards are not overlooked as incentives for continuing participation. A suggestion that results in substantial savings may rate a cash award under the company suggestion program, but all members of the circle share equally.

The Westinghouse Program[29]

In the spring of 1978, Westinghouse Corporation decided to use quality control circles at its Defense and Electronics Systems center in Baltimore. The word "control" was dropped from the title of the program (to eliminate the possible connotation of coercion), and the program was placed under manufacturing operations rather than under conventional quality assurance.

The new program required intensive orientation. Top executives were included in this effort, as well as middle managers and line supervisors. The leaders of the three unions representing hourly and salaried workers were informed about the aims and nature of the program and assured that their roles as representatives of employees in disputes over contractual matters and working conditions were not under challenge.

Training for supervisors and employees is an important element of the Westinghouse program. Each circle leader or supervisor was given an intensive two-day course in group problem solving. Next, all employees in work units where supervisors had volunteered to be circle leaders were introduced to quality control concepts and invited to become circle members. Ten volunteers from each unit were selected for one-hour training sessions over a period of six to eight weeks. Among the topics covered was the use of various measurement techniques familiar to industrial engineers for pinpointing product defects.

Westinghouse is satisfied with results. Only seven circles were formed when the program started in 1978. By 1981, the number had risen to 60. The favorable experience at the Defense and Electronic Systems Center has persuaded top management to extend the concept to the rest of the company's operations.

Benefits and Barriers

Whenever substantial benefits are claimed for change in industrial practice (in this instance, the introduction and use of quality control circles), two questions are appropriate. First, how do the realized benefits compare to the costs entailed in operating the installed program? Second, while the change is under contemplation, how do the expected benefits compare to the expected costs? Both of these questions involve reckoning in nonmonetary, as well as monetary, terms; and the nonmonetary reckoning is subjective, unpredictably different for labor and management and for the people who comprise these two categories.

Companies that have had satisfactory results with quality circles cite monetary and nonmonetary net gains, direct and indirect. At the end of its first three years of experience with quality circles, Lockheed estimated that the savings of the program were about four times the cost of operating it.[30] An attitude survey conducted at Westinghouse found unanimous support for continuation and extension of the circle program. In addition to the accomplishment of their explicit primary purpose, circles are credited with contributions to higher productivity, better methods of production, improved communications and morale, greater safety, fuller utilization of worker capabilities, and development of leadership skills transferable to other settings.

What about the second question, which is more important to the future of the quality circle movement in the United States? Despite the enthusiasms of "agents of change," those who have to carry the costs of change are cautious with good reason. These costs are, as already suggested, psychological and institutional, as well as financial. Labor and management are usually inclined to keep a *status quo* they understand; they, in Hamlet's words, would "rather bear those ills we have than fly to others that we know not of." Managers fear loss of authority, and unions commonly suspect that cooperative endeavors not originating with them could lure workers away in addition to yielding productivity gains in which workers do not sufficiently share. The costs of uncertainty and of power redistribution are reducible in some measure by advance cooperation of a company and a union in the planning of a program and in the selection of areas of most promising application. In the automobile and aerospace industries, this wise course has been pursued.

NOTES

1. *Labor-Management Committee: Planning for Progress,* Federal Mediation and Conciliation Service, Washington, 1977, pp. 16-17; and *Recent Initiatives in Labor-Management Cooperation,* National Center for Productivity and Quality of Working Life, Washington, 1976, p. 7.

2. *Characteristics of Major Collective Bargaining Agreements, January 1, 1978,* Bulletin 2065, U.S. Bureau of Labor Statistics, Washington, April 1980, p. 25.

3. *Thirty-Second Annual Report, Fiscal Year 1979,* Federal Mediation and Conciliation Service, p. 28. See documentary appendix for FMCS sample committee bylaws and contract.

4. C. L. Bowen, "Preventive Mediation," *Proceedings of the Twenty-First Annual Winter Meeting of the Industrial Relations Research Association,* 1968, pp. 160-164; and *Report and Recommendations,* National Committee on Industrial Peace, Washington, 1974, pp. 6-7.

5. J. J. Popular, "Relationships by Objective," in J. A. Loftus and Beatrice Walfish, *Breakthrough in Union-Management Cooperation* (Scarsdale: Work in America Institute, 1977), pp. 40-43.

6. *Directory of Labor-Management Committees (Spring 1978),* National Center for Productivity and Quality of Working Life, p. 79.

7. *Recent Initiatives,* pp. 25-27.

8. *Labor-Management Committees,* p. 65.

9. D. T. Hoyer, "A Program of Conflict Management: An Exploratory Approach," in *Proceedings of the Thirty-Second Annual Meeting of the Industrial Relations Research Association,* 1980, pp. 334-335.

10. Milton Derber and Kevin Flanagan, *A Survey of Joint Labor-Management Cooperation Committees in Unionized Private Enterprises in the State of Illinois, 1979, Part One* (Urbana: University of Illinois Institute of Labor and Industrial Relations, 1980), pp. 22-23.

11. J. W. Driscoll, *Labor-Management Committees in the U.S.: A National Survey* (Cambridge: Massachusetts Institute of Technology Sloan School of Management, 1979), p. 6.

12. *Ibid.,* p. 11.

13. *Starting a Labor-Management Committee in Your Organization: Some Pointers for Action,* National Center for Productivity and Quality of Working Life, Washington, 1978, ii.

14. Richard Balzer, *Clockwork: Life Inside and Outside an American Factory* (Garden City, NY: Doubleday, 1976), p. 328.

15. R. H. Clarke and J. R. Morris, *Workers' Attitudes toward Productivity,* Chamber of Commerce of the United States, Washington, 1980, p. 13.

16. R. A. Katzell, Daniel Yankelovich, and Associates, *Work, Productivity, and Job Satisfaction* (New York: The Psychological Corporation, 1975), p. 103.

17. See p. 35 of BLS report cited in footnote 2.

18. I. W. Abel, *Employment Security and Plant Productivity Committees: Ten Coordinating Steel Companies,* National Commission on Productivity and Work Quality, Washington, 1974, p. 2; and *The Joint Advisory Committee on Productivity,* United Steelworkers of America, AFL-CIO, Pittsburgh, 1971.

19. *Industry Week,* December 6, 1971; and *Recent Initiatives,* pp. 9-16.

20. For details of the new agreement and the experimental cooperation program, see documentary appendix. For progress under the agreement, see *Business Week,* July 29, 1981, pp. 132-136.

21. J. C. Eldred and Associates, "Worker Participation in Problem Solving—Community and Entrepreneurial Variations on a Theme," a paper presented at the 31st Annual Technical Conference of the American Society for Quality Control, Philadelphia, May 16-18, 1977.

22. *Ibid.,* pp. 5-6.

23. *Recent Initiatives in Labor-Management Cooperation, Vol. II,* (Washington: National Center for Productivity and Quality of Working Life, 1978), pp. 35-44.

24. R. D. Rosenberg and Eliezer Rosenstern, "Participation and Productivity: An Empirical Study," *Industrial and Labor Relations Review,* April 1980, pp. 355-367.

25. R. E. Cole, "Learning from the Japanese: Prospects and Pitfalls," *Management Review,* September 1980, pp. 22-42; and J. M. Juran, "International Significance of the QC Circle Movement," *Quality Progress,* November 1980, pp. 18-22.

26. Information supplied by Joji Arai, Japan Productivity Center, Washington.

27. Dudley Lynch, "Circling up Japanese Style," *American Way,* April 1981, p. 36.

28. W. S. Riecker, "Quality Control (QC) Circles—Tapping the Creative Power of the Workforce," in *Proceedings of the American Institute of Industrial Engineers 1976 Systems Engineering Conference,* pp. 90-94; R. E. Cole, "Made in Japan—Quality Control Circles," *Across the Board,* November 1979, pp. 72-78; and *Quality Control Circles: A Practical Guide* (Stamford: Productivity, Inc., 1981).

29. G. E. Swartz and V. C. Comstock, "One Firm's Experience with Quality Circles, *Quality Progress,* September 1979, pp. 14-16.

30. Riecker, "Quality Control (QC) Circles," p. 94.

7
Company-Level Arrangements: Worker Satisfaction, Well-Being, and Security

Roughly speaking, we may say that the arrangements treated in this chapter are *worker* oriented in the first instance, while those considered in the preceding chapter were *company* oriented in the first instance. The phrase "in the first instance" is not gratuitous; it is meant to imply a "second instance" in which something needs to happen if cooperation is to prove successful. Elaboration of this point follows.

A program intended, say, to enhance the quality of working life (QWL), to increase worker participation, or to "humanize" work ought also to offer some positive incidental payoff to a company, whether or not this prospect is initially advertised. This ulterior payoff may be an improvement in intracompany communication, in the climate of industrial relations, in rates of absenteeism and turnover, in efficiency of operations, or in product quality. Similarly, a program intended in the first instance to meet company needs of the kind just cited ought also to hold forth the likelihood of financial or other benefit to the worker in the shorter or longer run. Accordingly, many of the arrangements described below and in the preceding chapter ac-

139

quire a strong family resemblance as the total benefits to the two parties, immediate and ulterior, are taken into account.

This convergence is basic to successul cooperation. Each party should expect a benefit to accrue to the other as well as to itself; indeed, it should welcome this "double plus," since mutuality is a more dependable foundation for effective collaboration than is altruism or selfishness. An untempered adversary spirit is shortsighted in its indifference to the complementarity of benefits, in its aspiration simply for a gain to itself that leaves the other party to accommodate and to cope. This spirit is shortsighted in making demands for "rights" without also recognizing "duties" or "obligations," which really stand for the rights and benefits to which the second party and the public may reasonably feel entitled.

Adversarial language is often used as a face-saving cloak or disguise by labor or management as either takes tentative first steps toward cooperation. The tempering of the adversary spirit cannot always be comfortably conceded as awareness of the potential benefit of collaboration dawns. Whatever language is used, the most viable and rewarding of joint ventures are those that frankly seek benefits for both parties from the outset.[1]

Quality of Working Life

The term "quality of working life" (QWL) pays a price for popularity. The more widely it is used, like the term "productivity," the less definite is its meaning. It is used interchangeably with "humanization of work," "work reform," "work redesign," and "work improvement." It is too frequently used loosely to characterize almost any joint program that requires a committee, but it ought to be confined to joint ventures that in the first instance aim at satisfying workers' desires or needs for restructuring of the workplace.

This restructuring should allow greater participation in decisionmaking on the job, constructive interaction with one's fellows, and opportunity for personal development and self-realization.

The writings of many industrial psychologists, sociologists, and management theorists have inspired piecemeal efforts toward work reform (e.g., job enrichment and sensitivity training for foremen) without, however, offering a new integrated vision of work improvement, which is the original hallmark of QWL. According to one of the leading spokesmen of the QWL movement, "the systemic redesign of work systems involves the way tasks are packaged into jobs, the way workers relate to each other, the way performance is measured and rewards are made available, the way positions of authority and status symbols are structured, the way career paths are conceived."[2] Two other students of the participative "work culture" emphasize that a program of significant work improvement

requires a climate and structure that differs from the traditional hierarchical organization. It calls for an open style of management, such that information is shared and challenges or suggestions related to improving the existing *modus operandi* are genuinely encouraged. It also requires expeditious, respectful and appropriate responses to inputs of those kinds. Finally, it requires that the QWL improvements not be imposed from the top down. Rather it calls for a partnership between management people and representatives chosen by non-management people—or in unionized situations a coequal union-management structure—for planning, developing, and implementing the agreed-upon process and program. . . . Such a participative and responsive style of management provides a springboard from which a large variety of improvements in the design, structure and organization of work can be developed.[3]

From statements such as these, which are only two of very many that could be quoted, it is easy to anticipate frequent disappointment of expectations. Despite best laid plans, piecemeal improvement is far more probable than a holistic reconstruction of the work system within a relatively short period. Without prior preparation of a relationship of deep trust on both sides, the realization of any integrated cooperative vision is most unlikely; so the usual practical question is really how to develop that trust, no matter what collaborative scheme one has in mind. Furthermore, it is well to recognize that the worker may not be as dismayed by the current limitations of the workplace as the sociologist who cannot imagine himself in the same setting; and that the worker does not concentrate his total life on the work relationship, but may wholesomely regard the economic nexus as a means to consumption off the job, in leisure at home or in a tavern, with family, friends, television, etc. All things considered, perhaps a sound enough guide to what QWL means is provided in a definition included in a news report of an international conference that ended in Toronto in early September 1981: "many forms of new work organizations . . . involving workers in shop-floor decisions through problem-solving committees."[4]

Two Decades of Growing Interest

Experimental QWL projects initiated in the 1960s attracted wide attention in North America, United Kingdom, and Scandinavia. Europe is commonly regarded to have led the way. The principal techniques tested in the experiments of the 1960s required changes in the division of labor: the introduction of self-managed, autonomous work teams that take collective responsibility for performing a set of tasks; the organization of simple tasks into more complex wholes requiring more knowledge and skill; and the use of flexible assignment patterns, such as progressive movement of workers from one set of tasks to the next in order to master an increasing segment of the work of a team.[5]

In the 1970s, QWL experiments were started at the manufacturing plants of a number of large U.S. corporations. The plants, however, were not among the biggest, and newer ones were well represented. Two researchers have estimated that, between 1970 and 1976, 75-90 projects had been set up, mostly in nonunion plants of fewer than 500 employees. Of these, 25-30 were begun in new settings, where established work procedures did not have to be overcome.[6]

In addition to background factors cited for rising interest in QWL in the 1960s, corporate executives were responding in the 1970s to concerns over flagging productivity. Union leaders at the top tended to cling to their preference for bargaining as the best way to improve the work environment, but less rigidity was evident down the line. A survey conducted by Cornell researchers in 1975 showed that 63 percent of 211 local labor leaders and union activists favored joint action with management on QWL issues, while 52 percent favored a joint approach on productivity issues, and only 23 percent favored joint programs on traditional bargaining issues (e.g., wages, fringe benefits, hours, and job security).[7] In 1979, conferees from 20 international unions expressed a need for more challenge, satisfaction, and recognition in work; for more training within the union at all levels and more sharing of experience; and, above all, for greater union initiative in stimulating, planning, and implementing QWL improvement programs lest management act alone anyway.[8]

Few major labor figures have endorsed the view of a vice-president of the United Auto Workers that improvement of QWL "is essentially an extension of the basic goals of unionism."⁹ Nevertheless, some unions did, in the 1970s, cooperate with management to establish joint QWL projects, regarding such participation pragmatically as an adjunct to collective bargaining. Most notable for size and influence were the programs set up in the automobile, steel, and telephone industries (see Appendix A).

Symptomatic of the growing interest in QWL is the contrast between attendance at the Toronto conference in 1981 and attendance at the first international meeting at Harriman, New York in 1972. On this earlier occasion, delegates numbered 50, mostly from universities. In 1981, delegates numbered more than 1,500; and, of these, 200 were unionists and 750 represented management. Although labor participation in such meetings has usually been scant, this was not the case at Toronto. Local officers from the automobile industry were especially evident: "More than 80 union and company officials from Ford Motor Company alone were at the conference," a reflection of the fact that joint QWL efforts of varying levels were under way in about 100 manufacturing and assembly plants."¹⁰

General Motors Experience

Having just mentioned Ford, we should go on to consider the joint national program started by General Motors and UAW in 1973. This program originated out of a common concern about employee discontent with working conditions that could not be resolved through normal machinery of collective bargaining.

Union and management had long ago agreed that productivity improvement was a "sound and mutually beneficial objective." The contractual provision for an annual improvement factor, first introduced in 1948, stated that this wage gain "depends on technological progress, better tools, methods, processes, and equipment, and a cooperative attitude on the part of all parties in such progress." Management decisions on issues affecting productivity (such as the pace of the line), job security, health and safety, and shift work were often a source of disputes, but these could be resolved in the process of collective bargaining and grievance settlement.[11] But low morale and discontent with the work environment (reflected in high rates of absenteeism and turnover and in wildcat strikes that especially impeded productivity on production lines involving sequential operations) continued to trouble both the company and the union.

Experiments to improve communication were launched in the early 1970s by the director of organizational research and development, but without union participation. In 1973, at the UAW's request, a two-tiered arrangement for union-management cooperation at the national and local levels was formally established in a memorandum of agreement in the national contract.[12] This arrangement included a National Committee to Improve the Quality of Worklife, with two officials of the international union and two personnel officers. It operated as a catalyst in creating interest among local plant managers and union officials and providing information on the meaning and implications of the QWL concept; and it also monitored and evaluated local projects. The arrangement included a second tier at the local level: the union "shop committee" (which handled grievances and bargaining) plus local management. At this level, the groundwork was laid for pilot QWL projects; a climate of mutual respect was developed, and a commitment of both sides to the QWL concept was promoted. Instead of a separate QWL committee, the union shop committee was used to avoid "any conflict in determining which subjects fall within the purview of adversarial collective bargaining and which are subject to the cooperative effort of quality of worklife."[13]

As distrust lessened, both parties proceeded to organize pilot projects involving workers on a voluntary basis in problem solving and in decisionmaking with regard to the workplace. The guidelines, usually agreed upon in advance, assured that workers in the projects would not be subject to speedup or layoff and that the national bargaining agreement would not be violated. Third-party consultants, usually employed at company expense, facilitated establishment and operation of the projects.

Over 50 QWL projects have been started in General Motors-UAW bargaining units throughout the nation. The specific designs vary from plant to plant, according to the concerns and objectives of local unions and managements. The program has expanded steadily since 1973 despite several changes in top management.

A highly successful project was organized in 1975 at the Tarrytown, New York car assembly plant, which had one of the poorest records of labor relations and production in GM and was in danger of being shut down. With the support of top management and UAW officials, plant managers and officers of Local 664 undertook joint exploration and discussion of common goals. The upshot was participation of employees in planning a major plant rearrangement and in organizing a joint training program in team problem solving. By 1979, nearly all 3,600 employees had voluntarily participated. The program was followed by intense exchange of ideas among workers, supervisors, and technical people in the most efficient ways of setting up jobs on the assembly line to produce a radically new automobile model. After an investment of $1.6 million, both management and union believe that successful worker involvement will yield enormous long term advantages. The organizational benefits already derived—in efficiency, cost savings, lower absenteeism, and fewer grievances—are reported to be substantial.

The demonstration that QWL could work in an auto assembly plant stimulated other producers in the troubled industry to engage in joint projects with UAW. At Ford, a plant-level program similar to GM's was launched in 1980 under the guidance of a National Joint Committee on Employee Involvement (EI). The agenda of local EI committees included product quality as well as workers' attendance and worklife quality. By 1981, company and union spokesmen were already able to report significant gains in product quality.[14]

QWL at Harman International[15]

The Work Improvement Program at Harman International Industries, Inc. attracted considerable professional and media attention in the early 1970s as a pioneer experiment in cooperation at a unionized plant. Previous QWL experiments had taken place in nonunion settings, so one goal at Harman was to create a model acceptable to unions. Located at Bolivar, in a rural section of west Tennessee, the Harman plant employed about 1,000 workers in the production of auto mirrors under a collective bargaining agreement with the United Auto Workers.

The original impetus and plan for the project came from the company president, the UAW vice president, and a leading QWL consultant. All were strongly committed to an experiment in restructuring the work of the entire plant in accord with four principles—"job security, equity, worker democracy, and individuation." This commitment at the top was recognized as essential for the required substantial changes in attitudes, organization, and management practices.

A "shelter agreement" protected workers from possible adverse effects. The company and the union stated that "the purpose is not to increase productivity. If increased productivity is a by-product of the program, ways of rewarding the employees . . . will become legitimate matter for inclusion in the program." Funds from foundations, government agencies, and the company enabled employment of a team of behavioral scientists for technical assistance to both sides. In many circles, the whole program was regarded as idealistic and academic.

A committee including plant managers and local union leaders was set up to oversee the design of specific work improvements by small core groups of workers and foremen. In one instance, a core group decided that a task could be accomplished more quickly through teamwork; management agreed not to raise the production standard and allowed workers who finished early to go home. Another cooperative project involved union and management participation in establishing efficiency rates. Still other projects focused on worker participation in bidding on a particular product; in-plant training; and internal communication.

The progress of the Bolivar experiment was closely studied by University of Michigan researchers over a six-year period. They found that jobs became more secure; that productivity and product quality improved; that accidents decreased at a faster rate than the industry average; that minor accidents and short term absences due to illness declined, while minor illnesses increased; that machine downtime increased; and that employee earnings held steady. Some indicators of work satisfaction showed declines, but others indicated gains or showed no change. A large proportion of the employees did, however, express satisfaction with the QWL program, its impact, and their union's effectiveness in representing their concerns.

Rushton Coal Mine

A QWL project was started in 1973 at a small coal mine of the Rushton Company, employing 180 workers, in north central Pennsylvania. It was developed by a joint labor-management committee with the guidance of a team of university experts.[16] The president of the company had become interested in finding a system for giving miners more responsibility, autonomy, and influence over how they did their job; his aim was to attract younger workers to Rushton in the future. The president of the United Mine Workers endorsed the project since it was also concerned with improving safety conditions and practices. Because of its broad implications, the federal government provided the initial funding for the research team.

The experiment involved major restructuring of the way mine work was performed. Five goals were established: safety, increased productivity, higher earnings,   greater job skills, and greater job satisfaction. An experimental section was established in the mine with 27 volunteers, 9 to a shift. Responsibility for daily production and direction was assigned to the crew instead of to the foreman, whose primary responsibilities became safety and coordination. The crew, in effect, became an autonomous work group. Each member of the experimental crew was expected to learn the jobs of his fellow workers. All received the same top rate of pay since they could perform multiple tasks. A major part of the change effort was a training program on safety, ventilation, roof control, and the requirements of new legislation. Day-to-day oversight of the experiment was performed by a small joint group.

Intensive evaluation of the first 18 months of the experiment by an independent team of behavioral scientists found several positive gains: significantly fewer safety violations, increased jobs skills, higher pay, strong team spirit, greater feeling of responsibility, more interest in work, and more communication (vertical and horizontal). Productivity did not significantly increase, nor were labor-management relations improved. Supervisors and middle managers suffered increased stress, and conflict within the union over pay differentials broke out.

From the mine operator's point of view, the experiment proved the feasibility of a new form of work organization.

Despite a close negative vote by union membership, he decided to extend the system to the entire mine in 1976. Although the experiment continues at the Rushton mine, it has so far had no imitators in the industry.

Pros and Cons

General appraisals of the outcomes of experiments in work restructuring reveal the expected kinds of benefits, but cautions should also be observed. First, the good news reported in an assessment of 25 cases:

> Increases in productivity seem to result from about half the projects, while in the other half no change occurs. Most of them seem to create more skilled and flexible workforces. Most projects also seem to result in increases in job satisfaction and in feelings of personal growth, job involvement and organizational commitment. Absenteeism, turnover and lateness of arrival at work seem to be very much reduced with most of the projects; this tallies with the finding that job satisfaction increases.[17]

Another favorable evaluation, based on 36 projects, found them distributed "along a broad spectrum of effectiveness," but concluded that "the average effectiveness of these innovative work systems is higher than the average of more conventionally organized but otherwise comparable plants."[18]

Now, the bad news. A leading QWL researcher has emphasized the fragility of the new work systems. His review of various projects in operation at least five years disclosed that they, too, eventually succumbed, despite initial success. Among the causes of failure were the loss of key sponsors, conflict between organizational elements inside and outside the QWL project, insufficient commitment in the company as a whole, and decline through time in the attractiveness of available rewards and in the pristine excitement of novelty.[19]

Mention was made earlier of the wariness of labor, so it is appropriate to add that managers at the plant level also have doubts and qualms. A study of work restructuring projects in eight firms found managers concerned about possible deterioration of relations with labor, the high cost in terms of managerial time and effort, the risk of raising expectations of benefits that could not be sustained, and the exploitation of experimental results in the process of collective bargaining. Although first line supervisors recognized that they might continue to play a constructive role if they had been involved in the design of a project, they were fearful of loss of authority or of their jobs.[20]

At this juncture, it is well to observe that not all nonsupervisory employees would necessarily welcome the graduation of a QWL experiment to a plantwide norm. Many workers do not mind routine jobs under the present dispensation and would regard the changes required in the name of work improvement to be unduly stressful. For a majority of workers, the center of gravity of life does not lie in the shop; money income remains a very potent salve for the subcritical bruises endured by the psyche in the usual, less-than-ideal workplace.

Resistance to change from current systems of work is very evident in the startup phase of a new QWL project. Two researchers who have studied the dynamics of 10 such undertakings found that "the existing negative forces in a workplace are usually stronger than the forces that favor joint projects."[21] The obstacles include insufficient knowledge and experience; lack of a clear model appropriate to company conditions; threats to entrenched status and authority; uncertain impact on collective bargaining; and a lengthy and costly gestation period that may outlast initial enthusiasms. Where successful projects are nevertheless launched, the critical elements are typically supplied by the intervention of neutral, informed consultants acceptable to the two sides. These third parties provide needed information and guidance, serve as communications links, uncover common goals and effectively verbalize them, and allay understandable fears.

It is a healthy sign that "skeptics" were reported among the participants in the 1981 Toronto conference mentioned earlier. Although many delegates told of bilateral benefits of cooperative ventures (e.g., improvements in efficiency, costs, and even in the climate for bargaining), concern was also expressed "whether QWL will become just a passing fad or a long term commitment by both management and labor." In particular, in the automobile industry. where QWL has been taken very seriously, the willingness of the two sides to continue their collaboration with the restoration of profitability "in a year or two" is a matter of conjecture.

Flexible Work Schedules

"Flexitime," another recent innovation intended to meet the needs or desires of workers for greater autonomy in the workplace, has been eyed with favor by many employers as a device for reducing absenteeism, tardiness, and turnover.[22] In response to rank and file interest, a few unions have joined with management in efforts to develop flexible work schedules without impairment of operations.

A typical flexible work schedule allows an employee to begin work at any time within specified limits in the morning (7 A.M. to 9 A.M.), and to leave work at any time within specified limits in the evening (4 P.M. to 6 P.M.). All employees, however, are expected to be on the job during the core periods (9 A.M. to 11:30 A.M. and 1:30 P.M. to 4 P.M.). Lunchtime may also be left to the employee's discretion, the length being set by management.[23]

There are many variants, depending on the degree of flexibility permitted by company operations. Sometimes, hours in excess of, or fewer than, the contractual workweek may be carried to other days: looser systems allow employees to determine their own daily and weekly hours, provided a monthly target is met. Compressed workweeks of 4 days and 40 hours or 3 days and 36 hours have not been adopted widely.

Diffusion

After introduction at the Messerschmidt Research and Development Center in West Germany in 1967 as *gleitzeit* (gliding time), flexible work schedules were adopted rapidly by banks, insurance companies, and other white-collar employers in Western Europe.[24] It came to the United States in 1973 and since then has become fairly common. The Bureau of Labor Statistics estimated that, in 1980, over 7.6 million full-time employees, or 12 percent of the full-time labor force, were on some kind of flexible work schedule.

Although trade unions played a leading role in earlier reforms of worktime (e.g., introduction of the 8-hour day, the 5-day week, and paid vacations and holidays), they have, on the whole, taken an ambivalent position regarding flexible work schedules. At first, they opposed the idea on the ground that it threatened overtime pay provisions of the Fair Labor Standards Act. In 1978, leading representatives of six U.S. unions conferred with union officials and workers about flexible working hours and other job innovations at various worksites in England, West Germany, and Sweden; they then reported, in *Innovations in Working Patterns,* a recognition of potential benefits if unions are involved in initial discussions, planning, implementation, and evaluation. They also recommended that gains in productivity from flexible work schedules should be shared with employees through collective bargaining. They concluded that American unions ought to become aware of alternative working patterns, not only to protect employees from possible pitfalls but also to take advantage of new bargaining options.

Except for the Communications Workers Union, few unions in the private sector have become involved in cooperative experiments with flexible work schedules. The Communications Workers Union, having a high proportion of women clerical workers in its membership, has made flexibility of work schedules, where feasible and desired by employees, one of its goals in bargaining with the Bell System. Agreements on flexitime have been reached with Michigan Bell, Mountain States Bell, and Pacific Bell. These provide for joint committees to plan the introduction of changes in work scheduling.[25]

Assessments

As usual, bilateral benefits of flexitime are often realized, as intended, by both workers and employers, but failures and abuses are also reported. Case studies show reductions of absenteeism, lateness, and overtime, but little effect on turnover; and they also indicate gains in productivity and job satisfaction. Workers are better able to meet family responsibilities and to conduct personal business; they may also make better transportation arrangements and reduce the stresses of everyday living.[26]

Organizational efficiency can also be diminished if communications and continuity of operations are disrupted by injudicious scheduling or failure to honor the routines established. Some kinds of work can be performed more independently than others; typing, filing, accounting, computing, and many other office jobs are easier to perform with little or no interaction, while this is not the case for assembly line and other sequential blue-collar tasks. Flexitime is also difficult to apply to shift work.[27]

Experts in labor-management relations commonly endorse flexible work scheduling. For example, in the 1976 presidential address at the annual meeting of the Industrial Relations Research Association, an eminent scholar declared:

> From the standpoint of improving the quality of working life, nothing could be healthier than these exercises in manipulating working hours. The United States, with its highly decentralized systems of industrial relations and collective bargaining, is an excellent setting for this experimentation.[28]

Safety and Health

Three stages are discernible in the protection of workers against industrial hazards. First, employers assumed sole responsibility. Second, with the advent and growth of unions, occupational safety and health have been prominently treated in collective bargaining agreements. Third, labor and management have, in recent years, gone beyond earlier approaches to safety and health issues by establishing joint committees to discuss problems and to propose solutions. About one-third of the major bargaining agreements in force on January 1, 1978, covering 3 million workers, had provisions for such committees.[29] Federal legislation has played an important role in this evolution.

Although their alertness to occupational hazards has been rising, workers continue to assign highest priority to economic concerns. Rising health and safety consciousness has influenced, and been influenced by, the standards and regulations of the federal Occupational Safety and Health Administration. In the U.S. Department of Labor's 1977 Quality of Employment survey, 78 percent of responding workers noted one or more hazards in the workplace, compared to 38 percent in 1969.[30] When, however, workers were asked in 1977 to state their choice between a 10 percent pay raise and working conditions that were "a little safer or healthier," only 33 percent of the respondents preferred safety over pay. For workers exposed to serious hazards, the figure was 42 percent. By way of contrast, 66 percent of the surveyed workers expressed a preference for increased retirement benefits over a 10 percent pay raise. Furthermore, when unionists were asked where their organizations should concentrate, "handling grievances" ranked first, while "increasing worker input in business decisions" ranked tenth and last and "increasing occupational safety and health" ranked seventh.

Two Forms of Cooperation: Pledges and Committees

The statistics just cited reflect the priorities of people who are obliged to earn a living and to provide for old age and are used to working conditions that are far from ideal. They do not indicate indifference to safety and health so much as a need to put "first things first." Advocates of QWL experiments may find this fact of life—or of other people's lives—disappointing, but management and unions, fortunately, have drawn the socially useful conclusion that they have to exercise a responsibility of stewardship according to their capabilities. Evidence of acceptance of the challenge is offered in collective bargaining agreements.

About 16 percent of all major agreements in the BLS analysis of 1978 contain a pledge that the two parties will work together to achieve safe working conditions and that the union will participate in the operation of the company programs. Such programs usually provide for safety equipment, training, information, proper use of hazardous materials, accident reports, safety suggestions, etc. The initiative rests mostly on management, and unions have a relatively inactive and subordinate role.

A second type of cooperation, exemplified in about one-third of major contracts and covering 40 percent of employment, involves establishment of special union-management committees. These joint committees deal with safety and health problems on a continuous basis—in the primary metals, rubber, auto, and mining industries. Representation usually includes three union members and three management members. Meetings are held at least once a month, and full pay is commonly allowed for time spent on committee activities during working hours.

The joint safety committees have important advisory functions, and final approval of their recommendations is up to management. Recommendations are adopted by majority vote of committee members; they are likely "to involve negotiation and compromise, particularly if the management representatives must consider the effects of safety solutions on costs or efficiency."[31]

Indicative of the scope of joint committees is this description of the functions of the one established in the Fontana, California plant by Kaiser Steel Corporation and the United Steelworkers:

> The function of the safety committee shall be to advise with plant management concerning safety and health and to discuss legitimate safety and health matters. In the discharge of its function, the safety committee shall: consider existing practices and rules relating to safety and health, formulate suggested changes in existing practices and rules, recommend adoption of new practices and rules, review proposed new safety programs developed by the company, and review accident statistics and trends and disabling injuries which have occurred in the plant and make recommendations to prevent future recurrences.[32]

What Makes a Good Committee

Like other kinds of committees, those concerned primarily with safety and health vary greatly in robustness and activity. Outside influences are pertinent to effectiveness—for example, pressure for enforcement of OSHA regulations, the state of technical knowledge, and the vigor of research on problems affecting particular firms or industries. Some light on pertinent internal factors—such as the quality of committee members, ambient conditions, and modes of operation—is shed in a study made by three Cornell researchers of committees in about 50 New York State companies having contracts with the Machinists union.[33]

The Cornell study indicates that committees tend, as might be expected, to be more effective where the local union is strong, the rank and file care about matters of health and safety, and management is disposed to deal with these matters. They are able to operate on a higher plane if union representatives have a wide range of skills, if first line supervisors are included, and if management members have decisionmaking authority. They can also perform better if they meet monthly, precede meetings with walkaround inspections, review past recommendations and progress toward implementation, keep minutes, and have procedures for reporting results of committee recommendations to the rank and file as well as to top management.

Localization of OSHA

The role of joint safety and health committees may be expanded significantly by OSHA's decision to decentralize some of its operations in response to business criticism of, and reduced funding for, government inspection of workplaces. Where appropriate, federal inspection will presumably be replaced by self-inspection by labor-management safety and health committees. This innovation is being tested at a nuclear power project by Bechtel Corporation and the California Building and Construction Trades Council.[34] Instead of federal and state surveillance, a joint safety and health committee will conduct inspections for compliance with OSHA construction standards and try to assure that hazards are quickly corrected. Where the parties cannot agree, OSHA will make the final decision.

Labor-management cooperation is also being strengthened by OSHA's expanded support for the education and training of union safety and health officials. A joint program sponsored by the Construction Employers' Association of Chicago and the Chicago and Cook County Building and Construction Trades Council is training thousands of apprentices and journeymen in a variety of safety and health areas of an industry with one of the highest accident rates.[35]

Alcoholism and Drug Abuse

Over 4.5 million persons in the workforce are estimated to be suffering from alcoholism, and tens of thousands from drug dependency. The economic cost of problem employees to a firm, as well as to themselves and society, is considerable. Under many collective bargaining agreements, both parties agree that employees who report to work under the influence of alcohol or drugs, or who bring drinks or drugs into the plant, are subject to disciplinary action, including discharge.[36] Any employee who is disciplined has the right to file a grievance against the action. The local union representative usually tries to defend the worker against the employer's charges and to prevent dismissal. This adversary proceeding assures due process or fair play to employees charged with drunkeness but does little to solve their problems.

The shortcomings of disciplinary action have led some companies to establish supplementary rehabilitation programs without waiving their rights under the collective bargaining agreement. A basic premise of these recovery programs is that alcoholism and drug dependency are correctible illnesses—treatable, once detected, through education, counseling, and medical care.

While management often takes the main responsibility in introducing and operating recovery programs, joint planning and administration have been established in an increasing number of companies, notably in the steel and auto industries, and the postal service. Of the 1,724 major agreements in force in 1978, 53, covering about 1 million workers, provided for joint programs. Many additional programs have been established under memoranda or letters of agreement. Employees are more likely to participate in a recovery program proposed by management when a union can assure the protection of job security rights and the confidentiality of consultations with medical officials.

Guidelines for Cooperation

Broad guidelines for union-management programs have been developed by the Labor-Management Committee of the National Council on Alcoholism, which consists of seven union presidents and seven corporate leaders.[37] This body has recommended the formation of two kinds of labor-management committees in large multiplant corporations—at the corporate level and in each plant.

The principal functions of corporate committees are to establish a written policy on confidentiality, job security, insurance coverage, and the disease concept; develop an appropriate training program for all supervisors and union representatives; determine budgets for local committees; and act as a clearinghouse within the company on prevention and treatment. A full-time program coordinator, paid by the company, would carry out the committee's decisions.

The local plant is assigned the responsibility of developing procedures for supervisors and union representatives to follow in identifying and motivating workers to seek diagnosis and in referring diagnosed alcoholics to approved community treatment centers. The suggested procedures begin with interviews on job performance with the supervisor and the union representative. Employees who accept the offered professional services are assured of job security and confidential handling of their records. Plant union-management committees in some instances exert an important influence in strengthening community treatment and educational services for alcoholism and drug abuse.

Examples of Joint Programs

A number of joint union-management programs have been organized on the model proposed by the Labor-Management Committee of the National Council on Alcoholism. Among the early ones were those at American Motors and Deere (in cooperation with the United Auto Workers) and American Airlines (in cooperation with the Transport Workers Union).

A joint program of broad counseling services for "troubled employees" was organized in the 1970s at Kennecott Copper.[38] All employees and their family members were afforded the opportunity to obtain professional help, not only on alcoholism and drug abuse, but also on family, financial, and legal troubles, by telephoning a unit called INSIGHT.

One of the most extensive programs is the joint Substance Abuse Recovery Program developed by General Motors and the United Auto Workers. Originally called the Alcoholism Recovery Program, this effort was enlarged, as a result of the 1976 national negotiations, to cover drug abuse.[39] The local committee is called a "team." The union representative functions with no loss of pay under supervision of the plant medical department.

Although many thousands of GM employees have been helped by the Substance Abuse Recovery Program, one of its goals has remained elusive: unwarranted absenteeism continues. In response to complaints from members who resent burdens imposed by absentees, the UAW declared in 1979 that "unwarranted casual absenteeism is wrong," and it signed a "Memorandum of Understanding on Attendance" with General Motors to organize joint local pilot projects "to reduce and minimize unwarranted absences."[40]

Job Security and Reemployment Aid

The experience of plant shutdowns and employee shakeouts in the 1970s and the prospect of very much more of the same in the 1980s have alerted labor and management to the desirability of contingency arrangements.[41] The remainder of this chapter deals mostly with private efforts to provide for job retention and reemployment assistance through bargaining clauses, "redundancy plans," and buyout of plants marked for closing or divestiture by affected workers or communities. No account is taken of legislative proposals to prevent or slow down abandonment of obsolete or unprofitable facilities; or to require employers to give workers early notice of intent to shut down, to provide separation pay, to maintain health benefits, and to compensate communities for tax loss.[42]

Collective Bargaining Clauses

Under the National Labor Relations Act and various arbitration decisions, the unrestricted right of employers to relocate remains a controversial and unsettled issue. Various provisions in collective bargaining agreements seek to clarify the rights and obligations of the contracting parties in the event of significant technological change or shutdown. For example, employers may be required to: give advance notice of change; follow seniority rules in layoffs or transfer; provide severance pay, supplementary unemployment benefits, or relocation rights and allowances; and pay benefits to displaced workers who wish to retire early. Some contracts contain "no layoff" attrition clauses for reduction of the workforce in continuing plants by turnover.

Protection by contract, however, is spotty. For example, fewer than half of the workers covered by major agreements can draw supplementary unemployment benefits, severance pay, or relocation allowances. Only about 10 percent are covered by contracts with advance notice in plant shutdowns or relocation.[43] In a troubled and uncertain economy, employers have naturally been reluctant to extend contractual job security and eager to maintain maximum flexibility for themselves.

Redundancy Planning

A number of companies and unions collaborate in "redundancy planning," which involves anticipation of structural changes and preparation of retraining and job search programs for workers no longer needed.[44] Through such programs, companies can demonstrate social responsibility, protect prior investments in "human capital," and reduce outlays for severance pay, supplementary unemployment benefits, and tax payments under unemployment compensation merit-rating. Union participation is essential for protection of seniority rights of workers transferred to other plants.

Joint Planning for Technological Change. Since the introduction of the dial telephone in the 1920s, the Bell System has planned adjustments to minimize labor displacements due to technological change. Its plan featured advance notice, attrition, reassignment, relocation allowances, and early retirement.

In 1980, the Bell System and the Communication Workers Union agreed to establish a formal joint Technology Change Committee in each company of the system. These committees discuss the nature and impact of any impending major technological change at least six months in advance. They also plan and recommend programs to protect the job security and pay of employees and measures for retraining and reassignment. Covering over 300,000 employees, this venture in joint planning is one of the most extensive in the United States. (See documentary appendix for excerpt from agreement.)

In 1979, UAW and the major automakers agreed to establish National Committees on Technological Progress to consider adjustments required (e.g., in work assignments and skill training) by the introduction of new processes, methods, or equipment. The contracts obliged the companies to give advance notice of such innovations as early as possible. These committees, or their successors, will play an important role in the design of appropriate manpower measures for easing the changeover to robotization and other techniques intended to enhance the competitiveness of American cars.

Transfer and Retraining. The planned shutdown of a large tobacco plant of the Brown and Williamson Company in Louisville has occasioned "one of the most comprehensive and ambitious readjustment programs undertaken by a large U.S. company."[45] A three-year program for closing out an old plant with 3,000 employees and concentrating production in a new plant at Macon, Georgia was worked out in collective bargaining in 1979 with the Tobacco Workers Union and the Machinists.

The agreement required 18 months of advance notice of a plant closing. It also provided several standard types of financial assistance: graduated severance pay based on service, early retirement benefits for those 55 and over, and a guarantee of life and medical insurance up to six months after the shutdown. For employees desiring to transfer to the new Macon plant, the company paid moving expenses and offered a trial period of 60-90 days. Over 400 slots were reserved for Louisville employees.

More innovative were the provisions for training and placement assistance. Maintenance workers with skills unique to the tobacco industry were helped to take retraining courses for skilled jobs outside the industry. Others were given classroom training on company premises for the high school equivalency test. Group counseling was provided for all employees by persons from management and the union trained in appropriate techniques. The company also wrote to a large number of firms recommending its employees for vacancies and assisted in the preparation of resumes.The whole program was paid for by the company.

Outplacement Assistance. Several large companies, in cooperation with their local unions, have organized programs for improving the skills of displaced employees in searching and applying for jobs. Many blue-collar workers, having had work experience limited to one company or industry, feel handicapped in actively looking for jobs; they lack know-how in writing resumes, making telephone inquiries, and participating in interviews with prospective employees.

Shortly after Goodyear Tire and Rubber announced in September 1980, six months in advance, the shutdown of its Los Angeles and Conshohocken plants, it engaged an outside consultant to prepare a voluntary "career continuation program" for about 1,000 employees who were to be laid off.[46] This program covered a variety of informational, counseling, and training services. About 850 employees participated in a series of small workshops on skill and aptitude assessment, the labor market, self-awareness, job-targeting, hidden job markets, resume writing, and employment interviewing. Individual counseling was also offered with group followup for 60 days after plant closing. From the beginning, local leaders of the United Rubber Workers were consulted about the process although the program was outside the scope of the contract. According to the consultant, "this support from the union turned out to be very valuable in alleviating initial skepticism on the part of employees.[47]

The Dana Corporation often stated that "people had a right to expect continued employment with the corporation," but it was forced to shut down its Edgerton, Wisconsin plant in mid-1980 because of lack of orders for its light truck parts.[48] Since employees had considerable advance knowledge of the plant's difficulties at Edgerton from their participation in the corporation's Scanlon Plan, the decision was not wholly unexpected. Under a preferential hiring program negotiated with UAW, any employee permanently displaced had the right to a job in any other Dana plant, with a moving allowance and relocation assistance of two months' pay; but unfortunately, the shutdown of other Dana plants and layoffs elsewhere in the company limited this option.

An outplacement training program, similar to Goodyear's, was developed by Dana staff for all employees, covering a skills inventory, resume writing, and communication skills. In addition, advice on financial planning was offered. A unique feature of the program was the close working relationship established with the public job service of Wisconsin, which supplied information on work available in different parts of the country.

The whole process was facilitated by a long history of cooperative industrial relations and the firm commitment of management and the union to help displaced employees to find new jobs quickly. A survey of opinion after the shutdown found that workers still held favorable perceptions of Dana "due to the corporation's efforts to assist in the adjustment problem."[49]

Tripartite Cooperation in the Steel Industry. A unique program to assist dislocated workers was organized in 1979 by the steel companies, the union, and government agencies after a series of plant shutdowns. The Steel Tripartite Advisory Committee, discussed in chapter 3, acted as monitor of programs administered at the local level. Under the collective bargaining agreement, dislocated workers were entitled to unemployment and supplementary unemployment benefits, early retirement, and relocation and retraining allowances. Some workers were also eligible for benefits under the Trade Readjustment Assistance and CETA programs.

Shortly after the announcement by U.S. Steel and Jones and Laughlin, in the fall of 1979, of plant shutdowns affecting 13,000 workers at 15 sites, a Task Force of the Committee was sent to each site to review the progress of readjustment programs and to report on any obstacles and delays.[50] The Task Force was especially effective in coordinating local, state, and federal retraining efforts, in opening up communications among participating public agencies, and in breaking bottlenecks impeding needed training services. However, efforts of the Task Force to encourage local labor and management leaders to organize joint community committees achieved little success. In many cases, resentment over the shutdowns proved insurmountable.

A pilot project initiated by the Task Force at a plant of Crucible Steel involved outplacement assistance for workers scheduled to be permanently laid off. Job search training, along with intensive efforts to develop jobs by the employer and unions, was provided before the plant closed. The project was funded by Crucible Steel, the Steelworkers Union, state and local employment services, and CETA programs.

The work of the Task Force has contributed to a better understanding by government officials of how management, unions, and government agencies could cooperate in responding to plant closings, not only in the steel industry but in other industries as well. In its 1980 report to the president, the Steel Tripartite Advisory Committee recommended the assignment of a local federal adviser to work as a catalyst with local government, labor, and management officials in planning assistance to workers scheduled to be laid off.

Employee Ownership Plans. In a number of cases of threatened plant shutdown during the 1970s, employees and their unions departed from traditional accommodation and joined with local business and government leaders to prevent loss of jobs and tax revenues by purchasing the facilities and continuing operations. Most of these actions occurred in small towns, where alternative employment opportunities were scarce and where the plant or firm was a major tax-payer. The shutdowns generally represented divestitures by "absentee corporations"; the local plants no longer fitted in-to overall financial or product schemes.

The accompanying table shows ten cases of divestiture in which trade unions were involved in direct purchase—a small fraction of the thousand or so enterprises reported by the University of Michigan Institute of Social Research to have some form of direct worker ownership.[51] (Only a small percentage of the equity of these thousand firms,however, is owned by nonmanagerial employees. About 90 companies have been identified in which a majority of the assets are owned by employees, mainly under Employee Stock Owner-ship Plans (ESOP) described in the next chapter.)

A major problem of employee and community buyouts has been to convince outside investors that they were not risking their funds in "unprofitable" enterprises. In some cases, the appearance of failure might be in the eye of the beholder rather than in the balance sheet.[52] Conglomerates, for example, may divest themselves of subsidiaries despite profitability; they may originally have had unrealistic expec-tations of even higher profit, or they may have decided to change their output mix. Furthermore, gross mismanage-ment by absentee corporate owners cannot be ruled out; in such instances, transfer to local managers and employees could revive a failing entity. The experience of 16 employee-owned plywood plants in the Pacific Northwest in maintaining a level of productivity and profit higher than the industry average has been cited as evidence of the potential for success.[53] A still broader study by the University of Michigan's Institute of Social Research, of 30 firms, also found higher profit rates than for comparable companies in their respective industries.[54]

The main source of capital has been the savings of the employees whose jobs were at stake, but outside financing has also been necessary—with sales of stock to local banks, businessmen, and the public. In the case of the Mohawk Valley Community Corporation, which bought the Library Bureau from Sperry Rand, 70 percent of the stock was bought by investors outside the firm. The federal government has assisted in the financing of several employee plant purchases through low-interest loans or loan guarantees by the Small Business Administration, the Economic Development Administration, the Farmers' Home Administration, and the Housing and Urban Development Department.[55] Some states have also provided support through loan guarantees.

The case of the Campbell Works of the Youngstown Sheet and Tube Company illustrates the enormous difficulties confronting employees who try to buy a large-scale enterprise to protect their jobs.[56] The closing, which meant the loss of 4,100 jobs, led to formation of the Ecumenical Coalition of 200 religious leaders which, with the local steelworkers union, organized a campaign for community-worker purchase of the huge mill. Several private studies for the Coalition suggested that the reopened mill could become economically viable if workers, union, and management cooperated in a drive to reduce labor, energy, and material costs of production. The Economic Development Administration at first set aside $100 million in loan guarantes for one stage of the project; but, in March 1979, it decided to

Some Employee-Owned Unionized Firms

Firm & Location	Industry	No. of Employees	Year of Conversion	Union	Government Assistance
Bates Fabric Lewiston, Maine	Textile, bedspread	1,100	1977	Amalgamated Textile & Clothing Workers Union	Farmers Home Admin. guaranteed 90% of $8 million loan
Chicago & Northwestern Transportation Chicago, Ill.	Railroad	15,900	1972	13 railroad unions	None
Jamestown Metal Products Jamestown, N.Y.	Metal cabinets	100	1973	International Association of Machinists	$0.4 million loan by SBA
Mohawk Valley Community Corp. Herkimer, N.Y.	Library furniture	250	1976	International Union of Electrical, Radio & Machine Workers	$2 million EDA loan
Okonite Corp. Ramsey, N.J.	Wire and cable	1,700	1976	United Rubber Workers & International Brotherhood of Electrical Workers	$13 million EDA loan; $4 million loan guaranteed by N.J. Development Authority
Pacific Paperboard Products Stockton, Calif.	Cardboard box	900	1977	Association of Western Pulp & Paper Workers	$5.5 million EDA loan
Rich-SeaPak Corp. Brunswick, Ga.	Seafood processing	1,300	1977	National Maritime Union	$5 million EDA loan

Company	Industry	Year	Employees	Union	Financing
Rath Packing Co. Waterloo, Iowa	Meat packing	1980	3,000	United Food & Commercial Workers International Union	$4.6 million HUD loan
South Bend Lathe South Bend, Ind.	Machine Tool	1975	500	United Steelworkers	None
Vermont Asbestos Group Eden, Vt.	Asbestos Mining	1975	178	United Cement, Lime & Gypsum Workers International Union	SBA guaranteed $0.4 million loan; State authority guaranteed $1.5 million loan

SOURCE: Based on information from the New Systems of Work and Participation Program of the N.Y. School of Industrial and Labor Relations, Cornell University; and Karl Frieden, *Workplace Democracy and Productivity*, National Center for Economic Alternatives, Washington, 1980, pp. 75-78.

withdraw entirely from financing the venture on the grounds of infeasibility and high risk in a declining market for steel. The project was subsequently abandoned altogether.

Some Results. Employee and community buyouts of the 1970s appear to have succeeded in many instances in preserving jobs and in producing at a profit—at least for a while. For example, the Library Bureau earned a substantial profit in the first year, then wound up in the red in the next two years, and recovered in 1980.[57] The Vermont Asbestos Group prospered because of high labor productivity and a sharp increase in the price of asbestos.[58] Whether or not such enterprises survive in the long run depends not only on their own new capabilities but also on market, financial, and other conditions outside their control. In other words, the price of revival is to become as vulnerable in the future as any other competing firms.

Appraisals of the implications of employee ownership for worker involvement have varied widely. University of Michigan researchers found, in one study, better communication, higher morale, fewer grievances, and greater job satisfaction because of changes in managerial attitudes. Other studies, however, report disappointment that employee ownership has not led to greater worker and union influence over management decisionmaking. In some cases, the same executives have continued to direct operations with little change in style. In the Vermont Asbestos Group and the Library Bureau, employees sit on boards of directors with representatives of local banks and other shareholders, but they seem to have little or no control over decisions of the executive committee.[59] In negotiations to save firms and jobs, employees and unions appear generally to have paid little attention to devising arrangements to give employee stockholders a special voice in managing company affairs.

The role of unions becomes ambivalent in employee-owned firms. While unions have supported employee-ownership programs as a pragmatic means of saving jobs in areas with few alternatives, they have continued to represent the interests of employees in interactions with management on wages, hours, and working conditions.[60] They presumably could extend their value to employees *qua* stockholders by providing education programs on worker "rights" in relation to those of members of boards of directors—if workers really cared.

Against a historical background of organized labor's opposition (and general employee indifference) to worker ownership of enterprises, the attitude and behavior of local unions should occasion no surprise. The American Federation of Labor was organized partly as a result of the disenchantment of wage earners with the efforts of the Knights of Labor in the 1880s to form producer cooperatives.[61] Many small labor-sponsored enterprises in the shoe, mining, cigar, foundry, and other manufacturing industries were set up in those days to provide jobs to members blacklisted by employers after unsuccessful strikes. Although these cooperatives appeared successful at first, many later failed because of lack of capital, inefficient managers, and "injudicious borrowing of money at high rates of interest upon the mortgage of the plant."[62] Others that proved more successful became joint stock companies in which the wage earner was treated as in any other private enterprise.

NOTES

1. I. H. Siegel, "Productivity, Worklife Quality, and Common Sense," *Professional Engineer,* November 1977, pp. 23-24.

2. R. E. Walton, "Innovative Restructuring of Work," in J. M. Rosow, ed., *The Worker and the Job* (Englewood Cliffs: Prentice-Hall, 1974), p. 149. See also his chapter, "Criteria for Quality of Working Life," in L. E. Davis and A. B. Cherns, eds., *The Quality of Working Life, Vol I.* (New York: The Free Press, 1975), pp. 91-118. Collective bargaining, in Walton's view, has been concerned primarily with three of the eight issues he regards as pertinent to the quality of working life: adequate and fair compensation; safety and a healthy work environment; and constitutionalism and due process. The other five attributes that he discerns are: development of human capacities; advancement; human relations; "total life space"; and "social relevance."

3. P. D. Greenberg and E. M. Glaser, *Some Issues in Joint Union-Management Quality of Worklife Improvement Efforts* (Kalamazoo: The W. E. Upjohn Institute for Employment Research, 1980), p. 3.

4. "Quality of Work Life: Catching On," *Business Week,* September 21, 1981.

5. Walton, "Innovative Restructuring," pp. 151-153.

6. P. S. Goodman and E. E. Lawler III, "United States," in *New Forms of Work Organization, 1* (Geneva: International Labour Office, 1979), p. 1.

7. Lee Dyer, D. B. Lipsky, and T. A. Kochan, "Union Attitudes toward Management Cooperation," *Industrial Relations,* May 1977, pp. 163-172.

8. Greenberg and Glaser, *Quality of Worklife Improvement,* pp. 17-18.

9. Irving Bluestone, "Human Dignity Is What It's All About," *Viewpoint,* 3rd Quarter, 1978, pp. 22-23. See also his article, "Creating a New World of Work," *International Labour Review,* January-February 1977, pp. 1-10; and Greenberg and Glaser, *Quality of Worklife Improvement.*

10. *Business Week,* September 21, 1981, p. 72.

11. B. J. Widick, ed., *Auto Work and Its Discontents* (Baltimore: Johns Hopkins University Press, 1976), p. 93. This book, by five university researchers who worked for years in auto plants and also had experience as union bargainers, provides a realistic perspective on worker attitudes.

12. On the GM-UAW joint effort, see S. H. Fuller, "How Quality-of-Worklife Projects Work for General Motors," *Monthly Labor Review,* July 1980, pp. 37-39; and a companion article by Irving Bluestone, "How Quality-of-Worklife Projects Work for the UAW," pp. 39-41. See documentary appendix for text of memorandum of agreement.

13. Bluestone, "Quality-of-Worklife Projects," p. 40.

14. The Tarrytown case is covered by R. H. Guest, the co-author with C. R. Walker, of the famous study, *The Man on the Assembly Line* (Harvard University Press, 1952), in "Quality of Worklife—Learning from Tarrytown," *Harvard Business Review,* July/August 1979, pp. 76-86. The Ford EI program was described to the Joint Economic Committee, U.S. Congress, in *Hearings on Business Management Practices and the Productivity of American Industry,* May-June 1981, pp. 137-146.

15. For an evaluation of this joint union-management venture, see B. A. Macy in "The Quality of Worklife Project at Bolivar: An Assessment," *Monthly Labor Review,* July 1980, pp. 41-43; and "A Progress Report on the Bolivar Quality of Work Life Project," *Personnel,* August 1979, pp. 527-530, 557-559. For accounts by project consultants, see Michael Maccoby, "Changing Work: The Bolivar Project," *Working Papers,* Summer 1975, pp. 43-55; and M. M. Duckles, Robert Duckles, and Michael Maccoby, "The Process of Change at Bolivar," *Journal of Applied Behavioral Science,* July/August/September 1977, pp. 387-399.

16. An independent evaluation of the Rushton project was prepared for the Institute of Social Research of the University of Michigan by P. S. Goodman, *Assessing Organizational Change: The Rushton Quality of Work Experiment* (New York: Wiley-Interscience, 1979). The academic consulting team also prepared a report: Eric Trist, G. I. Sussman, and G. R. Brown, "An Experiment in Autonomous Working in an American Underground Coal Mine," *Human Relations,* No. 3, 1977, pp. 201-236. The director of the American Quality of Work Center who proposed the project also reported: Ted Mills, "Altering the Social Structure in Coal Mining: A Case Study," *Monthly Labor Review,* October 1976, pp. 3-10.

17. Goodman and Lawler, "United States," p. 168.

18. R. E. Walton, "Work Innovations in the United States," *Harvard Business Review,* July/August 1979, p. 93.

19. P. S. Goodman, "Quality of Worklife Projects in the 1980s," in *Proceedings of the 1980 Spring Meeting of the Industrial Relations Research Association,* 1980, p. 490.

20. L. A. Schlesinger and R. E. Walton, "The Process of Work Restructuring and its Impact on Collective Bargaining," *Monthly Labor Review,* April 1977, pp. 52-55.

21. E. E. Lawler III and J. A. Drexler, Jr., "Dynamics of Establishing Cooperative Quality-of-Worklife Projects," *Monthly Labor Review,* March 1978, p. 26. On the role of consultants, see Gerald Sussman, *The Role of Third Parties in Labor-Management Cooperative Endeavors,* National Center for Productivity and Quality of Working Life, Washington, 1978.

22. For a discussion of flexible working schedules in relation to the theory of participative management, see A. D. Elbing, Herman Gadon, and J. R. M. Gordon, "Flexible Working Hours: The Missing Link," *California Management Review,* Spring 1975, pp. 50-57; and A. S. Glickman and Z. H. Brown, *Changing Schedules of Work: Patterns and Implications* (Kalamazoo: The W. E. Upjohn Institute for Employment Research, 1974).

23. See J. W. Newstrom and J. L. Pierce, "Alternative Work Schedules: The State of the Art," *The Personnel Administrator,* October 1979, pp. 19-21; and A. L. Porter and F. A. Rossini, "Flexiweek," *Business Horizons,* April 1978, pp. 45-51.

24. For the European experience, see *Innovations in Working Patterns* (Report of the U.S. Trade Union Seminar on Alternative Work Patterns in Europe), Washington: Communications Workers of American and German Marshall Fund of the United States, 1978.

25. Maureen McCarthy, "Trends in the Development of Alternative Work Patterns," *The Personnel Administrator,* October 1979, p. 2. See documentary appendix for letter of understanding.

26. D. J. Petersen, "Flexitime in the United States: The Lessons of Experience," *Personnel,* January/February 1980, pp. 21-31. For case studies of programs in different private industries, see R. T. Golembiewski and R. J. Hilles, "Drug Company Workers Like New

Schedules," and M. A. Hopp and C. R. Sommerstad, "Reaction at Computer Firm: More Pluses than Minuses," *Monthly Labor Review*, February 1977, pp. 65-71. See also David Robison, *Alternative Work Patterns, Changing Approaches to Work Scheduling*, Report of a Conference Co-sponsored with the National Center for Productivity and Quality of Working Life (Scarsdale: Work in America Institute, 1976). About 280 organizations using flexible work scheduling and other programs are listed in *Alternative Work Schedule Directory, First Edition* (Washington: National Council for Alternative Work Patterns, 1979).

27. J. D. Owen, "Flexitime: Some Problems and Solutions," *Industrial and Labor Relations Review*, January 1977, pp. 152-160; and J. N. Hedges, "Flexible Schedules: Problems and Issues," *Monthly Labor Review*, February 1977, pp. 62-65; and W. M. Young, "Shift Work and Flexible Schedules: Are They Compatible?" *International Labor Review*, January/February 1980.

28. Irving Bernstein, "Time and Work," Presidential Address, *Proceedings of the Twenty-Ninth Annual Winter Meeting*, September 16-18, 1976, Industrial Relations Research Association, 1977, p. 8.

29. *Major Collective Bargaining Agreements: Safety and Health Provisions*, Bulletin 1425-16, U.S. Bureau of Labor Statistics, 1976, chapter 7, p. 3.

30. R. L. Frenkel, W. C. Priest, and N. A. Ashford, "Occupational Safety and Health: A Report on Worker Perceptions," *Monthly Labor Review*, September 1980, p. 11.

31. *Collective Bargaining Agreements*, p. 13.

32. *Ibid.*, p. 7.

33. T. A. Kochan, Lee Dyer, and D. B. Lipsky, *The Effectiveness of Union-Management Safety and Health Committees* (Kalamazoo: The W. E. Upjohn Institute for Employment Research, 1977); and T. A. Kochan, *The Role and Effectiveness of Union-Management Safety and Health Committees*, a paper presented at Symposium for Labor Educators on Occupational Health and Safety sponsored by University of Wisconsin School for Workers, October 15, 1979. Another quantitative study, based on 113 plants in Maine, found "modest support that specific programs (jointly administered with unions) developed over the 1971-1975 interval reduced lost days in plants with 300 or more employees." See W. H. Cooke and F. R. Gautsche III, "OSHA Plant Safety Programs and Injury Reduction," *Industrial Relations*, Fall 1981, p. 257.

34. *Daily Labor Report*, February 5, 1981, and *Wall Street Journal*, March 26, 1981. See documentary appendix for excerpt from agreement.

35. *Annual Construction Industry Report, April, 1981*, U.S. Department of Labor, Office of Construction Industry Services, 1981, p. 46.

36. *Collective Bargaining Agreements*, p. 37.

37. *A Joint Union-Management Approach to Alcoholism Recovery Programs* (New York, National Council on Alcoholism, 1976).

38. M. Sadler and J. F. Horst, "Company/Union Programs for Alcoholics," *Harvard Business Review*, September/October 1972, p. 155. A similar program at a paper company is reported by R. Witte and M. Cannon, "Employee Assistance Programs: Getting Top Management's Support," *The Personnel Administrator*, June 1979, pp. 23-26.

39. *Alcohol and Drug Abuse Recovery Program*, UAW Community Services Department, Detroit, April 1978. Also, Letter to all GM Local Unions on Substance Abuse Recovery Program Guidelines from Irving Bluestone, July 13, 1977.

40. Letter to all GM Local Unions from Irving Bluestone, October 2, 1979.

41. R. B. McKersie, "Plant Closed—No Jobs (Continued)" *Across the Board,* November 1980, p. 14; G. J. Felsten, "Current Considerations in Plant Shutdowns and Relocations," *Personnel Journal,* May 1981, pp. 369-372; and Arthur Shostack, "The Human Costs of Plant Closings," *AFL-CIO American Federationist,* August, 1980 pp. 22-25.

42. For a review of legislative proposals, see article by Audrey Freedman, " 'Plant Closed—No Jobs',"*Across the Board,* August 1980, pp. 12-18. Protective laws covering workers affected by federal regulation such as railroad, airline, redwood forest, and trade programs are studied in an article by B. H. Millen, "Providing Assistance to Displaced Workers," *Monthly Labor Review,* May 1979, pp. 17-21; also see resolution on plant closings adopted by the Executive Council of the AFL-CIO Industrial Union Department, April 30-May 1, 1981, in the *Daily Labor Report,* May 6, 1981. The AFL-CIO position was influenced by a report on *Economic Dislocation: Plant Closings, Plant Relocations, and Plant Conversions* (Policies and Programs in Three Countries: Recommendations for the United States), Joint Report of Labor Union Study Tour Participants, May 1, 1979; and by *Silicon, Satellites, and Robots: The Impacts of Technological Change on the Workplace,* edited by Dennis Chamot and J. M. Baggett, Department for Professional Employees, AFL-CIO, Washington 1979.

43. *Characteristics of Major Collective Bargaining Agreements,* pp. 100-101.

44. P. F. Drucker, "Planning for 'Redundant' Workers," *Personnel Administrator,* January 1980, p. 32. On planning in the automobile industry, see Ephlin's statement to Joint Economic Committee, cited earlier.

45. McKersie, "Plant Closed (Continued)," p. 15. Details are presented in *Plant Closure: A Case History,* by C. H. Teague, vice-president, personnel and labor relations, Brown and Williamson Tobacco Corporation. Testimony before the U.S. Senate Committee on Labor and Human Resources, Washington, September 17, 1980.

46. This account is based on articles by two participants: Tom Bailey, "Industrial Outplacement at Goodyear, Part 1: The Company's Position," and Tom Jackson, "Industrial Outplacement at Goodyear, Part 2: The Consultant's Viewpoint," *Personnel Administrator,* March 1980, pp. 42-48.

47. *Ibid.,* p. 47.

48. *The Dana Corporation: The Edgerton Experience.* A Presentation of Representatives from the United Auto Workers, the Dana Corporation, the Wisconsin Job Service, Department of Labor-White House Conference on Plant Closings, January 14-16, 1981, Washington, D.C. Statement by Phil Murphy, Director, Personnel Services, Dana Corporation, p. 2.

49. *Some Social Consequences of the Dana Corporation's Plant Closings in Edgerton,* Madison: Team for Analysis of Social Concerns, University of Wisconsin, December 1980.

50. Information supplied by W. L. Batt, director, Steel Task Force, U.S. Department of Labor. For guidelines for collaborative efforts on plant shutdowns, see publications by Gary Hansen and Marion Bentley of the Utah Center for Productivity and Quality of Working Life, Logan, Utah: *Life After Layoff: A Handbook for Workers in a Plant Shutdown,* and *Problems and Solutions in a Plant Shutdown: A Handbook for Community Involvement.* These handbooks were written in connection with a study of the shutdown of three sugar mills; see *Mobilizing Community Resources to Cope with Plant Shutdown: A Demonstration Project* (Logan, UT: Utah State University, 1981).

51. *Employee Ownership,* report to the Economic Development Administration, U.S. Department of Commerce, by the Survey Research Center, Institute for Social Research, University of Michigan, Ann Arbor, 1977, p. 2.

52. W. H. Whyte, Statement in Support of the Voluntary Job Preservation and Community Stabilization Act, Congressional Record, June 19, 1978, p. E-3326. This Act would have expanded the authority of the EDA to assist employees and community groups who want to buy plants being shut down because of divestiture.

53. The impressive productivity record of employee-owned plywood plants is reported in the following: K. V. Berman, *Worker Owned Plywood Companies: An Economic Analysis* (Pullman, WA: Washington State University, 1967); Paul Bernstein, *Workplace Democratization: Its Internal Dynamics* (New Brunswick, NJ: Transaction Books, 1980), pp. 13-26; "When Employees Run the Company—An Interview with L. J. Bennett," *Harvard Business Review,* January/February 1979, pp. 75-90.

54. Michael Conte and A. S. Tannenbaum, "Employee-owned Companies: Is the Difference Measurable?" *Monthly Labor Review,* July 1978, p. 25. The authors caution that these findings are tentative, based on limited data, and involve complex problems of comparing companies of different structure, etc.

55. See Daniel Zwerdling, "Employee Ownership: How Well is it Working?," *Working Papers,* May/June 1979, p. 20.

56. For a case study of Campbell Works Steel Mill, see Karl Frieden, *Workplace Democracy and Productivity* (Washington: National Center for Economic Alternatives, 1980), pp. 55-64; Daniel Zwerdling, *Democracy at Work* (Washington: Association for Self-Management, 1978), pp. 16-17.

57. R. N. Stern, K. H. Wood, and T. H. Hammer, *Employee Ownership in Plant Shutdowns: Prospects for Employment Stability* (Kalamazoo: The W. E. Upjohn Institute for Employment Research, 1980).

58. Zwerdling, "Employee Ownership," 53-62.

59. *Ibid.,* pp. 16, 74.

60. See Cornell study of experience of Vermont Asbestos Group by J. E. Johannesen, Statement before Subcommittee on Economic Stabilization, House Committee on Banking, Finance, and Urban Affairs, February 27, 1979.

61. J. R. Commons and Associates, *History of Labor in the United States, Volume II* (New York: Macmillan, 1926), pp. 430-438.

62. *Ibid.,* p. 437.

8

Company-Level Arrangements: Monetary and Quasi-Monetary Supplements

Supplements to wages and salaries (and to the ordinary fringes) are usable as inducements to employees to cooperate with management on behalf of company survival, autonomy, and profitability. Some of these supplements are monetary, paid as cash; others are quasi-monetary, paid as claims on company income. Some are currently realizable; others are deferred. All are contingent, rather than certain, as to payability at all or as to cash value. Four varieties of supplements are treated in the four sections that make up this chapter: group bonuses, profit sharing, employee stock ownership, and pensions.

Group Bonuses

Among the best-known group incentive programs are the Scanlon Plan, the Rucker Share of Production Plan, and Impro-Share.[1] The first of these has features that qualify it for special attention in a book on labor-management cooperation. It not only entails greater employee (or union) participation than do the other two but it also proceeds from a sincere philosophy of reconcilability of labor and management interests without disparagement of adversarial bargaining.

Group bonuses reward employees, not as individuals performing specific assigned tasks but as members of an aggregate responsible for a correspondingly broad concept of output. The group may be as large as the whole workforce of a plant or company, in which case prime emphasis is placed in bonus payment on final salable output or on total value added. The payment system is intended to overcome the disabilities that have plagued earlier programs of individual incentive pay. The latter fostered competition among workers, rather than cooperation, and discouraged information sharing. They often led to grievances and low morale, especially where difficulties in assessing individual contributions to output (e.g., in the chemical process industries and in sequentially dependent operations) impeded establishment of fair standards. An obvious virtue of the group bonus is that it keeps in constant view the "bottom line" of all productive activity: workers have to perform well in making their specific subproducts because, in so doing, they are also enhancing the output of end products, which are the source of company revenues and of their own extra compensation.

The Scanlon Plan

In the late 1930s, Joseph N. Scanlon, steelworker and local union president, had a vision of harmonizing management's concern for productivity with labor's for a fair share of the gains—within the framework of collective bargaining.[2] He tried out his idea in a small company that was hard pressed to make ends meet while paying union wages. During the rest of his short life, he refined his concept, first as head of the production engineering department of the national steel union and later as an associate of Massachusetts Institute of Technology.

The Scanlon Plan rests on three legs. First, employees are expected to generate and communicate ideas continually for improving the plant's total performance. Second, a suitable way of measuring the company's changing performance over time is required. Third, an acceptable formula is needed for determining the company's productivity surplus and for distributing this bonus pool between employer and employees.

The three legs must rest on a floor: the advance willingness of the two parties to agree to consider the plan and to adopt it on a trial basis. This initial impulse to cooperate is expected to find reinforcement in the subsequent experience of operating under the plan and to culminate in a *modus vivendi.* [3]

The two parties may first come to a Scanlon consultant to seek help after, say, an individual incentive program has become mired in sluggish productivity and poor morale. A committee of labor and management representatives is then set up to review other company plans in the next four to six months and to devise a version that is applicable to their own organization on a trial basis. For operational test of the trial plan for a limited period, the consultant is likely to require a positive vote of 80 percent of the employees. If the results of a trial are deemed satisfactory, the employees or their union sign a formal agreement with management to institute the plan. A sample contract is provided in the documentary appendix.

Joint Scanlon Committees

Two kinds of committees are utilized under the Scanlon Plan. Close to the rank and file are the production committees, which receive and discuss employee suggestions for improving methods, raising output quality, reducing costs, and so forth. Overarching these is a plantwide screening committee.

At plants of the Dana Corporation, which embraced the Scanlon concept relatively early, production committees comprised of elected workers and appointed managers were set up in every department for each shift.[4] In one of the Dana plants, as many as 16 committees have been known to exist at one time. An attempt is made to have every employee serve on a committee as well as to offer suggestions. UAW locals endorse the full participation of their members. The production committees meet monthly on company time to review the suggestions. Approved proposals requiring very small outlays are eligible for immediate implementation. More costly proposals of merit, or those impinging on more than one department or shift, are passed on to the higher-level screening committee. Rejected suggestions are returned with explanations or with requests for revision.

The screening committee has additional major tasks. Comprised of the plant manager and supervisory staff plus two representatives from each production committee, it provides a forum for discussion of company goals, the competitive situation, technological developments, and other matters affecting the health and viability of the enterprise. One more function of the committee is its most redeeming feature from the standpoint of the average employee: review of company accounting data to determine and announce the monthly productivity bonus pool.

Scanlon bonus. A major difference between Scanlon production committees and the joint productivity committees discussed in chapter 6 is that participants are promptly rewarded by cash bonuses based on measured performance of the enterprise as a whole. Since the main objective is to encourage teamwork and coordination to improve the productivity of the enterprise, bonuses based on departmental or individual performance are ruled out. The plan thus discourages "suboptimizing" rivalries among departments, shifts, maintenance and production workers, and engineers.

These rivalries are often inimical to "bottom-line" production. The bonus is distributed among all employees, including supervisors, managers, clerical, and service workers—groups usually excluded from individual incentive plans.

The bonus computation requires joint establishment of a simple quantitative standard or yardstick for determining whether any monthly gains have been made.[5] An outside Scanlon consultant often helps in deriving an acceptable measure from company accounts. The most commonly used standard is the ratio of payroll costs to sales value of production. Labor and management jointly determine the scope of company operations embraced in the standard ratio and select a representative past time period, when the ratio was fairly stable, to serve as the basing point. Payroll costs usually include total wages and salaries plus fringe benefits of both supervisory and nonsupervisory employees. Sales value of production covers the dollar value of sales plus or minus the change in inventory. Returns, allowances, and discounts are subtracted from sales value to encourage quality production. The base ratio is fixed at a level that does not jeopardize the firm's competitiveness and is also perceived as equitable to all.

The base-period ratio of payroll to sales is applied to the sales value in a given month to derive allowed payroll costs. If the actual payroll costs are lower than the allowed amount, the difference constitutes the available bonus pool for the month. From time to time, the base-period ratio may require adjustment to reflect changes in technology, product mix, degree of plant integration, prices, wages, and inventories. Some bargaining between labor and management is involved in all decisions relating to changes in the standard ratio.

Although the bonus is derived from data on financial performance expressed in "current" (rather than "constant") dollars, the Scanlon Plan is usually called a "productivity" incentive program. The payroll-to-sales ratio, however, is not a true measure of "physical" productivity (or strictly, of the reciprocal of labor productivity). Actually, changes in the dollar ratio of sales to payroll correspond to changes in physical productivity only if the ratio of average hourly earnings to the unit value or price of output remains constant over time.[6] While not a true productivity measure, the dollar ratio does have bilateral acceptance, and it does focus the attention of the entire workforce on cost items over which managers and employees have some control.

The Scanlon Plan provides a formula for distributing monthly savings in labor cost—the bonus pool—between employer and employees and also among the employees. Labor and management agree on the formula when the Plan is first installed. A reserve of one-quarter of the bonus fund is first set aside to cover possible deficits during the year or to be paid out as a year-end bonus. Of the remaining three-quarters, 75 percent is paid to employees and 25 percent to the company. Each employee receives a percentage increase in pay based on the percentage that the bonus fund comprises of the payroll. All employees receive the same percent bonus increase.

The monthly bonus payment is the linchpin that holds the Scanlon Plan together. Money is the "bottom line" for workers who are not yet sufficiently affluent or secure in affluence to give top priority to other rewards of work. In other kinds of joint arrangements, the *sine qua non* of a plan's survival is usually the continuance on the job of a key supportive manager or union official.[7] A monthly bonus check, on the other hand, provides everyone with a visible, measurable stake in the plan's continuation. Conversely, the failure to produce bonuses regularly, despite employee efforts, weakens credibility and may become the main factor for breakdown of the plan.

The bonus, incidentally, may be sizable. At a Dana plant in Wisconsin, monthly bonuses averaged 14 percent of payroll in 1974, 22 percent in 1975, and 20 percent in 1976. For the average worker, the bonuses amounted to $1,221 in 1974, $2,176 in 1975, and $2,153 in 1976.

While the bonus formula is intended to harmonize the goals of employees with the goals of the organization, the Scanlon Plan is not conceived as a substitute for collective bargaining. The determination of wage and fringe benefits, the definition of worker rights and obligations, and the handling of grievances are still subject to adversarial negotiations. The plan is explicitly kept out of the process of collective bargaining.[8] A union's bargaining strategy, on the other hand, may be tempered by a climate of amity and by a deeper knowledge of the firm's circumstances and ability to pay.

Advantages and obstacles. Case studies made over the past 30 years or so give high marks to the Scanlon Plan. A review of 22 studies made between 1947 and 1972, which covered the experience of 44 firms, found that 30 were apparent successes and 14 were failures.[9] This favorable rate may be somewhat overstated, however, since successful firms are more likely to allow their experience to be reported than those firms that fail. Consultants, in particular, are naturally more eager to talk of positive than negative results.

The tangible benefits of the Scanlon Plan, where effectively applied, appear to be substantial. Studies show rates of 50 to 80 percent of the workforce contributing suggestions; in contrast, a participation rate of about 30 percent is indicated for individual suggestion systems.[10] Furthermore, the quality of Scanlon suggestions, as measured by acceptance rates, seems to be at a higher level. Output per manhour presumably increases in response to brisk suggestion activity, which management may seek to sustain by feeding problems for solution by the productivity committees.

The intangible benefits are more difficult to document or measure, but they are real. Among these are greater cooperation among departments and between supervisors and employees, closer identification of employees with their firms, and higher job motivation.[11] Also to be expected in Scanlon companies are diminished resistance to technological change, a vigilant interest on the part of employees in better management and planning, and greater flexibility in the administration of collective bargaining contracts.

It would be wrong to overlook some disadvantages of the Scanlon Plan for individual employees. High performers under individual incentive plans may suffer losses in pay in shifting to a group bonus system. Highly productive groups under the Scanlon Plan, moreover, may resent payment of the same bonus percentage to service and other indirect workers whose contribution is not directly evident. Finally, individual employees who are less interested in cash bonuses than their fellow employees may be subjected to intense peer pressure to increase their pace of work. Such unavoidable inequities in group incentive plans require acknowledgment and explanation by union and management lest they become sources of serious discontent.

Despite the many publicized advantages of the Scanlon Plan, only about 400 firms use it.[12] Most firms cited in studies are unionized, with the steelworkers, machinists, auto workers, and rubber workers the principal partners. Herman Miller, Inc., an internationally known furniture company in Michigan which adopted the Scanlon Plan in 1950, is nonunion; it perceives the plan as "the central management process" for integrating the work of all employees to meet the company's economic objectives. In another nonunion company in Michigan, Donnelly Mirrors, the Scanlon Plan is part of a participative management program that features interlocking work teams, salaries for all employees, and a less hierarchical authority structure.[13]

The Scanlon Plan seems to flourish best in moderate-size and small manufacturing plants where communications are good and employees can see more readily the connection between their own job performance and the achievement of the firm's goals. The plan is also more workable where credible, simple performance measures can be derived; this criterion would rule out firms with frequent changes in product lines and costs. Furthermore, the company must be willing and able to pay substantial consulting, bookkeeping, and clerical costs, as well as bear the cost of time spent in committee meetings. Finally, and above all, a high degree of trust is essential; without such trust on both sides, management would be most reluctant to disclose cost data and to discuss business prospects with employee representatives.

Talking of trust brings us back to the fundamental requirement of good communications throughout a plant or company. A behavioral scientist has described the Scanlon Plan as "a complex means for improving intergroup relations" and has declared its effectiveness to be "directly related to the already existing maturity of relations within and between labor and management."[14]

In closing, we should note that internal conditions do not suffice to determine a plan's success. Adverse external business conditions can destroy a plan even more readily than it destroys a firm. In chapter 7, we referred to havoc wrought at Dana by the collapse of American automobile production.

Profit Sharing

Throughout the troubled history of American labor-management relations, an idyllic dream has frequently recurred: the blunting, if not elimination, of "class" antagonisms by conversion of the worker into a minor "capitalist." Company efforts to translate this dream into a workaday reality have actually been limited; and, where tried, they have hardly succeeded in bridging the economic and psychological (not to say social) chasm that separates employee from employer. On the other hand, where tried, they have certainly helped to strengthen the sense of mutuality that coexists with a latent, manifest, or sublimated disposition toward conflict. Perhaps, the reinforcement of mutuality in particular places at particular times is as much as ought to be expected from the regular administration of necessarily small doses of profit and equity ownership. After all, societies that have gone through major revolutions professing to transform workers into "collective owners of the means of production" have egregiously failed to instill an intended "confusion of genres" in the psyches of their sullen toiling masses.

In chapter 1, it was noted that, during the 1920s, employers astutely challenged the growing labor movement for the loyalty of workers. Among the devices used were programs of profit-sharing and stock ownership. Two authors of a standard text on labor-management relations look back on the experience of the decade as follows:

> Profit-sharing plans continued to manifest their traditionally high birth rate as well as their equally high death rate, and employee stock ownership, introduced on a wider scale than ever before, was expected to (and frequently did) cement the faith of the workers in the existing order, entrench their reverence for the institution of private property, inculcate the belief that strikes against the firms employing them were strikes against themselves, and convince them that the economic interests of the wage earners were fundamentally harmonious with those of the employing and investing class.[15]

Many of the programs collapsed during the Great Depression, which also saw a resurgence of unionism. Unions have seldom endorsed profit sharing, and they have also taken a generally negative view of employee stock ownership. In contrast, they have included the establishment and administration of private pension plans in their bargaining agenda.

Nature and Prevalence of Plans

Profit sharing plans are arrangements by employers to set aside a fixed percent of the annual net profits, if any, to distribute as a supplement, annually or eventually, to each employee's wage or salary. The plans usually do not involve employee participation in management decisionmaking or in shopfloor consultation. Since profits are highly volatile, subject to market forces and the competence of management as well as productive effort of the workforce, annual cash distributions have often proved disappointing.

A more popular type of profit sharing is the "deferred" plan,which is often adopted in place of, or as a complement to, a company pension program. Instead of making annual cash payments, the deferred plan accumulates an individual's shares of company profits in a fund usually invested in the company's stock and makes payouts upon retirement, death, disability, or resignation. Unlike a formal pension program, deferred profit sharing may not promise a definite set of benefits and need not rest on an actuarially sound basis of employer contributions.

The Profit Sharing Foundation has estimated that, as of the end of 1980, about 15 million employees were enrolled in some 286,000 deferred and combination plans and 80,000-100,000 cash plans.[16] Profit sharing is practiced in a wide variety of manufacturing and nonmanufacturing industries, in companies both large and small. It is obviously not applicable to public services and nonprofit organizations.

Only about 29 out of 1,550 major contracts studied by the U.S. Bureau of Labor Statistics in 1980 had provisions pertaining to profit sharing. Union leaders have generally preferred to concentrate on gains "in the pay envelope," and few seem to have followed Walter Reuther's suggestion that profit sharing might be a particularly useful noninflationary arrangement for unions "to get their full equity."

A unique case of profit sharing under collective bargaining is provided by the experience of the American Velvet Company and the Amalgamated Clothing and Textile Workers.[17] The company, the last major velvet producer in New England, employs about 500 people and has kept its plan in force since 1940. The plan requires 27 percent of net profits (before taxes) to be paid into a fund from which an annual bonus is distributed to eligible employees on the basis of each employee's annual earnings. One-third of the profit sharing bonus is paid in cash; another third is invested in a retirement trust fund; the final third is left to the employee's choice. The company has not missed a bonus since 1939. In addition to its profit sharing plan, American Velvet Company and the local union engage in a program of union-management cooperation that has fostered the communication of cost-saving ideas, intense loyalty, and sufficient productivity improvement to help the company remain competitive.

Appraisal

A seasoned observer of the industrial scene has listed a number of virtues of profit sharing. Plans do encourage "a more positive attitude by employees toward their work and their firm." Furthermore, they provide useful economic education: There is no such thing as a free lunch, rewards being distributable only "when they can be afforded." Finally, "profit sharing as a retirement plan can often provide adequate benefits under a more flexible method of financing than the usual funded plan with mixed benefits."[18] For a long-service employee, the benefits could substantially supplement those obtained through Social Security.

These remarks do not, of course, imply that the benefits to workers are economically exciting enough to inspire serious ideological defection. Besides, as already mentioned, a worker's effort is only one of many elements that determine the availability and size of his profit share; he may fail to obtain the supplement he thinks he has merited, in which case the program provides only a negative or doubtful incentive.

Employee Stock Ownership

Two eras or styles, which might be designated classical and modern, need to be distinguished in the discussion of employee stock ownership programs. The classical era began before the turn of the century. The modern era, marked by the enlistment of the federal government as a fiscal third party with a visible hand, began in the 1970s.

The Classical Approach

In 1893, the Illinois Central Railroad offered workers an opportunity to purchase company shares below market price on the installment plan. Until the end of World War I, relatively few other firms followed this lead. One that did was United States Steel, which established its huge stock ownership program in 1903.

During the 1920s, employers found stock ownership more appealing than profit sharing (the roots of which trace to the 1870s) as a means of linking together the fortunes of companies and their workers. By 1916, fewer than 50 companies were reported to have ownership plans in place; by the time of the stock market crash in 1929, the number had risen to more than 300, with perhaps 1 million employees participating as owners of shares estimated to be worth about $1 billion. Among the well-known corporations with stock purchase plans were Standard Oil of New Jersey, Pennsylvania Railroad, American Telephone and Telegraph, General

Motors, Firestone Rubber, Eastman Kodak, International Harvester, and Philadelphia Rapid Transit.[19]

The crash of the stock market taught workers that share ownership entails the risk of depreciation of asset values as well as the happier prospect of appreciation. Profit sharing programs, on the other hand, do not require workers to share losses. Fortunately, employees had so little equity in their new role as capitalists that they could not have lost sight of the continuing future importance of wages or salaries in their life plans. It is also pertinent to add that New Deal legislation (with respect to Social Security, unemployment compensation, housing, etc.) and the later G.I. bills for World War II and other veterans pointed to far more probable ways for a worker to improve his scale of living or even to build a modest estate.

Enter Federal Government as Sponsor

A new impetus was given to the formation of programs of stock ownership by federal legislation of the 1970s that made them financially attractive to employers via tax deductions. Among these laws were the Employee Retirement Income Security Act of 1974 (ERISA), the Tax Reduction Act of 1975, and the Tax Reform Act of 1976. The so-called ESOPs (employee stock ownership plans) spurred by these federal enactments already exceeded 5,000 by 1981.[20]

The new ESOPs do not necessarily require stock purchase by workers.[21] The basic model calls for establishment of a company trust to which a company makes payment of externally borrowed funds for the explicit purpose of acquisition of newly issued company stock. As the company repays the outside lender, the stock is retained in the trust. The company may elect to augment the trust's assets with additional payments of stock or cash. Each year, the trust's accruals are allocated to accounts of participating employees (according to their wages or salaries) for eventual distribution upon retirement or death.

The U.S. Treasury benignly supplies a subsidy in the form of "tax expenditures" (i.e., forgone revenues) to encourage the setup and operation of ESOPs. It allows two deductions from the employer's taxes—for interest paid to lenders and also for repayments of principal. The employee or his estate is not subject to tax until distribution.

A variant on this basic model is treated even more generously by the federal government. Under this version of ESOP, an employer may claim an additional investment tax credit of 1 percent for an additional equivalent setaside of its common stock; or an extra credit of one-half percent if employees match additional employer contributions. Employees are generally prohibited from withdrawing their own payments into an ESOP for seven years.

Federal sponsorship of ESOPs will broaden considerably as a result of liberal provisions of the Economic Recovery Tax Act of 1981. The net effect of the new changes in law will be to encourage more rapid acquisition by employees of larger percentages of company stock. One amendment alters the basis of employer contributions to ESOPs in 1983 from a small percentage of investment (qualified for the investment tax credit) to a smaller percentage of payrolls. This shift will make ESOPs as attractive to labor-intensive (e.g., white-collar) firms as they have been to capital-intensive enter-prises. Furthermore, employers will be able to carry back for 3 years and forward for 15 years any unused ESOP credit in a current year. Another change allows an employee to use an ESOP as an IRA (individual retirement arrangement); thus, beginning in 1982, he or she may purchase up to $2,000 of stock in an ESOP and take a personal income tax deduction for this amount.

Creative Uses of ESOPs

The ESOP concept is adaptable to many purposes, such as community development, the funding of producer cooperatives (which may include the combination of workers for the advancement of "workplace democracy"), the continuity of small family businesses experiencing loss of key members through retirement, or the defense of larger enterprises against hostile takeovers.[22] In 1981, however, the management and employees failed in their effort to keep Continental Airlines out of the grasp of another carrier. The joint strategy, foiled by lobbying on the state level, envisaged issuance of $185 million of new stock to an ESOP trust (enough for 51 percent control) to be "bought" through voluntary pay cuts and productivity improvements over a number of years. A board of directors would have included employees associated with three unions and one nonunion organization, three management representatives, and eight persons elected by all shareholders. If the scheme had succeeded, Continental Airlines would have become the second largest majority employee-owned company.

While unions are generally wary of ESOPs that are unilaterally established, stock ownership became a bargaining chip for the United Auto Workers in the deal with management to keep Chrysler operating. The Chrysler Loan Guarantee Act of 1980 required substantial wage concessions, but it also provided for the acquisition of 15 to 20 percent of the company's total stock by employees.

Cost and Benefits

The immediate cost of ESOPs in lost government revenues is impressively high. If such plans lead, say, to higher productivity, greater profit, and more stable employment than would otherwise obtain, the long term accounting picture would become far more favorable. In any case, estimated tax expenditures for investment credits claimed by corporations for ESOPs have been set by the Office of Management and Budget at $695 million for fiscal year 1980, $770 million for 1981, and $820 million for 1981.[23]

The short-run cost to stockholders could also be high. The issuance of new stock to an ESOP trust represents a dilution of the equity interest of current shareholders. At a minimum, this enlargement of the volume of outstanding shares means a reduction of dividends in the near term as well as a probable decline in market price.

For the employee also, the establishment of an ESOP may not constitute an unambiguous gain. Riskier returns of dividends and asset appreciation have to be weighed against greater wage increases and the probable alternative of a pension program.

Apart from tax advantages, the employer looks for other gains—for example, in motivation of workers, reduced absenteeism, and smoother labor relations.[24] The incentive effect may be small since stock or cash dividends are only a small fraction of total compensation. The worker also has no right, as a rule, to vote his stock; and doing so would have little effect on corporate policy anyway. Provision for employee participation in problem solving on the shopfloor would appear to have significantly greater motivational force. Where unions exist, labor-management relations could be adversely affected by suspicions that ESOPs are risky, cheap, unilaterally designed alternatives to sound pension plans; by appraisals that they tend to favor higher-paid managerial employees; and by fears that they accentuate the differences in concerns of older and younger workers in negotiations over wages, and that they may give employers another device for countering union attempts at further organization or for encouraging decertification petitions.

Pensions

The pioneer in private industrial pension plans was Baltimore and Ohio Railroad (1884), but it had few followers until the first two decades of the present century. In 1916, some 117 plans were noted in a government report, with 69 of them established between 1910 and 1916. The pace quickened after World War I, an exhaustive count showing a total of 466 plans in existence in the United States and Canada in 1927. A later estimate, for 1933, indicated over 600 companies in the United States with plans covering about 5 million employees.[25]

After World War II, the number of plans increased considerably as employers sought, in the presence of a broad new system of Social Security, to identify employee interests with the fortunes of particular companies. By 1977, the estimated number of private plans exceeded 450,000; they covered nearly 50 million current or retired workers, and their assets had a market value of more than $300 billion.[26]

Unions have recognized their members' concern for adequate retirement income and have sought to extend bargaining beyond its "normal" frontiers to include negotiation and joint consultation on pensions. The Labor-Management Relations Act of 1947 provided that all trust funds of multi-employer pension funds be placed under joint employer-union management. Joint boards with equal representation of the two parties are responsible for day-to-day administration; they deal with problems of eligibility, contributions, and benefits and try to settle conflicts between the parties.[27]

Single-employer plans, on the other hand, are usually designed and operated with little input from the unions. A report of the AFL-CIO Industrial Union Department, issued in 1980, recommended that unions "should use the collective bargaining process to obtain as much of a voice as possible in the management of benefit funds."[28] Jointly administered company funds might, for example, be directed more readily to investments in residential mortgages in communities where workers live, in firms that have large domestic workforces or that have good labor relations, and in many companies other than the one that has set up the pension plan.

The 1981 tax law has important implications for private pensions—and also for the relation of these to Social Security, which faces an uncertain future as a result of demographic changes, inflation, and the expansion of benefits with inadequate actuarial and tax provisions for financing. Under the new law, a company pension plan may qualify, just like an ESOP, for annual, voluntary, tax deductible, employee contributions up to $2,000. On the other hand, an IRA may be set up by a worker independently of any existing company plan. It is not unlikely that the new law signals a future tilt toward security in old age through greater reliance on federal tax expenditures and less on tax levies. In such a case, not only will state and local governments become increasingly involved in complementary programs but so will labor and management at the company level.

NOTES

1. The Rucker Plan, like the Scanlon Plan, provides for a suggestion system, employee committees and a plantwide gain sharing plan. The Rucker standard ratio, however, is calculated on the basis of value added instead of sales value of production, thereby encouraging savings in materials, supplies, and energy purchased, as well as labor. Much less emphasis is given to labor-management cooperation and employee participation. Improshare, which stands for "improves productivity through sharing," is a relatively new group incentive plan developed by Mitchell Fein, a leading industrial engineer; it bases bonuses on improvements in labor productivity of the entire plant. Usually, no formal committee structure or employee participation is involved. For description of these plans, see study by the staff of the General Accounting Office, *Productivity Sharing Programs: Can They Contribute to Productivity Improvement,* U.S. General Accounting Office, Washington, March 3, 1981, pp. 9-12. Also, on Rucker Plan, see T. H. Patten, *Pay, Employee Compensation and Incentive Plans* (New York: Free Press, 1977), pp. 423-425.

2. For an account of Scanlon's philosophy and objectives by his associates, see articles by Clinton Golden, Fred Lesieur, Douglas McGregor, Joseph Scanlon, and G. P. Shultz, in *The Scanlon Plan: A Frontier in Labor-Management Cooperation,* F. G. Lesieur, ed., (Cambridge: The MIT Press, 1958). Also reprinted in this classic book is the famous article by R. W. Davenport, "Enterprise for Everyman," from the January 1950 issue of *Fortune.* For a more recent interpretation, from a behavioral science viewpoint, see C. F. Frost, J. H. Wakely, and R. A. Ruh, *The Scanlon Plan for Organization and Development: Identity, Participation and Equity* (Lansing: Michigan State University Press, 1974).

3. For an account of Scanlon's method of enlisting the participation of management and employees in the development of the plan, see G. K. Krulee, "The Scanlon Plan: Cooperation Through Participation," *Journal of Business,* April 1955, pp. 100-113.

4. See *Recent Initiatives in Labor-Management Cooperation,* National Center for Productivity and Quality of Working Life, Washington, 1976, pp. 43-46; also see case study of Parker Pen Company, pp. 46-50.

5. For details on bonus calculations, see B. E. Moore and T. L. Ross, *The Scanlon Way to Improved Productivity: A Practical Guide* (New York: Wiley, 1978), pp. 45-96. Various alternatives to simple ratios are presented. See also E. S. Puckett, "Measuring Performance under the Scanlon Plan," in Lesieur, ed., *Scanlon Plan,* pp. 65-79.

6. See I. H. Siegel, *Company Productivity: Measurement for Improvement* (Kalamazoo: The W. E. Upjohn Institute for Employment Research, 1980), p. 87.

7. See W. L. Batt and Edgar Weinberg, "Labor-Management Cooperation Today," *Harvard Business Review,* January/February, 1978, p. 102.

8. The United Auto Workers has established guidelines for dealing with Scanlon Plans. See statement by Don Rand of the UAW in *Breakthroughs in Union-Management Cooperation,* (Scarsdale, NY: Work in America Institute, 1977), pp. 28-29.

9. *A Plant-Wide Productivity Plan in Action: Three Years of Experience with the Scanlon Plan* (Washington: National Center for Productivity and Quality of Working Life, 1975), p. 37. In addition to a detailed case study of the Scanlon Plan at the DeSoto Company paint factory, this report reviews published research studies of the Scanlon Plan.

10. *Ibid.,* p. 40. For case studies showing the positive impact of four Scanlon Plans on productivity, see Michael Schuster, *Labor-Management Productivity Programs: Their Operation and Effect on Employment and Productivity,* a report to the Employment and Training Administration, U.S. Department of Labor, 1980.

11. *Ibid.,* pp. 19 and 41. Also E. E. Lawler III, "Reward Systems," in J. R. Hackman and J. L. Suttle, eds., *Improving Life at Work* (Santa Monica: Goodyear, 1977), pp. 205-207.

12. *Productivity Sharing Programs,* p. 9.

13. See R. S. Ruch, *The Scanlon Plan at Herman Miller* (Zeeland, MI: Herman Miller, 1976); also, J. F. Donnelly, "Participative Management at Work," *Harvard Business Review,* January/February 1977, pp. 11-12.

14. See Lawler, "Reward Systems," pp. 206-207; also, C. P. Alderfer, "Group and Intergroup Relations," in *Improving Life at Work,* p. 289. A review of Scanlon Plan literature by a Michigan State University researcher concludes that a high level of success depends heavily on managerial support, employee participation and time. See J. Kenneth White, "The Scanlon Plan: Causes and Correlates of Success," *Academy of Management Journal,* June 1979, pp. 292-312.

15. H. A. Millis and R. E. Montgomery, *Organized Labor* (New York: McGraw-Hill, 1945), p. 158.

16. Information supplied by Bert L. Metzger, president of Profit Sharing Research Foundation, Evanston, Illinois.

17. *Improving Productivity: Labor and Management Approaches,* Bulletin 1715, U.S. Bureau of Labor Statistics, 1971, p. 19; also H. R. Northrup and H. A. Young, "The Causes of Industrial Peace Revisited," *Industrial and Labor Relations Review,* October 1968, pp. 31-47.

18. Peter Henle, *Worker Participation and Ownership in American Business* (Washington: Library of Congress, 1974), pp. 9-10.

19. This paragraph and the preceding one are based on C. R. Daugherty, *Labor Problems in American Industry* (Boston: Houghton-Mifflin, 1936), pp. 757, 758-761.

20. *Employee Ownership,* June 1981, p. 4. (This new periodical is published by the National Center for Employee Ownership, Arlington, VA.)

21. ESOPs are explained in two publications of the Senate Committee on Finance: *Employee Stock Ownership Plans: An Employer Handbook,* 1980, and *ESOPs and TRASOPs: An Explanation for Employees,* 1978. For background studies on ESOP legislation, see Robert Hamrin, *Broadening the Ownership of New Capital: ESOPs and other Alternatives.* A Staff Study, Joint Economic Committee, Congress of the United States, June 17, 1976; and *The Role of the Federal Government and Employee Ownership of Business,* Select Committee on Small Business, United States Senate, January 29, 1979.

22. Imaginative uses of ESOPs may be found in various issues of *Employee Ownership* (see footnote 20).

23. *Special Analysis, Budget of the United States Government, Fiscal Year 1982,* Office of Management and Budget, Washington, 1981, p. 228.

24. For a critique of ESOPs from various points of view, see G. M. Saltzman, *Employee Stock Ownership Plans (ESOP's): An Economic and Industrial Relations Analysis,* Office

of the Assistant Secretary for Policy, Evaluation and Research, U.S. Department of Labor, September 1979. For a strong advocacy of ESOPs, see speech by Senator Russell Long, sponsor of S. 1162, Expanded Ownership Act of 1981, in *Congressional Record,* May 12, 1981, pp. S4779-S4795. Part of S.1162 was incorporated in the Economic Recovery Tax Act of 1981.

25. Daugherty, *Labor Problems,* p. 745.

26. *Preliminary Estimates of Participants and Financial Characteristics of Private Pension Plans, 1977,* U.S. Department of Labor, Labor-Management Services Administration, 1981.

27. *Administration of Negotiated Pension, Health and Insurance Plans: Major Collective Bargaining Agreements,* Bulletin 1425-12, U.S. Bureau of Labor Statistics, 1970, p. 1.

28. *Pensions: A Study of Benefit Fund Investment Policies,* Washington: Industrial Union Department, AFL-CIO, 1980, pp. 4-5.

9
Public Sector Collaboration

Some Comparisons with Private Sector

Scope for labor-management cooperation in the public sector (federal, state, and local) appears even greater than in the private sector. Although unions and employee associations there include a larger proportion (over two-fifths) of the total number of workers (about 16 million) than in the private sector, they do not perform their negotiating functions as fully, freely, or surely.[1] Many of the labor organizations are relatively new and inexperienced. Collective bargaining, furthermore, is still unevenly accepted by public employers, in some instances having been rejected outright. The strike, too, is commonly forbidden in the public sector; the summary dismissal of federal air traffic controllers who walked off the job in August 1981 is bound to encourage or reinforce "hard-line" positions in other jurisdictions. Where strikes or other voluntary interruptions of service are legal or tolerated, the inconvenience and resentment felt by ordinary citizens may nevertheless act as a partial deterrent. Finally, machinery for impartial and binding arbitration is still not used routinely or as a last resort for the settlement of disputes that threaten to erupt into open hostilities.[2]

All these circumstances point to the desirability of labor-management forums for peaceful exploration and adjustment of differences and for the realization of mutual benefits at low cost to both sides. This chapter illustrates the variety of cooperative media already used in the public sector for consultation and problem solving. It takes special account of the Tennessee Valley experience, which has incorporated labor-management arrangements in a larger framework of regional development.

As in the private sector, the committees formed for joint consultation or problem solving in the public sector range widely, may overlap, and differ in vigor, efficacy, and longevity. Also as in the private sector, a bilateral disposition to temper the adversarial impulse is a prerequisite condition for constructive collaboration. This condition, though necessary, is not sufficient. It cannot be repeated too often that leadership, persistence, patience, knowledge, and skill are also required.

Many collective bargaining agreements already include provisions for labor-management committees. Indeed, such committees are far more prevalent than in the private sector, where they may be acknowledged in only about 5 percent of the major contracts. A study made by the U.S. Bureau of Labor Statistics (BLS) of 286 bargaining agreements in force in 1970 in 39 of the nation's larger cities showed provision for joint committees in 19 percent of the cases.[3] Another BLS study, for the federal agencies and a similar date, found a much larger incidence: 44 percent, or 314 of the 671 examined agreements.[4] Although many of the committees must have been only "paper" constructions, the figures nevertheless reflect an awareness of their potentials and a willingness to experiment.

Productivity Committees

The expansion of public needs and services, the concomitant increase in payrolls and staff, and the aggravation of normal taxpayer resistance by a relentless inflation—these developments have made productivity a lively issue of public debate since the late 1960s. Threats to solvency at all levels of government have inspired efforts to devise and apply means of economizing, such as the elimination of less essential services, reduction of waste, and improvement of personnel utilization and performance.[5]

At first, in the early 1970s, "productivity bargaining" seemed a practical way toward more effective use of workers. The idea was to allow management to "buy out" certain work rules as part of the wage settlement—and thereby to reduce unit labor cost and the upward pressure of cost on prices. In Nassau County (N.Y.) and elsewhere, projects were set up to improve performance and to consider the proper division of savings. Although clear benefits were discernible from work-rule reform, the design of mutually acceptable payoff formulas often proved elusive.[6]

An alternative approach to productivity advancement has entailed the establishment of formal committees through collective bargaining. Some of the committees engage in the estimation of savings attributable to productivity gain, but others do not have such duties. A few of the federal and local initiatives are briefly described below.

Federal Committees

In 1975-1977, joint productivity councils were set up at four defense depots.[7] Civilian employees at each of the facilities numbered about 6,000. In each case, local officials of the American Federation of Government Employees and the Laborers' International Union signed a memorandum of agreement with military commanders. These memoranda, developed with consulting assistance supplied through the National Center for Productivity and Quality of Working Life, outlined common goals, which had to be endorsed by high authority in union headquarters and in the Department of Defense.

Eight committee members selected by each council met weekly on government time to consider impediments to efficient performance. The recommendations of these committees were forwarded to commanding officers, who then advised the councils of their decisions. The committee deliberations were conducted with full appreciation that failure to achieve cooperative cost control could lead to contracting-out of in-house activities and a consequent loss of jobs.

Experience over several years has indicated both tangible and intangible benefits from the committee system. Performance standards were raised, absenteeism and abuse of sick leave were reduced, mutual trust between labor and management grew, and team work became more natural. Groundwork was laid for the later use of quality circles at various depots.

One exploratory study, relating to six joint undertakings in a large midwestern city in the early 1970s, reported favorably on the work of federal productivity councils and committees.[8] It particularly stressed the contribution of open channels of communication to reduction of labor-management disputes; the two-way flow of information provided a basis for effective problem solving.

Despite such positive features, another survey, made by the Office of Personnel Management, has disclosed a high mortality rate.[9] By 1980, only 4 out of 25 committees set up in the 1970s under collective bargaining agreements were reported to be still active. The remainder had either been abolished or had deteriorated as a result of labor-management conflict or indifference to their recommendations.

Local Government

Joint productivity committees have sprung up in various towns and cities caught between the tide of rising costs and the rocks of relatively static and uncertain revenues. The committees are typically confined to particular agencies or departments of government and may focus on particular facilities or activities.[10] Two examples are described briefly below for New York City, which attracted considerable national attention a few years ago as it teetered on the brink of bankruptcy—not alone, but very visibly.

New York Transit Authority. In the 1971 contract negotiations between the New York Transit Authority and the Transport Workers Union, the two parties agreed to establish a "special joint committee" for dealing with inadequate productivity in bus maintenance.[11] This activity, which engaged about 5,000 workers, had been the subject of long, intense contention.

The committee was chartered to review work practices and schedules, the adequacy of materials and tools, and so forth. It had an impartial chairman empowered to make binding decisions in case of disagreement. Initial success in projects involving bus maintenance encouraged establishment of similar committees in other departments. As productivity improvements led to reduction of manpower requirements, workers were transferred to other jobs without loss of pay and more repair work was done in-house rather than contracted out.

Both sides agreed that good results had been obtained under the joint program but felt that fuller rank and file participation was essential for maximum benefit. Union fears that workers would resist employment savings proved unwarranted. The program prepared the Transit Authority for participation in the citywide venture described next.

COLA-Productivity Linkage in New York. A broader-based program of cooperation was introduced and pursued as New York City's financial prostration neared irreversibility. Sweeping readjustments were required in pay and in union-management relations affecting some 250,000 employees. Piecemeal approaches to productivity stimulation had proved inadequate. More thorough reform became a prerequisite to federal and state assistance and to continuing credit-worthiness in general.

The new citywide program, begun in the latter 1970s under the eye of a state monitoring board, has entailed a stay of wage increases, lowering of employment ceilings (through attrition rather than layoffs), and defrayal of COLA (cost-of-living adjustments) through productivity gains and other cost savings rather than reduction of services. Top city and union officials make up a Joint Labor-Management Productivity Committee that is chaired by a representative of the public and sets broad policy guidelines. Lower tiers of similar committees were established for 26 city departments to plot the conservation of cash outlays without dilution of services.[12]

A survey of program participants conducted in 1977 found that sufficient money savings were frequently achieved for payment of the cost-of-living allowances.[13] It was felt, however, that the incentive effect would be of short duration and that commitment would flag as a sense of crisis diminished. Union officials voiced the expected criticisms that the program infringed on collective bargaining, paid insufficient attention to improvement of employee morale as a route to productivity gain, and was shaped primarily by management.

At each of 16 major public hospitals included in a city administration employing a total of about 35,000 workers, a labor-management committee proposed revenue-yielding projects to meet COLA goals.[14] Among the successful initiatives requiring no increases in personnel were the installation of more rigorous systems for collection of fees for outpatient services, major expansion of auxiliary pharmacy business, and the more economical use of medical supplies. A top level labor-management committee provided information and technical assistance to individual hospitals in addition to setting common policy and acting as coordinator.

The contracts negotiated in 1978 between the city and municipal unions cut the link of COLA and productivity, but the committee structure was retained. Attention shifted to matters like training and absenteeism, which, of course, also bear on productivity.

Despite the city's financial straits and the invocation of cooperative arrangements, the adversarial spirit has remained very much alive. A fresh example is provided by the comments made on a cost-of-living award to some 35,000 transit workers in October 1981; the award was based on a program designed to yield $16.9 million in savings.[15] The mayor opined that the decision of the three-man productivity panel to approve the payment was a "sham." The head of the Transit Authority, who was one of the three panel members, also had grave misgivings even though he cited savings in car cleaning, consolidation of operations in one of the shops, and a substitution of trucks for trains in picking up fares collected at train stations. The productivity panel concept, he stated, was "flawed." Credits, he felt, were being given where no tangible saving occurred and where workers carried only the workload expected under approved job assignments. The union head, also a panel member, was satisfied with the decision, claiming that it justified the contention that the workers had "earned and paid for" the full COLA. Savings were cited in the use of energy and in car maintenance. The neutral member considered the decision "fair" in the light of contract provisions and the facts on cost-savings and productivity disclosed in a review lasting "several weeks."

Quality Circles

From defense contractors in the aerospace industry, quality circles quickly spread to the contracting agencies themselves. A survey made in 1980 by the Office of Personnel Management found them in existence at regional or field installations of the Air Force, the Navy, and the Federal Aviation Agency.[16] As in industrial practice, the circles comprise small voluntary groups of about eight employees, led by supervisors, who meet weekly. All group members receive formal training in problem solving. Reported accomplishments usually feature reductions in rework, error rates, fuel consumption, and other specific sources of cost.

At the Norfolk Naval Shipyard, which has 12,000 employees, 36 circles are expected to be in operation in 1982. In the initial year, the program included only nine. Although the program was developed entirely by shipyard management, union representatives sit on the committee that directs it.

Worker Satisfaction and Well-Being

Labor-management arrangements that are directed toward worker concerns and needs are at least as necessary in the public sector as in the private. First, as already mentioned earlier in this book, such arrangements may have favorable spillover effects on productivity. The activity of government is typically labor-intensive, making heavy use of services to create and deliver other services, so worker morale and motivation have an important bearing on output quantity and quality. Furthermore, the products are usually not sold, so feedback from the marketplace is minimal. The products also often are intangible, preventive, or contingent, so it is easy for a government worker to lose a vivid sense of the realities of the competitive external environment of the customer. Finally, since pay is regular and the job relatively secure, the daily discontents and frictions of the internal workplace acquire great psychological moment.

Before such irritations can manifest themselves in indifferent service or disruptive "job actions," they may be detected for joint address by means of attitude and opinion surveys. One study, for example, completed for the National Center for Quality and Working Life in 1978, cited public worker doubts about the competence of management and discontent with lack of recognition for good performance—while managers appeared satisfied.[17] Another example, a survey made by University of Michigan researchers for the U.S. Department of Labor and reported in 1980, found Michigan teachers more unhappy than American workers in general over various aspects of their jobs. The researchers concluded that "school effectiveness may be enhanced if increased resources are used to establish appropriate problem solving structures (e.g., strong channels for vertical communication) and those channels are actively used by school personnel to solve problems (e.g., instructional methods)."[18]

Quality of Working Life

Two experiments conducted in municipalities in the 1970s, in which consultants to the Quality of Worklife Program at Ohio State University's Center for Human Resource Research assisted, illustrate the collaboration of unions and management to upgrade work, the workplace, and the worker with benefit to performance.

Springfield Project. In 1974, the district director of the union (AFSCME) representing municipal employees proposed a project to defuse tense labor-management relations in Springfield, a city of 80,000 people.[19] The union saw an opportunity to improve the public perception of organized government employees, while the city manager saw an opportunity to provide better service. A written agreement, ratified by 470 union members, established guiding principles: twin goals of improving the work environment and delivered services; avoidance of issues belonging to the domains of collective bargaining and grievance handling; setaside of contract provisions for the duration of the project only if both parties agree; and avoidance of layoffs or downgrading as a result of the project.

A central committee, half top management and half union leaders, moved to involve rank-and-file workers in five departmental mini-committees. These mini-committees, in turn, coordinated work groups at the worksites. Under the supervision of a foreman, each work group met weekly, over a month, to identify problems of common concern and to make recommendations. Over 300 people took part in this self-examination. The work groups fed back their reports to the mini-committees, which analyzed the data and presented the results with recommendations to employees in their departments.

The system permitted more open communication and information exchange throughout the city government and gave workers a chance to advise on the purchase of equipment used in their jobs. It also permitted work restructuring, with more responsibility and autonomy for teams—and concomitant increase in productivity, reduction of overtime, and shortening of the actual workday. It allowed enlargement of the jobs of motor equipment operators to include training in welding for in-house repair work instead of contracting out.

Columbus Project. The Springfield venture led the regional director of the government workers' union (AFSCME) and the Ohio State University consultants to propose a similar project to the mayor of the much larger neighboring city of Columbus. The mayor readily assented, and a two-year agreement was signed (see documentary appendix). Necessary funds were supplied by the city, the union, and the U.S. Department of Health, Education, and Welfare.[20]

Both sides pledged to keep adversarial issues outside the project. Management guaranteed that no reduction of jobs or pay would be sought, that time for meetings would be compensated, and that needed training would be provided. Furthermore, it agreed to work with the union to develop a plan for sharing with employees any productivity gains achieved through the project. The union pledged to make every effort "to resolve any grievances filed in contract items set aside for trial periods outside the formal grievance procedure."

The same structure was adopted as in Springfield—a top level committee, mini-committees, and unitary work groups. Again, communication was greatly facilitated, and problem solving at the group level was encouraged. It was recognized that broad participation in decisionmaking conduces to broad acceptance of the emerging decisions.

Many different aspects of worklife quality were addressed during the first two years of the Columbus program. Among these were: improvement of employee lunchrooms, procedures for equalization of overtime (as required by the collective bargaining contract), design of a system for evaluating performance, and experimentation with flexible work scheduling for maintenance personnel. More important than the concrete results was the demonstration by the Columbus and Springfield projects that cooperation could create an atmosphere and the instrumentality for investigating alternative modes of organizing work in public services with advantage to both employee satisfaction and productivity.

Skill Improvement

Both parties have long recognized that skill improvement through training of employees could be a win-win game. In a number of cities with strong unions and sophisticated management, innovative training programs have been jointly planned and organized. These efforts, however, do not appear to have been as widely imitated as they presumably deserve to be.

An early venture was one sponsored in 1968 by the district council of a union of local government employees and New York City officials for upgrading workers in municipal hospitals.[21] This joint undertaking, which depended heavily on federal funds, provided in-service training for low-rank employees, enabling some to move into licensed occupations without interruption of their employment or jeopardy to their seniority and other rights. It dramatized the possibility of career development for the disadvantaged in public institutions.

A more recent example is the joint program set up in Troy, Michigan by the Department of Public Works and Parks and the AFSCME local.[22] The proposal originated with management; it started with a general idea about productivity improvement, but, in the discussion that ensued, training in health and safety came to the fore as a matter for primary emphasis. A survey of employees convinced the joint Job Enrichment and Productivity Committee to accord priority to training in first aid, the operation of equipment, and supervision. Further development of this training initiative followed a detailed work analysis of each job by the personnel department and a review of employee recommendations for improvement. The union withdrew from co-sponsorship for lack of direct benefit, but it continued to participate with the Department in furtherance of membership training.

Flexible Work Schedules

By 1980, according to the Bureau of Labor Statistics, a fifth of the employees in public administration were eligible for some type of flexible work scheduling. Impetus to the spread of novel arrangements that allow for worker convenience without impeding organizational operations was given by passage of the Federal Employees Flexible and Compressed Work Schedules Act of 1978 (P.L. 95-390). This law authorized a three-year period of controlled experimentation for federal civilian employees to determine the advantages and disadvantages of various alternatives to traditional uniform work schedules. This experimentation was accommodated by temporary modification of certain premium pay, overtime pay, and scheduling provisions of the Fair Labor Standards Act.

About 1,500 experiments, involving about 325,000 workers, were under way in federal agencies throughout the country by 1982. The most popular plans allowed maximum carryover of hours from one pay period to the next; a shorter workweek with longer hours per day (4 days, 10 hours per day); and alternation of the standard and shorter workweeks.

Although union headquarters have looked askance at flexible work schedules (as potential threats to hard-won standards respecting premium pay and as arrangements that ought to be accommodated within the existing legal framework), local unions at federal agencies have been less circumspect. They have participated with management in selecting plans and sites for experimentation. In the U.S. Department of Labor, at least one labor-management task group has met regularly to monitor the program's effect on productivity and to work out answers to technical questions raised by employees.

In 1981, the Office of Personnel Management found widespread approval of flexitime among employees and supervisors after three years of experience, but continuation of the program was not assured. A view strongly held in the new federal administration is that flexitime should be limited to cases in which clear benefits in productivity or service to the public would result.

Health and Safety

Since the Occupational Safety and Health Act does not cover public employees, their protection on the job and against alcoholic disablement has been an important topic of labor-management cooperation. Two urban examples are briefly considered below.

In the District of Columbia, joint committees exist in at least two departments of the local government under the umbrella of collective bargaining.[23] A comprehensive and continuing joint program seeks to eliminate dangerous equipment, to improve safety in the workplace, and to promote safety consciousness in the repair shop of the Service Department. Significant reductions of accidents and injuries have been reported as well as gains in productivity. The union and management also cooperate in dealing with tardiness, absenteeism, and morale, with the union taking major responsibility for helping problem workers. In another D.C. department, concerned with water supply, the union and management have cooperated in counseling and rehabilitation programs for workers afflicted with alcoholism. This condition, described as a major deterrent to productivity, has affected about 15 percent of the workforce. In the same department, a joint safety committee is said to have been noticeably successful in accident prevention.

In the city of Memphis, labor-management committees were set up in 1971 to combat health and safety hazards in the sanitation, public works, and public service departments, employing about 2,600 workers.[24] Since high accident rates were ascribed mainly to poor maintenance of equipment, joint committees promoted the timely reporting of malfunctions, stricter inspection of city vehicles, rigorous investigation of accidents, and installation of safety devices. In the opinion of both parties, the committees have had constructive influence.

Employment Security

The fiscal travail of the 1970s exposed the vulnerability of "secure" jobs in the state and local "civil service." The 1980s will apparently underscore the same insecurity in federal employment. Bargaining contracts in the public sector have seldom provided for severance pay; and, in a period of government retrenchment, the general public and elected politicians are much more inclined to seek the retention of customary services than the jobs of the "bureaucrats" performing them. Accordingly, some interest has developed in joint programs to anticipate and to alleviate the problems faced by public sector personnel when budgets are cut and work is extensively reorganized.

New York State Committee

As an example of the kind of cooperation entailed, we briefly consider the program established by the State of New York and the Civil Service Employees Association in 1976.[25] A key role in this program was given to a joint committee for "continuity of employment." This committee included five management representatives, five union representatives, and a neutral academic chairman (assisted by a staff of two). Its work was regarded as adjunct to, and parallel with, the collective bargaining process. The committee's charter was set forth in the bargaining agreement, as in the case of the Armour automation committee described in chapter 5. Its assignment was to:

a) Study worker displacement problems arising from economy RIFs, programmatic reductions and curtailments, closedowns, relocations, consolidations, technological changes, and contracting out; and

b) Make recommendations for the solution of these problems, including but not limited to the use of normal and induced attrition (e.g., early retirements), sharing of available state job opportunities (e.g., transfers) indemnification (e.g., severance pay), and transition to work in the labor market beyond state employment (e.g., retraining).

In its first three years, the committee studied the status and adjustments of 10,000 workers already laid off, proposed remedial actions, made policy recommendations on job security, and conducted several demonstration projects on avoidance of layoff by workforce planning and reassignment.

The committee's efforts to help laid off workers were only "minimally effective." Of the 10,000 in the original cohort, 1,200 remained unemployed or were underutilized. A center was accordingly set up, at state expense, to assist through counseling, referral retraining, and outplacement in the private sector. The target group, however, was not generally receptive; it consisted largely of older workers, and only about 10 percent clearly benefited.

The committee was more successful in devising an alternative to the state's layoff policy. It proposed workforce reduction through attrition and the offer of retraining for other jobs in the same area at comparable grades. These concepts were subsequently applied to state efforts to deinstitutionalize mental health care.

In 1979, New York State and the Civil Service Employees Association agreed to extend the scope of cooperation beyond continuity of employment. A Committee on the Work Environment and Productivity was established with nine members, representing labor, management, and the general public. The enlarged responsibilities included study and recommendations concerning performance evaluation, productivity, and quality of working life. A major goal set for 1979-1982 was "enhancing the lives of employees at the workplace and improving productivity through cooperative labor-management committees."[26] A sum of $2 million was appropriated for demonstration projects, employee surveys, etc.

Pensions

Provision for retirement income now exists for public employees at all levels of government. The contributory federal program for civil servants was enacted in 1920. (Federal pension and related benefits for war veterans trace back to 1792.) The first city pension plan, set up in New York in 1857, was confined to policemen. New York City was also the site of the first mutual aid program for teachers, established in 1869; employer contributions did not begin until 1898. Among the states, Massachusetts led the way in setting up a pension program for *all* its employees (1911). With the growth of the merit system, the scope and number of public plans has increased steadily during the present century.[27]

The expansion of public pension plans in the past two decades has been enormous, especially at the state and local levels. Public employee unions have been active in seeking pension gains as part of total compensation. By 1975, 6,698 public plans were in force, including 68 at the federal level; and over 90 percent of public employees were covered (10.4 million full-time and part-time state and local employees and 5 million others on federal civilian and military payrolls).[28] Union officials are included in retirement boards that administer state and local plans; they participate in investment decisions.

Fiscal difficulties at all levels of government have invited closer scrutiny of pension benefits, financing, and administration. Unions have negotiated with administrators and legislators on proposed changes intended to reduce costs. Studies of the management of state and local pension funds—assets amounting to more than $46 billion in 1976—have revealed widespread inadequacies tending to reduce investment income and accordingly to increase the burden on taxpayers.[29]

In the mid-1970s, when New York City could no longer sell its bonds on the open market or refinance existing debt without guarantees from the state and federal governments, municipal unions approved the use of employee pension fund money for purchase of large amounts of the city's notes and bonds. According to a leading industrial relations scholar, "this made the unions *de facto* partners in the management of the city." He also noted, however, that "there is little evidence that unions in New York City have abandoned, or even diluted, in a significant way their aggressiveness and intensity of effort in collective bargaining."[30]

Tennessee Valley Authority

To developing nations, the Tennessee Valley Authority (TVA) has, for almost half a century, served as a model of integrated planning for the economic and social development of a "backward" region. In the United States, attitudes toward this gem of the New Deal has been ambivalent and inconstant—except, perhaps with regard to its brilliant record of labor-management cooperation over several decades. This record commands our attention not only because of the durability of the collaboration but also because of the size of the organization (more than 40,000 employees), the number of unions and states involved, and the extensive tie-ins with the private sector. Very recently, in 1981, the historic harmony appeared ready to end in bitter discord; and this development, too, is reason for taking special notice of the TVA phenomenon.

Committee System

The design for cooperation at TVA proceeded from a visionary idealization of economic democracy, but it also took account of a worldly precedent: the B&O plan discussed in an earlier chapter. A guiding premise was that collective bargaining and cooperation are not only compatible but also essential to effective operation.[31] Article X of the contract negotiated between TVA and the Trades and Labor Council of 16 craft unions in 1940 called for a two-tier committee structure:

1. TVA and the Council, having recognized that cooperation between management and employees is indispensable to the accomplishment of the purposes for which TVA has been established, maintain and support a Central Joint Cooperative Committee and local joint cooperative committees as an effective means by which to foster such cooperation.

2. These cooperative committees give consideration to such matters as the elimination of waste; the conservation of materials, supplies, and energy; the improvement of quality of workmanship and services; the promotion of education and training; the correction of conditions making for misunderstandings; the encouragement of courtesy in the relations of employees with the public; the safeguarding of health; the prevention of hazards to life and property; and the strengthening of the morale of the service. The committees shall, however, not consider and act upon subjects or disputes the adjustment of which is provided for by Articles VI, VII, and VIII of this agreement (jurisdiction, grievances, wages).

Later, similar provision was made in the agreement with unions representing white-collar workers (e.g., the TVA Engineering Association and the Office and Professional Employees International Union). Additional information on the committee system is given in the last entry of the documentary appendix.

In 1980, the Central Policy Committee oversaw 119 entities—64 "conferences" including white-collar workers, 15 "committees" including workers in the 16 building trades, and 40 "groups" including both blue-collar and white-collar workers. Each of these entities has 15-30 members (both labor and management), and each member represents 8-15 employees. Meeting monthly, each committee or conference deals with proposed solutions to problems of morale, productivity, quality, housekeeping, etc. that cannot be settled by the bargaining process.

The committees and conferences solicit suggestions for improvement (from managers as well as hourly workers!). Many of the suggestions are offered by groups of employees. Approved suggestions do not earn cash awards; instead, they are given wide publicity. Most of the suggestions relate to work methods, quality of service, and waste; others relate to safety, health, training, morale, and the work environment.[32]

Relation to Collective Bargaining

In principle, the committees and conferences are required to steer clear of matters subject to formal contract negotiation, like pay, and grievances for which machinery already exists. In practice, however, these extra-normal entities have naturally engaged in discussions of issues that eventually are decided in contract negotiations. In 1975, the contracts were amended to allow recommendations on negotiable matters.

Negotiations concerning wages and fringe benefits, while conducted separately from committee-conference deliberations, are not intensely adversarial as a rule. TVA employees are supposed to be paid according to area prevailing pay rates. Surveys of these scales are conducted jointly—a procedure that has normally reduced, even if it does not eliminate, the acrimony so common in conventional bargaining.

A Quality of Worklife Venture

In 1974, a joint experiment was begun to expand the scope of, and to create more interest in, the cooperative conferences of white-collar employees.[33] The Chattanooga office of the Division of Transmission and Engineering was selected as the site; it employed 300 persons, including engineers, draftsmen, supervisors, and office workers. The aim of the project was to determine organizational changes that would create a more satisfying work environment and conduce to higher productivity.

With the assistance of independent consultants, the committee in charge conducted interviews, made surveys, and held meetings and workshops to encourage interest in projects that could lead to greater employee influence over daily work. As might be expected, first-line supervisors at first resisted, fearing transfer of decisionmaking authority on technical matters to their staffs. Some projects were stimulated on work restructuring, flexible scheduling, recognition of merit in pay, and performance evaluation. An important result of the venture was to enlarge the scope of cooperative conferences in all TVA divisions.

In addition to the committee-conference system, there are programs for joint address of special topics of mutual interest. Thus, joint training committees develop and administer courses for operators and apprentices. A joint health insurance committee monitors the medical insurance plan. A joint committee exchanges ideas on job classification.

The New Disharmony

While officials of TVA and the many unions involved have consistently and strongly supported the committee-conference system, the era of good feeling may have come to an end in 1981. In September, the TVA Board and five white-collar unions, representing 17,500 employees, sharply disagreed over new contract terms affecting pay and promotion. Pro-strike sentiment was tempered by fresh memory of the fate of federal air traffic controllers, who were summarily dismissed after their August walkout.[34] A settlement was finally reached, but the unions decided to cancel their participation in the voluntary program of cooperative conferences begun in 1947. For the time being, the blue-collar workers continued to support their cooperative committees.

The unusual bitterness of the dispute reflected a major shift in labor-management styles over the past few years. Inflation and budgetary constraints have motivated greater management stress on productivity and cost-cutting. Unions appear to have become less inclined to cooperate in these regards and more inclined to concentrate on "maintaining gains won during the past through the only effective mechanism available—collective bargaining."[35]

NOTES

1. Michael Grace, "The Chaos in Public Sector Bargaining," *The AFL-CIO American Federationist,* July 1981, p. 9.

2. See R. W. Fleming, "Public-Employee Bargaining: Problems and Prospects," *Proceedings of the Thirty-First Annual Meeting, August 29-31, 1978,* Industrial Relations Research Association, p. 15. See Arvid Anderson, "The Trilateral Shape of the Eighties," *Proceedings of the 1980 Spring Meeting, April 16-18, 1980,* p. 454. Mention should be made of the establishment of a joint labor-management committee by statute in Massachusetts for resolving police and firefighter disputes.

3. *Municipal Collective Bargaining Agreements in Large Cities,* Bulletin M59, U.S. Bureau of Labor Statistics, 1972, p. 14.

4. *Collective Bargaining Agreements in the Federal Service, Late 1971,* Bulletin 1789, Bureau of Labor Statistics, 1973, p. 62.

5. For brief analysis of the problem, see *Improving Productivity in State and Local Government* (New York: Committee for Economic Development, 1976).

6. See R. B. McKersie, "An Evaluation of Productivity Bargaining in the Public Sector" in *Collective Bargaining and Productivity,* Gerald Somers, ed. (Madison: Industrial Relations Research Association, 1975), pp. 55-60. Also, Sam Zagoria, *Productivity: A Positive Route* (Washington: Labor-Management Relations Service of the U.S. Conference of Mayors, 1978), p. 10.

7. See G. H. Kuper, "Labor-Management Councils: No One Loses!" *Defense Management Journal,* April 1977, pp. 59-64.

8. J. E. Martin, "Union-Management Committees in the Federal Sector," *Monthly Labor Review,* October 1976, p. 32.

9. See *Survey of Quality Circles and Labor-Management Committees in the Federal Government,* Office of Productivity Programs, Office of Personnel Management, Washington, 1980, p. 6.

10. For examples, see *Labor-Management Committees in the Public Sector: Experiences of Eight Committees* (Washington: National Commission on Productivity and Work Quality, 1975). For a comprehensive account of how joint committees are organized and operated, see G. I. Susman, *A Guide to Labor-Management Committees in State and Local Government,* U.S. Department of Housing and Urban Development, Washington, 1980. Also, Susan Clark, *Executive Report on Guide,* U.S. Department of Housing and Urban Development, Washington, 1980.

11. *Labor-Management Committees,* pp. 11-20.

12. For detailed account of the system, see A. C. Goldoff with D. C. Tatge, "Union-Management Cooperation in New York," *Public Productivity Review,* Summer/Fall 1978, pp. 35-47.

13. A. C. Goldoff, "The Perceptions of Participants in a Joint Productivity Program," *Monthly Labor Review,* July 1978, pp. 33-34.

14. For an account of the experience, see *Improving Productivity and Quality of Working Life in the Public Sector: Pioneering Initiatives in Labor-Management Cooperation,* A

Final Report on "Project Network" (Philadelphia: University of Pennsylvania, Management and Behavioral Science Center, Wharton School, 1980), pp. 75-93.

15. *New York Times,* October 2, 1981.

16. *Survey of Quality Circles,* pp. 8-11.

17. *Employee Attitudes and Productivity Differences between the Public and Private Sector* (Washington: National Center for Productivity and Quality of Working Life, 1978).

18. Hyman Kornbluh and R. A. Cooke, *The Quality of Worklife of Teachers,* Report to the U.S. Department of Labor, ASPER, Washington, 1980.

19. See case study in *Recent Initiatives in Labor-Management Cooperation,* Vol. II (Washington: National Center for Productivity and Quality of Working Life, 1978), pp. 53-62.

20. See case study in *Improving Productivity,* pp. 17-41; also. Marty Jenkins, "Columbus, Ohio Continues Structured Approach to QWL," *Labor-Management Relations Service Newsletter,* October 1979, pp. 2-3; and Don Ronchi and Roger Wilkens, *Productivity in Perspective: The View from a Refuse Team* (Columbus: Ohio State University, Center for Human Resources Research, 1977).

21. Sumner Rosen, "Union-Management Cooperation: Is There an Agenda for Tomorrow?" *Proceedings of the Twenty-First Annual Winter Meeting, December 29-30, 1968,* Industrial Relations Research Association, pp. 85-86.

22. *Improving Productivity,* pp. 139-149.

23. *Labor-Management Committees,* pp. 5-10; and pp. 47-52.

24. *Ibid.,* pp. 39-46.

25. For a full account, see R. B. McKersie, Leonard Greenhalgh, and Todd Jick, *Report of the Continuity of Employment Committee for the Period 1976-79* (Albany: Governor's Office of Employee Relations, 1980). See documentary appendix for committee bylaws.

26. *Report to the Legislature on Expenditures and Activities for Joint Labor-Management Committees* (Albany: Governor's Office of Employee Relations, 1981).

27. This paragraph is based largely on J. J. Corson and J. W. McConnell, *Economic Needs of Older People* (New York: Twentieth Century Fund, 1956), chapter 8.

28. A. H. Munnel and A. M. Connolly, *Pensions for Public Employees* (Washington: National Planning Association, 1979), p. 3.

29. *Ibid.,* p. 92. See, also, Arden Hall and Hal Hovey, "State and Local Government Retirement Systems: Problems and Prospects," *National Tax Journal,* September 1980, pp. 377-378.

30. T. A. Kochan, *Collective Bargaining and Industrial Relations* (Homewood, IL: Irwin, 1980), p. 439. See, also, Damodar Gujarati, *Pensions and New York City's Fiscal Crisis* (Washington: American Enterprise Institute for Public Policy Research, 1978).

31. For a detailed description of the whole system, see, *Guidelines for Union-Management Cooperative Program,* Tennessee Valley Authority, Knoxville, April 1971.

32. For evaluations, generally favorable, see S. H. Slichter, J. J. Healy, and E. R. Livernash, *The Impact of Collective Bargaining on Management* (Washington: Brookings In-

stitution, 1960), p. 863; A. S. Tannenbaum, "Systems of Formal Participation," in *Organizational Behavior Research and Issues* (Madison: Industrial Relations Research Association, 1974), p. 96; and Martin Patchen, *Participation, Achievement, and Involvement on the Job* (Englewood Cliffs: Prentice-Hall, 1970).

33. See case study by P. S. Goodman and E. E. Lawler III, "United States," in *New Forms of Work Organization* (Geneva: International Labour Organization, 1979), pp. 159-162.

34. *Business Week,* September 21, 1981, pp. 31-32.

35. M. L. Brookshire and M. D. Rogers, "Productivity and Collective Bargaining in the Public Sector," in *Proceedings of the 1981 Spring Meeting, April 29-May 1, 1981,* Industrial Relations Research Association, p. 479.

10
Looking Ahead

This brief chapter comments on the near term outlook for labor-management cooperation in the light of past developments and current signs. Accordingly, it leans heavily on the content of earlier chapters. On the whole, it suggests a considerable quickening of the tempo, and extension of the range, of collaborative activity at the industry, enterprise, and community levels.

We should recall first what amounts to a necessary, but not sufficient, condition for the quickening and extension just mentioned: the American style of industrial relations has already proved hospitable to pragmatic, even creative, probings for collaborative opportunity. The preceding chapters (and the documentary appendix) amply attest to the trial and practice of many varieties of joint activity that have counterparts in West Europe and Japan. They also should alert the reader to the possibility of underestimating the actual level of labor-management cooperation in the United States—because of the prevalence, open-endedness, and adaptability of decentralized collective bargaining.

The American style of industrial relations promises to become still more hospitable to collaboration in the near future as: (1) its usual adversarial thrust is restrained (not abandoned) and (2) the federal government abdicates or at-tenuates various roles it had assumed in the past few decades as a third party representing the perceived "public interest." The moderation of the adversarial spirit (which animates the "normal" competition and conflict of labor and manage-ment in the United States) and the federal retreat will leave greater scope for the co-existing voluntaristic impulse to joint endeavor.

Future reinforcement of the voluntary disposition to cooperate is suggested by a number of pervasive cir-cumstances. Among these are:

1. A proneness to (a) intolerable rates of price inflation and (b) wage increases far in excess of productivity gains.
2. Slow, uncertain, and uneven economic growth in a set-ting of very high interest rates and huge defense demands.
3. Intense foreign competition for markets in the United States as well as markets abroad.
4. Aging of the labor force, which will (for this and other reasons) become more security-oriented.
5. Attrition of the economic base of once-prosperous areas and regions of the country.
6. More determined automatization and robotization of production, threatening various conventional skills and ex-isting jobs.
7. Budgetary stringency at the state and local levels, diminishing the bargaining power of public service unions.

Efforts to reduce drastically the federal presence in "regulation" and in social welfare arrangements may be ex-pected to encourage labor and management to (1) minimize disturbance to existing equilibria and to (2) expand the cur-rent range of topics for negotiation and cooperation. Presumably, the two parties will wish to limit the new uncer-tainties surrounding the devolution of federal responsibilities to lower jurisdictions and nongovernmental bodies. They will also have to fill gaps left by the weakening of federal commitment to worker health and safety, pollution control, training, and so forth. Incidentally, the shifting of burdens from the federal government to local jurisdictions will contribute to the budgetary stringency cited in the preceding paragraph.

The seven pervasive circumstances listed above may be expected to promote collaboration along these lines:

1. The sharing of financial and cost information with unions by companies in dire straits (a conditional "opening of the books").

2. The placement of labor leaders on more company boards of directors.[1]

3. Retention, insofar as practicable, of otherwise laid off workers for training in problem solving techniques and in occupations needed for future productive activities.[2]

4. Promotion of company, industry, and area products and lobbying for import limitations.

5. Borrowing from pension funds to help ailing local governments.

6. Company assistance to employees in the acquisition of relinquished facilities (e.g., through stock ownership plans) and also in the operation of them for short initial periods (e.g., through supply or sales contracts).

7. Grudging acquiescence of unions in wage concessions, work-rule changes, etc., intended to cut costs and save jobs—in return for future profit sharing.[3]

8. Increased agreeableness of unions, as they become less able to win substantial gains in wages and fringe benefits, to cater to the interests of younger and better educated workers in QWL, participative, and problem solving programs.

9. Greater readiness of unions and employers to enter, under appropriate conditions, into joint programs for raising productivity, improving product quality, and safeguarding health and safety.

10. Greater willingness of national labor leaders to participate in a credible price-wage stabilization program in the event of a federal reversal of proclaimed policy.

Despite the anticipated quickening of the tempo of collaboration and the anticipated extension of the range, difficulty will continue to be experienced at the enterprise, industry, and community levels in starting up, maintaining, or expanding specific joint programs. Enthusiasm of the two parties for cooperation is far more relevant than the enthusiasm of academic observers and media commentators.[4] It is easier to assert the basic requirement of mutual trust than to show the two parties how to revise their attitudes fundamentally. Where mutual trust has already led to cooperation, a recession can wreck a successful program—e.g., by forcing the layoff of workers in quality circles or other problem solving programs whose jobs were supposed to be protected.[5] This cautionary paragraph could be extended to point to other problems, such as the uncertainty of getting sustained top-level leadership and commitment. External economic pressures and federal retreat, however, will improve the probability of attitudes and behavior favorable to meaningful cooperation.

NOTES

1. Douglas Fraser, "Labor on Corporate Boards," *Challenge,* July/August 1981, pp. 30-33.

2. See remarks by R. J. Conklin and S. P. Rubinstein in *Business Week,* January 11, 1982, pp. 108-109.

3. While this book was being processed for publication, UAW concluded new agreements with Ford and GM that could greatly assist revival of the American automobile industry. The agreement negotiated with Ford and approved by union members in February 1982 is included in the documentary appendix.

4. Ivar Berg, Marcia Freedman, and Michael Freeman, *Management and Work Reform: A Limited Engagement* (New York: The Free Press, 1978), pp. 260-261.

5. The remarks cited in footnote 2 appear in an article titled "Will the Slide Kill Quality Circles?"

Appendix

Appendix A
Documentary Appendix

For easy reference, the 25 selected documents that follow are arranged in five sections: the national scene (I), the industry level (II), the community level (III), the company level (IV), and the public sector (V). Some items appearing in one section, however, could reasonably have been classified in another—as the next paragraph makes clear.

Two categories of documents are distinguished in the first section. One category (illustrated by three items marked with the prefix IA) refers to cooperative entities established under public or private auspices to deal with broad policy issues of national import. The documents in the second category (ten designated by the prefix IB) emanate from a national body—public (e.g., the Congress) or private (e.g., a national association or nonprofit foundation)—but really focus on coopeation at the level of the company or a plant. Accordingly, a reader interested in the documents grouped in IV may also wish to consult those in IB.

Contents of Documentary Appendix

I. The National Scene
  IA:1 A Presidential Advisory Committee (1981)
  IA:2 A Private Policy Group (1981)
  IA:3 An Earlier Presidential Committee (1961)
  IB:1 National Productivity and Quality of Working Life Act of 1975
  IB:2 Comprehensive Employment and Training Act Amendments of 1978
  IB:3 Full Employment and Balanced Growth Act of 1978
  IB:4 A Joint Economic Committee Report

235

IB:5   A Policy Statement of the National Commission on
       Productivity and Work Quality
IB:6   Guidance for Company Committees—National Center
       for Productivity and Quality of Working Life
IB:7   Sample of Committee Bylaws—Federal Mediation and
       Conciliation Service
IB:8   Sample of Committee Contract—Federal Mediation
       and Conciliation Service
IB:9   A Policy Recommendation on Alcoholism
IB:10 A Policy Statement of a Committee to Fight Inflation

II.   Industry Level
      II:1   Letter of Cochairmen of Steel Tripartite Advisory
             Committee
      II:2   Outline of Agreement on Retail Food Committee
      II:3   Memorandum of Understanding on St. Louis
             Construction
      II:4   Agreement on a California Nuclear Project

III. Community Level
      III:1 Report on Jamestown (N.Y.) Committee

IV.   Company Level
      IV:1   GM-UAW Letter of Agreement on Quality of Worklife
             Program
      IV:2   United States Steel-United Steelworkers Agreement
             on Participation Teams
      IV:3   AT&T-CWA Agreement of 1980
      IV:4   AT&T-CWA Statement of Principles on Worklife
             Quality
      IV:5   Mountain Bell-CWA Letter of Understanding
             on Flexitime
      IV:6   Scanlon-Plan Agreement at Midland-Ross
      IV:7   UAW-Ford Agreement, February 1982

V.   Public Sector
      V:1   Bylaws of Committee of New York State and Civil
            Service Employees Association
      V:2   Columbus-AFSCME Agreement on Quality of
            Worklife Committee
      V:3   TVA-Tennessee Valley Trades and Labor Council
            Agreement on Cooperative Committees

Section I
The National Scene

IA:1
Executive Order
Establishing the National Productivity
Advisory Committee (1981)

By the authority vested in me as President by the Constitution of the United States of America, and in order to establish in accordance with the provisions of the Federal Advisory Committee Act, as amended (5 U.S.C. App. I), an advisory committee on strategies for increasing national productivity in the United States, it is hereby ordered as follows:

Section 1. **Establishment.** (a) There is established the National Productivity Advisory Committee. The Committee shall be composed of distinguished citizens appointed by the President, only one of whom may be a full-time officer or employee of the Federal Government.

(b) The President shall designate a Chairman from among the members of the Committee.

Section 2. **Functions.** (a) The Committee shall advise the President and the Secretary of the Treasury through the Cabinet Council on Economic Affairs on the Federal Government's role in achieving higher levels of national productivity and economic growth.

(b) The Committee shall advise the President, the Secretary of the Treasury and the President's Task Force on Regulatory Relief with respect to the potential impact on national productivity of Federal laws and regulations.

(c) The Committee shall advise and work closely with the Cabinet Council on Economic Affairs (composed of the Secretaries of the Treasury, State, Commerce, Labor, and Transportation, the United States Trade Representative, the Chairman of the Council of Economic Advisers, and the Director of the Office of Management and Budget), the Assistant to the President for Policy Development, and other governmental offices the President may deem appropriate.

(d) In the performance of its advisory duties, the Committee shall conduct a continuing review and assessment of national productivity and shall advise the Secretary of the Treasury and the Cabinet Council on Economic Affairs.

Section 3. **Administration.** (a) The heads of Executive agencies shall, to the extent permitted by law, provide the Committee such information with respect to productivity as it may require for the purpose of carrying out its functions.

(b) Members of the Committee shall serve without compensation for their work on the Committee. However, members of the Committee who are not full-time officers or employees of the Federal Government shall be entitled to travel expenses, including per diem in lieu of subsistence, as authorized by law for persons serving intermittently in government service (5 U.S.C. 5701-5707).

(c) Any administrative support or other expenses of the Committee shall be paid, to the extent permitted by law, from funds available for the expenses of the Department of the Treasury.

(d) The Executive Secretary of the Cabinet Council on Economic Affairs shall serve as the Executive Secretary to the National Productivity Advisory Committee.

Section 4. **General.** (a) Notwithstanding any other Executive Order, the responsibilities of the President under the Federal Advisory Committee Act, as amended, except that of reporting annually to the Congress, which are applicable to the advisory committee established by this Order, shall be performed by the Secretary of the Treasury in accordance with guidelines and procedures established by the Administrator of General Services.

(b) The Committee shall terminate on December 31, 1982, unless sooner extended.

RONALD REAGAN

THE WHITE HOUSE,
November 10, 1981.

IA:2
New Labor-Management Group Formed (1981)

a) Press Release

WASHINGTON, D.C., March 4—The formation of a newly constituted Labor-Management Group was announced today at a press conference here. The new group represents an attempt by both business and
labor to maintain a continuing dialog.

John T. Dunlop, Harvard Lamont University professor and former
Secretary of Labor, is coordinator of the group. Lane Kirkland, president of the AFL-CIO, is chairman of the labor group and Clifton C.
Garvin, Jr., chairman of the Exxon Corporation, is chairman of the
management group.

Both the labor and management members of the new group have
agreed upon a Statement of Purpose which will guide the group's activities. (Note: Statement attached to this press release.)

In addition to Mr. Kirkland, the labor leaders who have been involved
are: Thomas R. Donahue, secretary/treasurer, AFL-CIO; John H.
Lyons, president of the Iron Workers; Lloyd McBride, president of the
United Steel Workers of America; Martin J. Ward, president of the
United Association of Journeymen & Apprentices of the Plumbing &
Pipe Fitters Industry of the U.S. & Canada, and William H. Wynn,
president of the United Food and Commercial Workers. Additional
labor members will be added.

In addition to Mr. Garvin, the business leaders who have been involved are: James H. Evans, chairman and CEO of the Union Pacific Corporation; Philip M. Hawley, president and CEO of Carter, Hawley,
Hale Stores, Inc.; Dr. Ruben F. Mettler, chairman of TRW, Inc.; Irving
S. Shapiro, chairman of the board, E. I. duPont deNemours & Co.;
George P. Shultz, president of the Bechtel Group, Inc.; Roger B. Smith,
chairman and CEO, General Motors Corporation; John F. Welch,
chairman-elect of the General Electric Company, and Walter B.
Wriston, chairman of CitiCorp.

b) Statement of Purpose

The U.S. faces a period in its history when non-inflationary economic
growth and full employment are essential to the maintenance of a free
and healthy society.

American labor and business see these as necessary mutual goals to provide our society with new and expanded job opportunities, increased living standards, international competitiveness in an interdependent world and the capacity to meet social commitments.

With these objectives in mind, the Labor-Management Group will meet on a voluntary basis to search for solutions to a wide range of issues.

The principal focus of the Group's discussions will be in the area of economic policy in which its collective experience is widely based. In framing its discussions, the Group is mindful that it is but one of many groups whose opinions may be sought in shaping the nation's policies. The Group's recommendations must consider its obligations to the aspirations of all Americans, including the just demands for equity by minorities, women and those for whom social justice is still a dream.

The national interest requires a new spirit of mutual trust and cooperation, even though management and organized labor are, and will remain, adversaries on many issues.

The uniqueness of America lies in the vitality of its free institutions. Among these, a free labor movement and a free enterprise economy are essential to the achievement of social and political stability and economic prosperity for all. It is destructive to society and to business and organized labor, if in our legitimate adversarial roles, we question the right of our institutions to exist and perform their legitimate functions. In performing these functions, we recognize that both parties must respect deeply held views even when they disagree.

One recognition of the legitimacy of our respective institutions is demonstrated in the process of free collective bargaining. We believe that both the democratic right of employees to determine the issue of representation and the process of collective bargaining must not be threatened by occasions of excessive behavior by employers or unions.

The Group will use the wider relationships its individual members have in the business and labor communities to broaden its knowledge of issues, to improve the overall labor-management climate and to communicate the results of its deliberations to its respective associates.

The complexity of issues suggests the Group may not find complete consensus on all the issues it explores. When it does, it will communicate its views publicly. Otherwise, the participants reserve to themselves the privilege to address issues in their individual capacities.

The Group intends to look closely at the issues it knows best and how they are affected by public policy. These are the issues that grow out of our experiences in industries and localities. Further we intend to explore a wide range of issues with particular emphasis on revitalizing the nation's economic base, rebuilding the private and public infrastructure on which our productive capacity as a nation depends, and stimulating safe and efficient means for meeting the nation's energy needs.

February 3, 1981

IA:3

Executive Order No. 10918

Establishing The President's Advisory
Committee on Labor-Management Policy

By virtue of the authority vested in me as President of the United States, it is ordered as follows:

Section 1. There is hereby established the President's Advisory Committee on Labor-Management Policy (hereinafter referred to as the Committee). The Committee shall be composed of the Secretary of Labor, the Secretary of Commerce, and nineteen other members who shall be designated by the President from time to time. Of the nineteen designated members, five shall be from the public at large, seven shall be from labor, and seven shall be from management. The Secretary of Labor and the Secretary of Commerce shall each alternatively serve as chairman of the Committee for periods of one year, the Secretary of Labor to so serve during the first year following the date of this order.

Section 2. The Committee shall study, and shall advise with and make recommendations to the President with respect to, policies that may be followed by labor, management, or the public which will promote free and responsible collective bargaining, industrial peace, sound wage and price policies, higher standards of living, and increased productivity. The Committee shall include among the matters to be considered by it in connection with its studies and recommendations (1) policies designed to ensure that American products are competitive in world markets, and (2) the benefits and problems created by automation and other technological advances.

Section 3. All executive departments and agencies of the Federal Government are authorized and directed to cooperate with the Committee and to furnish it such information and assistance, not inconsistent with law, as it may require in the performance of its duties.

Section 4. Consonant with law, the Department of Labor and the Department of Commerce shall, as may be necessary for the effectuation of the purposes of this order, furnish assistance to the Committee in accordance with section 214 of the act of May 3, 1945, 59 Stat. 134 (31U.S.C. 691). Such assistance may include detailing employees to the Committee, one of whom may serve as executive officer of the Committee, to perform such functions, consistent with the purposes of this order, as the Committee may assign to them, and shall include the furnishing of necessary office space and facilities to the Committee by the Department of Labor.

JOHN F. KENNEDY

THE WHITE HOUSE
February 16, 1961

IB:1
Section 204 of the National Productivity and Quality of Working Life Act of 1975 (P.L. 94-136)

This section stated 15 "functions" of the new National Center for Productivity and Quality of Working Life that it established. Two of these functions are particularly relevant to this book, viz., to:

(6) encourage, support, and initiate efforts in the public or private sector specifically designed to improve cooperation between labor and management in the achievement of continued productivity growth: *Provided, however,* That no activities of the Center involving consideration of issues included in a specific labor-management agreement shall be undertaken without the consent and cooperation of the parties to that agreement;

(12) encourage and coordinate the efforts of State and local governments, and institutions of higher education, to improve productivity;

IB:2

Section 6 of Comprehensive Employment & Training Act Amendments of 1978 (CETA)

Assistance to Plant, Area, and Industrywide Labor Management Committees

Sec. 6 (a) This section may be cited as the "Labor Management Cooperation Act of 1978."

(b) It is the purpose of this section—

(1) to improve communication between representatives of labor and management;

(2) to provide workers and employers with opportunities to study and explore new and innovative joint approaches to achieving organizational effectiveness;

(3) to assist workers and employers in solving problems of mutual concern not susceptible to resolution within the collective bargaining process;

(4) to study and explore ways of eliminating potential problems which reduce the competitiveness and inhibit the economic development of the plant, area or industry;

(5) to enhance the involvement of workers in making decisions that affect their working lives;

(6) to expand and improve working relationships between workers and managers; and

(7) to encourage free collective bargaining by establishing continuing mechanisms for communication between employers and their employees through Federal assistance to the formation and operation of labor management committees.

(c) (1) Section 203 of the Labor-Management Relations Act, 1947, is amended by adding at the end thereof the following new subsection:

"(e) The Service is authorized and directed to encourage and support the establishment and operation of joint labor management activities conducted by plant, area, and industrywide committees designed to improve labor management relationships, job security and organizational effectiveness, in accordance with the provisions of section 205A.".

(2) Title II of the Labor-Management Relations Act, 1947, is amended by adding after section 205 the following new section:

"Sec. 205A. (a) (1) The Service is authorized and directed to provide assistance in the establishment and operation of plant, area and industrywide labor management committees which—

"(A) have been organized jointly by employers and labor organizations representing employees in that plant, area, or industry; and

"(B) are established for the purpose of improving labor management relationships, job security, organizational effectiveness, enhancing economic development or involving workers in decisions affecting their jobs including improving communication with respect to subjects of mutual interest and concern.

"(2) The Service is authorized and directed to enter into contracts and to make grants, where necessary or appropriate, to fulfill its responsibilities under this section.

"(b) (1) No grant may be made, no contract may be entered into and no other assistance may be provided under the provisions of this section to a plant labor management committee unless the employees in that plant are represented by a labor organization and there is in effect at that plant a collective bargaining agreement.

"(2) No grant may be made, no contract may be entered into and no other assistance may be provided under the provisions of this section to an area or industrywide labor management committee unless its participants include any labor organizations certified or recognized as the representative of the employees of an employer participating in such committee. Nothing in this clause shall prohibit participation in an area or industrywide committee by an employer whose employees are not represented by a labor organization.

"(3) No grant may be made under the provisions of this section to any labor management committee which the Service finds to have as one of its purposes the discouragement of the exercise of rights contained in section 7 of the National Labor Relations Act (29 U.S.C. 157), or the interference with collective bargaining in any plant, or industry.

"(c) The Service shall carry out the provisions of this section through an office established for that purpose.

"(d) There are authorized to be appropriated to carry out the provisions of this section $10,000,000 for the fiscal year 1979, and such sums as may be necessary thereafter.".

(d) Section 302(c) of the Labor Management Relations Act, 1947, is amended by striking the word "or" after the semicolon at the end of subparagraph (7) thereof and by inserting the following before the period at the end thereof:"; or (9) with respect to money or other things of value paid by an employer to a plant, area or industrywide labor management committee established for one or more of the purposes set forth in section 5(b) of the Labor Management Cooperation Act of 1978".

(e) Nothing in this section or the amendments made by this section shall affect the terms and conditions of any collective bargaining agreement whether in effect prior to or entered into after the date of enactment of this section.

REPEALER

Sec. 7. Section 104 of the Emergency Jobs and Unemployment Assistance Act of 1974 (Public Law 93-567) is hereby repealed.

IB:3

Excerpt from Full Employment and Balanced Growth Act of 1978* (P.L. 95-523)

a. Section 109 amends Employment Act of 1946 by adding a new Section 8, of which 8(c) (4) cites this "structural policy" to "reduce the rate of inflation":

(4) encouragement to labor and management to increase productivity within the national framework of full employment through voluntary arrangements in industries and economic sectors.

b. Section 111 adds a new Section 9 to the Employment Act of 1946 that calls for "advisory boards" to the President, the Council of Economic Advisers, and federal agencies:

9(b) Such advisory board or boards shall include appropriate representation of labor, small and large businesses and industries, agriculture, commerce, State and local officials, and the public at large, and shall advise and consult with respect to matters related to this Act, the Full Employment and Balanced Growth Act of 1978, and other appropriate matters related to national economic programs and policies.

---

*Also known as Humphrey-Hawkins Act.

IB:4

Excerpt from *The 1981 Midyear Report: Productivity*, Report of the Joint Economic Committee, Congress of the United States, July 23, 1981

Recommendation No. 9: Encourage Labor and Management to Cooperate in Improving Long-Run Productivity and Competitiveness.

Cooperative activities by labor and management may significantly enhance government efforts to smooth adjustment problems and promote more effective uses of human resources. In hundreds of individual plants as well as several dozen industries and local communities, committees composed of worker and employer representatives have been formed to find acceptable solutions to issues of common concern.

At the plant level, for example, labor-management committees have arranged for training programs to meet changing skill requirements of employers and to alleviate labor bottlenecks. In other cases, labor and management have worked together to redesign production processes or deal with special workplace problems such as absenteeism. Community-wide committees have sought to encourage cooperative activities in local plants and create conditions that foster economic development. Labor-management committees in the retail food and steel industries have dealt with regulatory problems; in the railroad industry, cooperative projects have experimented with manpower and other changes to increase the efficiency of certain routes. While the scale, mix of activities, and success has varied from committee to committee, the initiatives have helped to improve productivity and strengthen labor-management relations in a variety of industrial settings.

IB:5

Excerpt from *A National Policy for Productivity,* A Statement by the National Commission on Productivity and Work Quality, October 1975

Labor-Management Relations

The Commission believes that greater cooperation between labor and management offers significant and mainly untapped potential for increasing productivity in all sectors of the economy. "Cooperation" in this context refers to an open exchange of ideas between labor and management, occurring outside the formal collective bargaining process and in a nonadversary environment. Improved cooperation requires, on management's part, a recognition that labor can contribute important know-how, imagination, and ingenuity in such areas as increasing output, reducing waste, improving morale and job satisfaction, and reducing counterproductive behavior such as absenteeism or alcoholism. Of equal importance, a cooperative approach to productivity improvement requires an acceptance by labor of its responsibility for sharing in the effort to improve productivity.

Collective bargaining has proved to be an effective mechanism for resolving differences between labor and management; however, the Commission believes that opportunities also exist for labor and management to identify and pursue common objectives outside the collective bargaining process, and that the pursuit of these objectives can serve their mutual interests without threatening the viability of collective bargaining.

The identification and promotion of areas of cooperation should prove equally useful in those sectors of the economy where employees are not represented by unions, and where no other formal mechanism exists for communication between management and employees on productivity issues.

In promoting the potential of expanded labor-management relations to achieve productivity improvement, the Commission feels that our national policy should place particular emphasis on the public sector. The public sector (Federal, State, and local government) now accounts for approximately one-fifth of the total national employed work force. However, many units of government lack administrators with adequate skills, training, and experience in labor relations. In addition, collective bargaining is often new and quite fragmented and many public service unions have less experience than their counterparts in the private sector. Therefore, the Commission believes that opportunities to improve labor-management procedures—including grievance-settling methods and communications on productivity improvement issues—and to expand the skill levels of those responsible for labor relations should be vigorously pursued.

In addition, the Commission believes that managers in almost every area of the economy can take more initiative and can contribute more to the process of productivity improvement. Accordingly, efforts to promote the value of increased productivity and to disseminate techniques for improving productivity should involve every employee. This is especially true in the public sector, where the need for administrators to take an active role in productivity improvement is not as widely understood as it might be.

. . . .

Quality of Working Life

In its broadest sense, the concept of quality of working life embraces many of the areas covered elsewhere in this statement—labor-management relations, job security, the quality of education and training provided to workers, and other factors associated with maintaining the capacity and motivation of the American work force. In this broad sense, the Commission believes that quality of working life is vital to our national productivity.

In addition, increased national attention has been focused recently on experiments designed to improve quality of working life in the more specific sense of the atmosphere in which work is conducted. The Commission endorses these efforts and believes that they offer promise in providing an atmosphere conducive to productivity improvement. In the view of the Commission, further experimentation should place more emphasis on seeking a better understanding of the relationship between productivity and the quality of a worker's environment and on learning more about which concepts of "quality of working life" seem most conducive to stimulating productivity improvement.

IB:6

Excerpt from *Starting a Labor-Management Committee in Your Organization: Some Pointers for Action,* National Center for Productivity and Quality of Working Life, 1978

Ten Summary Points for an Effective Labor-Management Committee

- Both parties share mutual interests in the long-term survival and success of the enterprise and the community, even though they may have conflicting goals in other matters.

- Both sides want to make the labor-management committee work and have realistic expectations of what it can accomplish. Participation in regular sessions symbolizes this commitment, which is known throughout the organization.

- Labor members of the joint committee are believed and trusted by the rank and file; the management members have sufficient status and authority.

- Maximum voluntary participation is encouraged; employees, including supervisors, are kept informed and involved in matters considered by the labor-management committee and have opportunities to express their views on its recommendations.

- The joint committees do not take up matters which infringe on the rights of either party as established under the collective bargaining agreement or the grievance procedure.

- Job security is recognized as basic to the program's success.

- The parties have a mature, open relationship. Each is willing to listen to the other side. Both agree to concentrate on finding answers to problems at hand and discovering opportunities for collaboration.

- The joint committees are promptly informed about the status of their recommendations. If they are not, the committees will lose interest and stop operating.

- Numerous channels of communication are encouraged, and an atmosphere of mutual respect prevails. However, communications must be accompanied by substantive recommendations.

- New ideas are encouraged, and their value weighed objectively. Concrete problems of interest to both management and labor must be pursued by the committee if it is to continue to function productively.

IB:7

Excerpt from *Labor-Management Committee: Planning for Progress,* Federal Mediation and Conciliation Service, 1977—Sample Format of Committee Bylaws

Joint Labor-Management Committee

Purpose

To investigate, study, and discuss possible solutions to mutual problems affecting labor-management relations.

Representation

Union

Five members: president, business agent, secretary-treasurer, and two stewards.

Company

Five members: Top management representatives, department head, two industrial relations representatives, and one other operating member from the departments working under the union contract.

The company's general manager and the international representative of the union are ex-officio members.

Substitutes may be chosen by mutual consent, but it is recognized that a continuity of membership is required. The operating members from management and the two representatives from the union, other than the president, business agent, and secretary-treasurer, will be rotated every 12 months.

Chairmanship

Chairmanship shall alternate monthly between the union and management. Each party will determine whether it will have a permanent chairman or rotating chairmen.

Reporting

Topics will be recorded as they are discussed. Any procedures or recommendations developing from these meetings will be communicated to the proper group; i.e., Operating Department, Joint Standing Committee, Negotiating Committee, etc.

Drafts of the minutes of meetings will be refined by one designated representative from each party.

Date and Time of Meetings

Meetings shall be held once a month, and they shall be limited to two hours. An agenda shall be submitted 48 hours prior to the meetings to both parties. At the first meeting, a specific day and time shall be selected for future meetings. Every attempt shall be made to keep such a schedule, realizing that some flexibility is necessary.

Topics not on the agenda shall not be discussed but rather shall be placed on the following month's agenda. The agenda shall include a brief description of each item to be discussed. Emergency items may be added to the agenda by mutual consent.

Discussion of agenda topics will be alternated, with the party occupying the chair exercising the right to designate the first topic.

General Guides

1. It is recognized that recommendations growing out of these meetings are not binding.
2. No grievances shall be discussed and no bargaining shall take place.
3. Topics that could lead to grievances may be discussed.
4. Each person wishing to speak shall be recognized by the chairman before speaking.
5. The chairman shall recognize a motion from either party to table a topic for further study.
6. Either party may initiate a request to the Federal Mediation and Conciliation Service for assistance.
7. Each topic shall be discussed fully and action reached before proceeding to another topic. Topics requiring further study may be tabled. Where mutually satisfactory decisions are not reached, the topic shall be cancelled, reverting to its proper place in the labor-management relationship—for instance, grievance procedure, negotiations, etc.

IB:8

Excerpt from *Labor-Management Committee: Planning for Progress,* Federal Mediation and Conciliation Service, 1977—Sample Format of Contract Language

Sec. 2   Joint Study Committee

2.51   The Company and the Union, desiring to foster better day-to-day communications, and to achieve and maintain a mutually beneficial relationship through the use of a continuing communications program to effectively maintain stable labor-management relations and avoid controversies, do hereby establish these bylaws for a Joint Study Committee.

2.52   The purpose of the Committee is to discuss, explore and study problems referred to it by the parties to this Agreement. The Committee, by mutual agreement, shall be authorized to make recommendations on those problems that have been discussed, explored and studied.

2.53   In order to have a frank and open discussion, the Committee shall have no authority to change, delete or modify any of the terms of the existing Company-Union Agreement, nor to settle grievances arising under the Company-Union Agreement. Committee discussions shall not be publicized except for those recommendations that have been mutually agreed upon.

2.54   The Committee shall be composed of ten members, five representing the Union and five representing the Company. The Union Committee shall include the President of the Local Union, the International Representative or Business Agent and the three Chief Stewards. The Company Committee shall include the General Manager, Industrial Relations Manager, Manufacturing Manager and two other Management representatives appointed by the Company.

   A representative of the Federal Mediation and Conciliation Service may be invited to attend and participate in Committee meetings.

2.55   The Chairmanship of the Committee shall alternate between a representative appointed by Management and a representative appointed by the Union. The representative appointed as Chairman shall serve a term commencing with the close of the meeting at which his appointment is announced and continue under the end of the next meeting.

Meetings shall be held on a day designated by the Chairman during the first full calendar week of the month. However, interim meetings may be held if mutually agreed to by the Committee.

Meetings shall be conducted in the plant unless otherwise agreed to.

Meetings shall begin at a time agreed upon by the parties.

The Chairman shall cause an agenda to be prepared for the meeting and distributed to all members at least two working days prior to the meeting.

IB:9
Model Joint Union-Management Statement of Policy on Alcoholism Recommended by the Labor-Management Committee of the National Council on Alcoholism

Joint Union-Management Statement of Policy

Judging by the combined experience of the most successful programs, the following principles should be considered for inclusion:

(1) Alcoholism is recognized as a disease for which there is effective treatment and rehabilitation.

(2) Alcoholism is defined as a disease in which a person's consumption of any alcoholic beverage definitely and repeatedly interferes with that individual's health and/or job performance.

(3) Persons who suspect that they may have an alcoholism problem, even in its early stages, are encouraged to seek diagnosis and to follow through with the treatment that may be prescribed by qualified professionals, in order to arrest the disease as early as possible.

(4) Any persons having this disease will receive the same careful consideration and offer of treatment that is presently extended, under existing benefit plans, to all those having any other disease.

(5) The same benefits and insurance coverages that are provided for all other diseases, under established benefit plans, will be available for individuals who accept medically approved treatment for alcoholism.

(6) This policy is not concerned with social drinking, but rather with the disease of alcoholism. The concern is limited to those instances of alcoholism which affect the job performance of the individual. The policy is designed solely to achieve restoration of health and full recovery.

(7) It will be the responsibility of all management and union personnel to implement this policy and to follow the procedures which have been designed to assure that no person with alcoholism will have either job security or promotional opportunities jeopardized by a request for diagnosis and treatment.

(8) Neither supervisors nor union representatives have the medical qualifications to diagnose alcoholism as a disease. Therefore, referral for diagnosis and treatment will be based on job perfor-

mance, within the terms, conditions and application of the union-management agreement.

(9) The decision to request diagnosis and accept treatment for alcoholism is the personal responsibility of the individual.

(10) An individual's refusal to accept referral for diagnosis or to follow prescribed treatment will be handled in accordance with existing contractual agreements and union-management understandings with respect to job performance.

(11) The confidential nature of the medical records of individuals with alcoholism will be strictly preserved.

(12) Persons participating in this program will be expected to meet existing job performance standards and established work rules within the framework of existing union-management agreements. Any exceptions to this requirement will be by mutual agreement between the union and management.

(13) Nothing in this statement of policy is to be interpreted as constituting a waiver of management's responsibility to maintain discipline or the right to take disciplinary measures, within the framework of the collective bargaining agreement, in the case of misconduct that may result from alcoholism.

IB:10

Excerpt from *A Policy Statement* Issued by a Bipartisan Committee to Fight Inflation* through American Enterprise Institute for Public Policy Research, June 23, 1980

We urge that other feasible means be adopted to increase the productivity of our economy. These should include larger private and public outlays for research and development; more carefully designed manpower training programs; productivity councils in individual plants, shops, and offices in communities across the country, in which employees and employers can pool their ideas for improving the efficiency with which their tasks are discharged; and other means of encouraging cooperative efforts of labor and management in furthering their common interest in greater efficiency.

---

*The Committee included 5 former Secretaries of the Treasury, 2 former Chairmen of the Board of Governors of the Federal Reserve System, 1 former Undersecretary of the Treasury, 1 former Chairman of the Council of Economic Advisers, and 4 former members of Congress.

Section II
Industry Level

II:1

Letter of Co-Chairmen Transmitting Summary of Findings and Recommendations of the Steel Tripartite Advisory Committee, September 25, 1980

Dear Mr. President:

In our capacity as joint chairmen of the Steel Tripartite Advisory Committee we herein summarize the findings and recommendations of the Committee and transmit its working papers for your review and consideration.

The Steel Tripartite Advisory Committee was established on July 26, 1978, in conjunction with the Administration's acceptance of the recommendations of the Solomon Report. The purpose of the Committee is to serve as a mechanism to ensure a continuing cooperative approach to the problems and prospects of the American steel industry. Its current membership includes:

Government

Secretary of Labor Ray Marshall
Secretary of Commerce Philip M. Klutznick
United States Trade Representative Reubin O'D. Askew
Environmental Protection Agency Administrator Douglas M. Costle
Assistant Secretary of Treasury for Economic Policy Curtis A.
  Hessler

United Steelworkers of America

President Lloyd McBride
Vice President Joseph Odorcich
Director Paul Lewis
Director Edgar L. Ball
Director Buddy W. Davis
Director Frank J. Valenta
Director Howard Strevel
Assistant to the President John Sheehan

Steel Industry

William J. DeLancey, Chairman, Republic Steel Corp.; Chairman,
  American Iron and Steel Institute

Harry Holiday, Chief Executive Officer, Armco Steel Corp.
Edgar F. Kaiser, Jr., Chairman, Kaiser Steel Corp.
William H. Knoell, President, Cyclops Corp.
Robert B. Peabody, President, American Iron and Steel Institute
David M. Roderick, Chairman, U.S. Steel Corp.
George A. Stinson, Chairman, National Steel Corp.
Donald H. Trautlein, Chairman, Bethlehem Steel Corp.

Shortly after it was established, the Committee concluded that the fundamental problems of the industry could best be addressed by focusing on five areas: capital formation, trade, environmental and regulatory matters, worker and community adjustment, and technology. Working groups were established in each area and assigned the task of developing findings and recommendations. The results of the working groups were then reviewed by the full Committee members. Our report is based upon this process.

On behalf of the Committee we have endeavored to summarize the condition of the industry, its basic problems, objectives to guide action, and the major findings and recommendations Committee members believe are necessary to revitalize the steel industry. All represent tripartite views. The summary of the findings and recommendations is organized according to the five working groups mentioned above. Although there has not been agreement on all matters, we have been impressed by the substantial consensus that has emerged among labor, business, and government members of the Committee.

At the outset we wish to emphasize four points that we believe are central to understanding how to improve the performance of the domestic steel industry.

First, steelmaking constitutes a foundation for a substantial portion of our industrial base. Metals continue to be essential to industrial production, and steel represents about 90% of all metals consumed.

Second, the problems of th steel industry, although varying from firm to firm, are fundamental. At the same time, the inherent strength of the industry as a whole provides major opportunities for long-term progress.

Third, the problems of the industry reflect failings on the part of government, management, and labor. None has been sufficiently responsive to the changes affecting the industry. All share responsibility for contributing to a more vital industry.

And fourth, remedying the problems of steel will require a substantial period of time. A coordinated and integrated set of initiatives, maintained for a 3 to 5 year period, or longer, will be necessary to set the industry on a new path.

We believe that the conclusions of the Steel Tripartite Advisory Committee provide useful guidance towards developing policies and programs that will foster modernization of the American steel industry.

_____   _____
Secretary of Labor   Secretary of Commerce

II:2

Description of the Initial Objectives and Proposed Activities Agreed upon by Union and Management Leaders at Formation of the Joint Labor-Management Committee of the Retail Food Industry, March 29, 1974

(1) The Committee shall serve as a forum for initiating and maintaining wage and benefit data collection programs and for the exchange of information to strengthen the ability of the industry (labor and management) to reach constructive decisions in collective bargaining. Labor, management, public and government representatives recognize that the information presently available on collective bargaining settlements, wage rates and wage patterns, fringe benefits, noneconomic contract clauses, and bargaining time tables is not always as accurate, available or useful to all parties as it should be. This can be improved. Programs in this area have already been initiated, with the help of the Cost of Living Council, and these should be refined, continued and expanded. The Cost of Living Council is prepared to defray the costs of assembling the information and of designing ways, with the assistance of managements and the unions to present the data in a useful and understandable form.

(2) If the Committee is to make a constructive contribution to the industry, it will have to be sensitive to interference with normal collective bargaining and respect the autonomy of the individual organizations. The Committee cannot and should not be a mandatory industry settlement organization. However, with reliable data that is kept current and utilizing its role in encouraging open communication and exchange of information on a national basis, the Committee may be able to assist the industry in key contract discussions that might otherwise lead to major confrontations. Such procedures as encouraging early discussion of difficult problems, supplying information for such discussions, and bringing to bear national experience on local problems should be a part of this function. These kinds of procedures have increasingly been used by a variety of other industries to encourage constructive and responsible collective bargaining. All of this activity must be closely coordinated with the Federal Mediation and Conciliation Service.

(3) The Committee shall be a national forum for discussions of a variety of longer range industry problems that often surface in local negotiations and which may benefit from national attention to

secure mutually beneficial results. Among these problems, but by no means an exhaustive list, are the following:

(a) Relationship between top management and the international unions—the need for a better understanding of the scope and limits of authority and responsibility on both sides.

(b) International and local unions' relations with rank and file.

(c) Understanding lines of management and union authority at the bargaining table.

(d) Technological change.

(e) Government regulation.

(f) Management and union work practices.

(g) Fragmented bargaining.

(h) Contract administration.

(i) New types of dispute settlement mechanisms.

The parties have themselves indicated that most of these items have a high priority on their list of concerns.

(4) Overriding all of the above, and implicit in the fundamental work of the Committee, would be to use the Committee as an ongoing forum to broaden the base of communication between labor and management at all levels and on all subjects of mutual concern to labor and management. Therefore, in setting priorities the agenda must reflect the role that individual members play outside of the Committee and the concerns of those that do not participate in its regular meetings—the local and regional representatives on both sides.

(5) The international unions and the major national retail chains have expressed their willingness for a period (such as the rest of 1974) to cooperate with the above procedures, to serve on the operating committee, to meet regularly, and join in a procedural voluntary agreement to this effect.

II:3

Memorandum of Understanding Signed by Union, Contractor, and Other Groups, Construction Industry, St. Louis, 1977

I. Preamble:

The parties signatory to this Understanding recognize the problems confronting the construction industry in the Eastern Missouri Area and pledge their cooperation and support to the provisions of this Understanding and other mutually agreed upon policies and programs which will tend to eliminate these problems and promote a healthy growth of the construction industry in this area.

II. Customers:

1. Owners shall continue to show increasing personal interest in their construction before and after their contracts are let. Wherever possible, owners agree to conduct prebid conferences to explain what is expected of contractors and prejob conferences to resolve possible jurisdictional disputes.

2. Owners shall pursue more thorough job design to insure that jobs can be built economically and efficiently with a minimum of changes.

3. Owners shall set completion dates as realistically as possible. Owners shall enforce the terms of the contract and work with prime contractors for best possible results. Owners shall make every effort to render prompt decisions.

4. Wherever possible, owners shall avoid and discourage scheduled overtime or other actions that mitigate against effective and economical construction.

III. Designers:

1. Architects and Engineers will provide professional services to Owners in the most feasible way within the limitations of the Owners needs and established budget.

2. Architects and Engineers will prepare plans and specifications which will clearly define the scope and details of the project necessary for bidding and construction. For convenience of reference and to facilitate letting of subcontracts by the Contractor, these documents will conform with general building practice relating to jurisdictional matters.

3.   Architects and Engineers will consult with the Owner advising him of reasonable bidding and construction time schedules in accordance with local construction industry practices.

4.   Architects and Engineers will recommend that Owners follow recognized industry standards and procedures for bidding projects, award of contracts, observation of the work and progress payment procedures. Wherever possible changes resulting in extra costs and multiple punch lists will be minimized.

IV. Contractors:

1.   All Contractors shall make installations in accordance with plans and specifications and recognized contract procedures.

2.   All Contractors shall exercise their management rights. These rights shall include planning, directing, hiring, firing, layoff, transferring, appointing foremen and general foremen and otherwise directing the work force.

3.   As part of the planning and execution of management procedures, all Contractors shall provide their craftsmen with necessary plans, employer furnished tools, equipment and materials in order for the craftsman to perform his duties in the most efficient and expeditious manner.

4.   Prime contractors shall be responsible for the job progress of their subcontractors and they shall coordinate and support the project operations of their subcontractors.

5.   All Contractors shall follow all recognized and ethical standards and procedures in bidding on, soliciting bids and performing all work.

V. Unions (Craftsmen):

1.   The importance of workmen remaining on a job from start to completion is recognized by both parties. Contractors must be able to give reliable completion dates to contract letting agencies and owners. To meet this objective, it is pledged that illegal work stoppages and strikes will not occur.

2.   Unions further pledge that no picketing or strikes will be used in jurisdictional disputes. After obtaining all necessary facts the parties involved will resolve the dispute off the job site as expeditiously as possible. If necessary, the Council of Construction Employers and the Building Trades Council will render all assistance in these discussions. If the dispute cannot be settled in this manner, the applicable contract provisions for settlement of jurisdictional disputes will be followed.

3. Alleged violations of union contracts or disputes over interpretations of union contracts will not be the grounds for unions to picket or strike until the following occurs: (1) The parties in this dispute will meet off the job site to resolve the disputes. (2) The Council of Construction Employers and the Building Trades Council will be given opportunity to participate in the discussions. Failure to settle such disputes in this manner will necessitate the use of the grievance procedure and/or arbitration provisions in the applicable labor agreement.

4. Increased productivity is the key to putting contractors who employ union workmen in a more competitive position. To accomplish this objective, the individual workman shall be made to realize the importance of his role in the Construction Industry through both oral and written communications from the Employers, Employer Associations, the Building Trades Council and the Union. Workers will be made aware of their responsibility. The necessity of performing a day's work for a day's pay will be emphasized.

5. Where stewards are appointed by respective unions, the steward shall be a qualified workman performing the work of his craft who shall exercise no supervisory functions. There shall be no non-working stewards.

6. Workmen shall be at their place of work at the regular starting time and shall remain at their place of work until quitting time. There shall be no limit on production by workmen nor restrictions on the use of tools or equipment other than that which may be required by safety regulations.

VI. Joint Contractor-Union:

1. Unions and contractors will work in harmony with the objective of demonstrating to contract letting agencies and owners, that organized labor and their employers will strive to produce the best quality installation for the money spent by the consumer.

2. It is recognized that prolonged periods of overtime tend to reduce productivity and, therefore, is undesirable and not in the best interest of the industry, the craftsman and the consumer. Therefore, except in unusual circumstances, overtime will not be worked. Where unusual circumstances demand overtime, such overtime will be kept to a minimum.

3. Unnecessary and/or inefficient work practices, where they exist, shall be eliminated. Slowdowns, standby crews and work rules which cause same and featherbedding practices increase costs and place the contractors who employ union labor at a competitive disadvantage. Elimination of these inefficient work practices is a necessity and will be diligently pursued by both parties.

VII. Suppliers:

1. Suppliers will, to the best of their ability, seek to deliver materials and equipment according to project schedules.

2. Suppliers will counsel with owners, architect-engineers or contractors so as to advise the appropriate party of necessary procedures and requirements leading to order placement, so that project schedules may be maintained.

3. Suppliers will work in close harmony with their contractual partner on the project so as to provide the most economical price for materials necessary to meet project requirements.

4. Suppliers will expedite erection plans, shop details, and installation instructions for approval and project distribution to insure project schedules.

5. Suppliers will furnish materials of a quality to meet or exceed mutually agreeable plans and specifications.

6. Suppliers will attempt to maintain stock items which are used on a regular basis, to minimize delays in obtaining such items.

A harmonious working relationship between all parties using this Understanding as a guide should result in the healthy growth of the construction industry in the Eastern Missouri Area.

The Memorandum of Understanding will be developed and implemented in accordance with the various existing labor agreements and will be fair and equitable to both labor and management, as well as the property owners and the public in general.

Signed this 28th day of November, 1977.

Council of Construction Employers

St. Louis Building & Construction Trades Council

Consulting Engineers Council of Missouri

St. Louis Chapter, American Institute of Architects

St. Louis Area Construction Users Council

St. Louis Chapter Producers' Council, Inc.

II:4

Excerpt from National Constructors Association/ California Building & Construction Trades Council Joint Voluntary Cal/OSHA Self-Inspection Program for the San Onofre Nuclear Generating Station, Units 2 & 3 at San Clemente, California

Introduction

It has been shown that governmental inspection/enforcement programs alone are not effective in reducing job injuries and illness; hence, a significant percentage of such occurrences are not inspection preventable by routine compliance inspections.

Therefore, The National Constructors Association/The California Building & Construction Trades Council have jointly agreed to a pilot program which will enable a joint Labor/Management Committee, comprised of persons employed on the project, to function in such a manner so as to provide a continuing assurance that compliance with the Cal/OSHA Construction Safety Orders is maintained.

Voluntary Self-Inspection Program

The purpose of the jobsite committee is to assist the employer, as required, in the implementation of the Voluntary Self-Inspection Program. The committee will function as outlined below. The committee's activities will be monitored by the National Constructors Association/California Building and Construction Trades Council Joint Committee on Voluntary Self-Inspection.

Organization of Jobsite Voluntary Program Safety Committee

1. A four-member committee, comprised of two employer representatives and two employee representatives will be established.
2. All committee members must be current employees on the project.
3. All employee committee members will be appointed by the local Building Trades Council having jurisdiction.
4. Employee committee members may not be union stewards.
5. Employer members shall have field supervisory responsibility excepting the employer Safety Representative who shall be a permanent member of the committee.
6. Committee members will be permitted to perform committee business.

7. Participation on the committee shall not preclude discharge for cause or reduction in force for valid reasons. Participation on the committee does not guarantee continued employment.

Functions of the Jobsite Committee

1. The committee shall meet on a weekly basis at a time and place agreed by the membership.
2. The committee will assist in the implementation of the Voluntary Self-Inspection Program at the SONGS 2 & 3 site.
3. As an adjunct to the on-going safety programs, the committee shall conduct inspections to assure continuing compliance with the Cal/OSHA Construction Safety Orders. General (project-wide) inspections shall be conducted on a monthly basis. Other inspections will be conducted as required by committee action. The abatement measures taken on violations noted during inspections will be reviewed by the committee.
4. The committee shall review all Report of Safety Problem forms submitted by employees to the contractor's safety department since the last meeting. The follow-up action taken by the employer will be reviewed by the committee.
5. Other outstanding or unsolved safety matters relating to compliance with the Cal/OSHA Construction Safety Orders will be considered.
6. Minutes will be kept of each committee meeting.

Notification of Voluntary Self-Inspection Program to Project Employees

1. Current employees will be advised through a printed notice disseminated to each employee at the tool box meeting prior to the effective date of the program. The program will be the principal topic of this meeting.
2. New hires will be given a printed notice at time of hire. The Voluntary Self-Inspection Program will be discussed thoroughly at the new hire safety orientation meetings.
3. Copies of the printed notice will be posted in conspicuous locations.
4. The program will be discussed periodically in all safety meetings.
5. The function of the program will be reviewed with each newly assigned foreman and supervisor.

Monitoring of Voluntary Self-Inspection Program

1. The National Constructors Association/California Building and Construction Trades Council Joint Committee will monitor the implementation of the Voluntary Self-Inspection Program through periodic on-site audits of the jobsite committee's activities.

2. Cal/OSHA will monitor the program through periodic on-site audits by designated personnel.

Documentation of Committee Activities

1. Minutes will be kept of each meeting.
2. Compliance inspection reports, noting violations of Cal/OSHA Safety Orders will be forwarded to management for review and action as necessary. Corrective actions/abatements will be reviewed by the committee.
3. Report of Safety Problem forms submitted to the Safety Department will be reviewed.

Notice of Safety Problem Form

This procedure is intended to be utilized after a verbal notification of the alleged problem/condition has been made to responsible personnel, or when extenuating circumstances exist.

1. Copies of the Notice of Safety Problem will be available in the Safety Department, in the change rooms, and from craft stewards.
2. The notice will be logged in upon receipt, reviewed by the Safety Department, appropriate action taken, and the results documented.
3. Those employees who elect to identify themselves will be advised of actions taken.
4. The jobsite committee will review all Notice of Safety Problems received by the Safety Department.

Section III
Community Level

III:1

Excerpt from *Commitment at Work*, the Five Year Report of the Jamestown Area Labor-Management Committee (1977)

Community Programs—A Comment

The original basis for the Jamestown Labor-Management Committee was as a community level program. It was believed that sufficient progress could be made in altering the industrial relations climate at the community (leadership) level so that a genuine change in the image and attractiveness of Jamestown would induce a new generation of private industrial development. This belief has proven to be supported by the arrest in the outmigration of plants, the attraction of Cummins Engine Company, the refinancing of five local companies which otherwise would have disappeared, and many subsequent plant expansions and modernizations.

Nevertheless, the community basis as the sole approach for effective labor-management cooperation was rejected by the leaders of the committee in 1973. They made an explicit decision to expand and decentralize the participation in the committee, through their support for both the in-plant committee structure and the skills development programs. While the in-plant work has matured sufficiently into a program in its own right, the skills development program remains as the cornerstone of the community-based activities. It is this program which pulls together organizations in the community, such as Jamestown Community College, the County Manpower office, the Manufacturers Association of Jamestown, and the County Industrial Development Agency. In a very real way, the continuing need to pull these organizations together serves as a "reality check" on the efficacy of the entire Jamestown operation. Meetings, feedback, and action plans which would otherwise be pursued on a unilateral basis are, through the medium of skills development, coordinated within this diverse set of organizations. The process appears effective and is one of the most compelling features of the Jamestown experience upon which visitors comment.

New initiatives on the community basis include the following:

— Training of secondary school teachers in a model curriculum of labor-management cooperation and quality of working life approaches to industrial organizations.

— Planning of a regular series of monthly workshops and seminars on topics of current interest.
— Regular exchange, both formal and informal, of approaches developed in in-plant committees. This exchange is exemplified by visits of union and management leaders to other plants within the Jamestown area.
— Community based documentation is planned, using videotaping as a method. This was suggested by the union president of Local #27, I.B.F.&O., Carborundum, in March, 1977.
— Distribution of a bi-monthly newsletter to members of the Jamestown Labor-Management Committee. The first newsletter was distributed in December, 1976.
— Broadening of participation in the regular dinner meetings and annual conference. The Fourth Annual Conference took place March 31-April 2, 1977.
— Technical assistance to director of Y.W.C.A. Child Care Center. The Jamestown area desperately needs additional child care facilities, especially in light of the findings of the *Manpower Overview* report produced by Larry Carter, Labor-Management Committee staff consultant, which points out the likelihood of a severe manpower and skills shortage in the Chautauqua County area in approximately 1981-82. It is expected that this shortage will increase the demand for child care by working mothers who will be attracted to the job openings.
— Technical assistance to a unique energy conservation program whose initial phase was a thermography based study of existing energy losses in Jamestown industry.
— Participation in the planning of a major industrial corridor rehabilitation program, being planned by the City of Jamestown, and likely to be funded by the Economic Development Administration. This program will include a process of "self design", in which participating manufacturers, located along the Chadakoin River in Jamestown, will design changes in the immediate physical environment of their plants which will help them in their operation. Examples include changing traffic patterns to facilitate better shipping and changing the slope of city streets to eliminate water run off problems.

In summary, the community based programs continue to reflect both the credibility and the relevance of the Labor-Management Committee as a focal organization for community redevelopment.

Section IV
Company Level

IV:1

Letter of Agreement between General Motors Corporation and United Auto Workers Establishing Quality of Work Life Program, 1979

GENERAL MOTORS CORPORATION

September 14, 1979

Mr. Irving Bluestone:
Vice President and Director
General Motors Department
International Union, UAW
Solidarity House
8000 East Jefferson Avenue
Detroit, Michigan 48214

Dear Mr. Bluestone:

During the course of the current negotiations, General Motors and the International Union, UAW reaffirmed the matter of the Corporation's letter of November 19, 1973, regarding the National Committee to Improve the Quality of Work Life. The text of that letter is as follows:

"In discussions prior to the opening of the current negotiations for a new collective bargaining agreement, General Motors Corporation and the UAW gave recognition to the desirability of mutual effort to improve the quality of work life for the employes. In consultation with Union representatives, certain projects have been undertaken by management in the field of organizational development, involving the participation of represented employes. These and other projects and experiments which may be undertaken in the future are designed to improve the quality of work life, thereby advantaging the worker by making work a more satisfying experience, advantaging the Corporation by leading to a reduction in employe absenteeism and turnover, and advantaging the consumer through improvement in the quality of the products manufactured.

"As a result of these earlier discussions and further discussions during the course of the current negotiations for a new collective bargaining agreement, the parties have decided that a Committee to Improve the Quality of Work Life composed of representatives of the International Union and General Motors will be established at the national level.

"This Committee will meet periodically and have responsibility for:

1. Reviewing and evaluating programs of the Corporation which involve improving the work environment of employes represented by the UAW.

2. Developing experiments and projects in that area.

3. Maintaining records of its meetings, deliberations and all experiments and evaluations it conducts.

4. Making reports to the Corporation and the Union on the results of its activities.

5. Arranging for any outside counselling which it feels is necessary or desirable with the expenses thereof to be shared equally by the Corporation and the Union.

"The Corporation agrees to request and encourage its plant managements to cooperate in the conduct of such experiments and projects, and recognizes that cooperation by its plant floor supervision is essential to success of this program.

"The Union agrees to request and encourage its members and their local union representatives to cooperate in such experiments and projects, and recognizes that the benefits which can flow to employes as a result of successful experimentation is dependent on the cooperation and participation of those employes and the local union representatives."

Very truly yours,

George B. Morris, Jr.
Vice President

IV:2

Memorandum of Agreement between United States Steel Corporation and the United Steelworkers of America, Establishing Labor-Management Participation Teams, August 1, 1980:

The following understandings have been agreed upon regarding an Experimental Agreement for Labor-Management Participation Teams.

The strength and effectiveness of an industrial enterprise in a democratic society require a cooperative effort between labor and management at several levels of interaction. The parties hereto recognize that if steelworkers are to continue among the best compensated employees in the industrial world and if steel companies are to meet international competition, the parties must pursue their joint objectives with renewed dedication, initiative and cooperation.

Collective bargaining has proven to be a successful instrument in achieving common goals and objectives in the employment relationship between steel labor and steel management. However, there are problems of a continuing nature at the level of the work site which significantly impact that relationship. Solutions to these problems are vital if the quality of work for employees is to be enhanced and if the proficiency of the business enterprise is to be improved.

The parties recognize that a cooperative approach between employees and supervision at the work site in a department or similar unit is essential to the solution of problems affecting them. Many problems at this level are not readily subject to resolution under existing contractual programs and practices, but affect the ongoing relationships between labor and management at that level. Joint participation in solving these problems at the departmental level is an essential ingredient in any effort to improve the effectiveness of the company's performance and to provide employees with a measure of involvement adding dignity and worth to their work life.

In pursuit of these objectives, the parties believe that local union and plant management at a plant can best implement this cooperative approach through the establishment of Participation Teams of employees and supervision in departments or similar units at the plant. Accordingly, it is agreed that the following experimental program will be undertaken with respect to Participation Teams.

1. The Company and the International Union will select a plant, or plants, on a pilot basis to be covered by this Experimental Agreement and will determine the date, or dates, during the term of this

Basic Labor Agreement on which the program shall commence. These determinations shall be made in consultation with local plant management and the local union and subject to their concurrence.

2. A Participation Committee will be established at the plant level to coordinate the activities of the Participation Teams at department or unit level. A Participation Team will be made up of a management co-chairman, an employees' co-chairman, and employee and supervision members of the department or unit. Employee members and supervision members need not be equal in number, and may be rotated periodically to permit broader employee involvement. The employees of the department or unit will select their Participation Team co-chairman and members.

3. Each employee member of a Participation Committee or a Participation Team shall be compensated for time spent away from work in Committee or Team activities at his average straight-time hourly rate of earnings as calculated under Section 11-D-1.

4. Participation Team meetings shall be called by the co-chairmen during normal working hours as often as the employee and supervision members agree. A Participation Team shall be free to discuss, consider and decide upon proposed *means to improve department or unit performance, employee morale and dignity, and conditions of the work site.* Appropriate subjects, among others, which a Team might consider include: *use of production facilities; quality of products and quality of the work environment; safety and environmental health; scheduling and reporting arrangements; absenteeism and overtime; incentive coverage and yield; job alignments; contracting out; and energy conservation* and *transportation pools.* The Participation Committee and the Participation Teams shall have no jurisdiction over the initiation of, or the processing of, complaints or grievances. The Participation Committee and the Participation Teams shall have no authority to add to, detract from, or change the terms of the Basic Labor Agreement.

5. A Participation Team shall be free to consider *a full range of responses to implemented performance improvement,* including, but not limited to, such items as *bonus payments or changes in incentive performance pay.* A Participation Team may also consider *one-time start-up bonuses for employees on new facilities who reach target levels in specified periods.*

6. To facilitate the establishment of these Participation Committees and Participation Teams, and to assist them, a Participation Team Review Commission will be established comprised of a headquarters representative of the International Union and a headquarters representative of the Company.

IV:3

Excerpt from 1980 Agreement between the Communication Workers of America and the American Telephone and Telegraph Company

Technological Displacement*

If during the term of this agreement, the Company notifies the Union in writing that technological change (defined as changes in equipment or methods of operation) has or will create a surplus in any job title in a work location which will necessitate reassignments to regular employees to different job titles involving a reduction in pay or to locations requiring a change in residence, or if a force surplus necessitating any of the above actions exists for reasons other than technological change and the Company deems it appropriate, any regular employee --

- who is in the affected job titles and work locations; and
- who is not eligible for a service pension may elect not to accept such reassignment to a job title involving a reduction in pay or to a location requiring a change in residence and shall be paid termination allowance. Any such regular employee who refuses to accept a transfer to a job title having the same or greater rate of pay and which does not require a change in residence shall not be paid a termination allowance.

*Western Electric Manufacturing lateral transfer and bumping procedures in universes with multiple titles at the same grade level already provide multiple protection for employees under similar circumstances. Western Electric Manufacturing will follow its regular contractual procedures. However, the reassignments to locations requiring a change residence would apply.

Technology Change Committee

The Company and the Union recognize that technological changes in equipment, organization, or methods of operation have a tendency to affect job security and the nature of the work to be performed. The parties, therefore, will attempt to diminish or abolish the detrimental effects of any such technological change by creating a joint committee to be known as the Technology Change Committee to oversee problems and recommend solutions of problems in this area as set forth below.

It is agreed that a Technology Change Committee be constituted in each Company. Such Committee will consist of not more than three representatives of the Company and not more than three representatives of the Union. Such Committee may be convened at the option of either party at mutually agreeable times.

The purpose of the Committee is to provide for discussion of major technological changes (including changes in equipment, organization, or methods of operation) which may affect employees represented by the Union. The Company will notify the Union at least six (6) months in advance of planned major technological changes. Meetings of the Committee will be held as soon thereafter as can be mutually arranged. At such meetings, the Company will advise the Union of its plans with respect to the introduction of such changes and will familiarize the Union with the progress being made.

The impact and effect of such changes on the employees shall be appropriate matters for discussion. The Company will discuss with the Union:

(a) What steps might be taken to offer employment to employees affected:
1. In the same locality or other localities in jobs which may be available in occupations covered by the collective bargaining agreements between the parties;
2. In other occupations in the Company not covered by the collective bargaining agreement;
3. In other Bell System companies:

(b) The applicability of various Company programs and contract provisions relating to force adjustment plans and procedures, including Supplemental Income Protection Plan, Reassignment Pay Protection Plan, termination allowances, retirement, transfer procedures and the like.

(c) The feasibility of the Company providing training for other assignments for the employees affected. (Example: sponsorship of typing training on Company time)

The Committees shall not formulate policy or arrive at binding decisions or agreements, but rather shall be charged with the responsibility to develop facts and recommendations so that the Company can make well-informed decisions regarding the matters covered by this provision.

Occupational Job Evaluation Committee

In the changing environment resulting from technological and organizational developments, the Company and the Union recognize the need to create new jobs, job titles, and classifications, as well as to restructure and redefine existing ones as necessary. They further recognize that employees performing such new jobs, as well as existing jobs, should be fairly compensated based on the work they do.

Accordingly, the Company and the Union agree to form a committee to be known as the Occupational Job Evaluation Committee. The membership of such committee will consist of six persons, three each to be designated by the Union and the Company.

The purpose of such committee is to research, develop and recommend a job evaluation plan using common measurements of work that can be uniformly applied so that all job titles and classifications (both existing and newly created) in the bargaining units can be properly evaluated. The Committee will be charged with the responsibility to develop and make recommendations regarding a job evaluation plan and its implementation to the respective bargaining representatives of the Union and the Company who shall constitute an overall policy and advisory group for the Committee. The final recommendations and report of the Committee shall be delivered not later than June 1, 1981. Such recommendations will not be binding on either the Union or the Company, but will be for the purpose of allowing such representatives to form well-considered and intelligent opinions regarding the adoption and implementation of a job evaluation plan.

If the Committee determines it to be advisable, it may contract with consultant(s) to assist it in developing a Plan and an implementation procedure to be recommended. The cost of any such consultant(s) shall be borne one-half by the Company and one-half by the Union.

This provision and the responsibilities of the Committee do not encompass or apply to job titles or grades or the job evaluation plans in the Western Electric Company.

. . . . .

Joint Working Conditions and Service Quality Improvement Committee

Recognizing the desirability of mutual efforts to improve the work life of employees and enhance the effectiveness of the organization, the Company and the Union express their mutual belief that activities and experiments initiated and sponsored jointly by management and the Union can prove beneficial to all employees and the Company, and that by encouraging greater employee participation, work can be made more satisfying and organizational performance and service quality can be improved.

The parties agree to continue cooperation in developing a spirit of mutual trust and respect and establishing structures to support cooperative participation by creating, at the national level, a Joint Working Conditions and Service Quality Improvement Committee, composed of three representatives each of the Union and the Company. The committee will meet periodically and have responsibility for:

1. Encouraging and assisting local Union officials and Company managers to understand and implement the principles on which this agreement is based.

2. Developing and recommending principles and objectives relative to working conditions and service quality improvement which will guide experiments or projects such as quality circles, problem solving teams, and the like, in various work situations. These should be designed to encourage teamwork, to make work more satisfying, and to improve the work operations.

3. Reviewing and evaluating programs and projects which involve improving the quality of the work environment.

4. Maintaining records and making reports to the Union and the Company on its activities.

5. Arranging for any outside consultants which it feels are necessary or desirable to assist it. The expenses thereof will be shared equally by the Company and the Union.

The parties agree that organizational and technological innovations are necessary and desirable; that every individual has the ability to contribute to the objectives of the organization; and that work should satisfy personal needs for self-respect and fulfillment as well as service and financial objectives.

The parties recognize that voluntary involvement by management and the Union is essential for the success of mutual efforts. The Company and the Union agree to encourage all levels of their respective organizations to cooperate in the design, development, and implementation of participative experiments, projects, and programs, in a spirit of mutuality and responsible leadership.

IV:4

Statement of Principles on Quality of Work Life
from the
CWA/AT&T National Committee
on Joint Working Conditions
and Service Quality Improvement

The 1980 National Memorandum of Understanding between CWA and AT&T states - - - "recognizing the desirability of mutual efforts to improve the work life of employees and enhance the effectiveness of the organization, the Company and the Union express their mutual belief that activities and experiments initiated and sponsored jointly by Management and the Union can prove beneficial to all employees and the Company, and that by encouraging greater employee participation, work can be made more satisfying and organizational performance and service quality can be improved."

The following principles provide the framework for the activities of the joint Union/Management National Committee to encourage and support the spread of the kind of activities referred to above:

(1)   The essential component of a Quality of Work Life (QWL) effort is a process which increases employee participation in the decisions which affect their daily work and the quality of their work life. Specific local concerns and local problem-solving should be the basis of QWL efforts.

(2)   The goals of QWL efforts are:
(a)   to employ people in a profitable and efficient enterprise.
(b)   to create working conditions which are fulfilling by providing opportunities for employees and groups at all levels to influence their working environment.

The pursuit of these goals is guided by the basic human values of security, fairness, participation and individual development.

(3)   QWL holds as a basic tenet that employees are responsible, trustworthy, and capable of making contributions when equipped with the necessary information and training. Management and the Union seek to better acknowledge, employ and develop the potential of all employees and are committed to providing the necessary information and training to encourage maximum contribution to the success of QWL.

(4)   QWL efforts must be viewed as a supplement to the collective bargaining process. The integrity of the collective bargaining process, the contractual rights of the parties and the workings of the

grievance procedure must be upheld and maintained. The process of implementing an improved quality of life at work shall not infringe upon existing employee, union, or management rights.

(5) Authorized representatives of the Union shall participate in the planning, development, implementation, and evaluation of specific QWL activities which involve Union-represented employees.

(6) Voluntary involvement by Management, the Union, and employees is essential to the success of mutual efforts. Participation in specific QWL activities shall be voluntary. Individuals shall have the right to participate in or to withdraw from such activities without penalty.

(7) Innovations which result from the QWL process will not result in the layoff of any regular employee or negatively affect the pay or seniority status of any Union eligible employee, whether he or she is a participant in the process or not.

(8) The success of QWL efforts requires a spirit of mutual respect and trust among employees, Management and the Union. Each party must give serious attention and consideration to the needs and values of the other parties. Management, the Union and employees must respect one another's legitimate needs and constraints. The success and maintenance of Quality of Work Life requires flexibility and continuing support and leadership from Management, Unions and employees at all levels.

(9) Quality of Work Life is not a "program": there is no universal or one best approach. It is a process which has great potential, but it can't be the answer to all the problems of employees, the Union, or the Company.

April 17, 1981

IV:5

Letter of Understanding between Mountain Bell and Communications Workers of America, District 8, Establishing "Flextime" Program

Mountain Bell

930 Fifteenth Street Room 1060
Denver, Colorado 80202
Phone (303) 624-4287

Robert D. Thompson
Assistant Vice President

August 13, 1977

Mr. J. E. Murphy
Assistant to the Vice President
Communications Workers of America
District 8
8085 East Prentice
Englewood, Colorado 80110

Dear Mr. Murphy:

This letter is intended to set out our understanding of the future application of the concept known as "flex-time" in work groups made up of employees represented by the CWA during the term of the August 13, 1977 Collective Bargaining Agreement.

Management will decide when and under what circumstances "flextime" will be allowed. The nature of the business is such that "flextime" is inappropriate for certain units and specific employees within a unit. For example, twenty-four hour shift operations cannot operate efficiently under the "flex-time" concept. In addition, a supervisor must be present in the unit or nearby in the office or building. This serves to insure that questions can be answered and a safe working environment maintained. After Management has analyzed the operating requirements of the office or work group to determine what hours of work are required and what levels of coverage are necessary within a given time frame, if "flex-time" is to be allowed, the following will apply:

1. The supervisor will determine the earliest and latest time employees will be permitted to work. Normally, these hours will be between 7:00 a.m. and 7:00 p.m., although service requirements may require other hours.

2. There is certain "core-time" during the day when all employees must be present. The supervisor will determine these hours during which all employees must be present. Included within this "core-time" will be one fifteen minute break in each half tour of the day. These break periods may not be taken consecutively so as to provide a half hour break; neither can they be taken consecutively with a one half hour lunch period which will be provided during the "core-time" period.

3. The difference between the time that employees will be permitted to work and the "core-time" will be the flexible time allowable. The "flex-time" at the start of the shift will be equal to that at the end of the shift.

4. Each employee is given freedom and responsibility in deciding upon reporting-in and checking-out time. The employees must work a full tour of duty during each day and will be considered late if they have not reported at the start of the "core-time".

5. No differential will be paid for any tour unless the "core-time" begins before 7:00 a.m. or ends after 7:00 p.m. Under no circumstances will a split shift differential be paid as the result of "flex-time" schedule.

6. "Core-time" may be changed by giving 24 hours' notice to employees.

If this letter accurately sets out our understanding, please initial in the space provided and return one copy for our files.

Yours very truly,

Assistant Vice President
Labor Relations & Employment

CONCURRED:

Assistant to the Vice President
Communications Workers of America
District 8

IV:6
Memorandum of Understanding between Midland-Ross Corporation, Electrical Products Division, Athens, Tennessee, Plant and Local Union No. 175, International Brotherhood of Electrical Workers (AFL-CIO)—Agreement to Establish a Scanlon Plan

This agreement is a supplement to the basic labor agreement between the company and the union, and can in no way invalidate or conflict with any of the provisions therein.

I. Plantwide Incentive Plan

This memorandum of understanding establishes a plantwide incentive plan designed to enable all employees of the Athens, Tennessee, plant of Midland-Ross Corporation, Electrical Products Division, up to and including the plant manager, but excluding over the road truck drivers, to benefit from their increased cooperation and efforts as reflected in increased productivity.

In order to assure full participation in the benefits of the increased productivity which should result from the employee-management cooperation plan, a plantwide monthly productivity bonus shall be applied, effective July 19, 1974, to remain in full force and effect for a trial period of one (1) year, after which time its continuance will be subject to the approval of both the management and the union.

II. Basis of the Plan

The Productivity Ratio

Records for the twelve (12) month period ending June 21, 1974, were used in the development of a ratio of 29.31 cents in payroll costs to each dollar in standard cost production value. Therefore, in each month 29.31 percent of each dollar of standard cost production value will represent the allowed payroll cost. Whenever the adjusted actual monthly payroll is less than the allowed payroll, the difference will constitute the bonus pool. However, in order to protect the company's interest in any month when the adjusted actual payroll exceeds the allowed, causing a deficit, a reserve will be accumulated in months when bonuses are earned. For this purpose twenty-five (25) percent of the bonus pool will be set aside. If this reserve fund should, in twelve (12) months' time, exceed the amount required to restore the ratio to the established norm in the deficit months, the excess shall then be distributed as a "year-end bonus," to be shared in the same manner as the monthly bonus. If the deficits for the Scanlon Plan trial period exceed the amount in the reserve fund, this deficit shall be terminated at the end of the Scanlon Plan trial period and shall not be charged against any bonus earnings of the next year. After the reserve has been set aside, the balance of the bonus pool shall be divided, with seventy-five (75) percent going to the participants and twenty-five (25) percent being retained by the company.

In calculating the distribution of the participating employees' portion, their aggregate share will appear as a certain percentage of their total earnings for the month. This percentage will indicate the bonus earnings of each participant. As required by Fair Labor Standards legislation, total earnings for the month will include all straight time hourly earnings and any shift bonuses and/or overtime premium paid. Vacation pay, holiday pay, funeral leave, and jury duty pay will be considered as earnings for bonus distribution. For purposes of bonus distribution, however, total earnings will *not* include the following: (1) earnings of new employees who have not yet been in the employ of the company for sixty (60) days; and (2) lost-time earnings of employees whose pay goes on while they are sick or absent for personal reasons.

The productivity bonus ratio is derived from the record of performance for the twelve (12) month period ending June 21, 1974. Substantial changes in the conditions which prevailed (with respect to such variables as wages, standard cost of production, product mix, technology, etc.) in establishing the ratio may necessitate changing this ratio in order to protect the equity of either party. Accounting practices and procedures may ascertain the adjustment to be made.

The plan is designed to compensate all employees for their ideas and efforts. Technological change requiring capital expenditures may alter the ratio by reducing labor costs without any increase in productive efficiency on the part of the participants. It is understood that in the event the employee representatives suggest mechanical changes which eliminate a job or jobs, the employees and the company will meet and make an earnest effort to place the employees affected on other jobs.

Substantial fluctuations in the product mix, with its various labor content proportions, may create inequities requiring a ratio revision. However, not every change in the variables affecting the ratio should require a ratio adjustment, since the development of the ratio itself reflects certain fluctuations which prevailed in the base period with respect to wage structure, labor turnover, product mix, standard costs, etc.

When the bonus amounts to less than 2 percent, payment will be deferred and added to subsequent bonuses and paid when the accumulation equals or exceeds 2 percent. However, at the end of the Scanlon year any bonus, even if less than 2 percent, will be paid out.

III. The Committee Structure

The heart of this plantwide incentive plan is participation implemented by the creation of joint committees of management and employees to promote increased productive efficiency. The committee structure includes production committees and a screening committee.

Production Committees

There shall be a production committee established for each of the following plant divisions or departments:

1. Stamping
2. Finishing
3. Assembly
4. Die Casting, Secondary, and Screw Machines
5. Fittings Assembly
6. Material Handling
7. Maintenance
8. Tool and Die, Machine Development
9. Office Department

Composition: Production committees shall each be composed of one management and two or more union or employee representatives. Union or employee representatives chosen in the first election shall serve for the trial period of the plan. It is desirable to have experienced committeemen serving on the production committees at all times, consequently, after the trial period of the plan, a method to alternately elect representatives to the production committees will be instituted.

Functions: Production committees shall meet in their divisions at least once each month, or more often if deemed necessary, for the specific purpose of discussing ways and means of reducing waste and increasing productive efficiency. Every effort will be made to schedule in advance of such meeting a specific production problem which will be placed on the agenda for discussion. Committee members may call upon those employees in their division who are most familiar with the specific problem outlined to participate in the scheduled meetings. In no event, however, may a committeeman call in more than *two* members. It shall be the responsibility of the production committeemen to record and explain all suggestions intended to increase productive efficiency or reduce waste which are made to them by the employees in their division.

The production committees shall keep accurate minutes of their meetings showing all suggestions designed to increase productive efficiency or reduce waste together with their disposition of the same. An approved copy of the minutes shall be transmitted immediately to the screening committee.

The functions of the production committees shall in no way conflict with the responsibilities and duties of the duly-elected grievance committees. The grievance committeeman may, if he deems it advisable, attend all meetings of the production committee conducted in his department or the unit to which he belongs.

The Screening Committee

Composition: The screening committee shall consist of seven management and nine union or employee representatives. The chief steward, by virtue of his office, shall be a member of this committee. The remaining eight members of the screening committee shall come from the production committees. Each production committee shall elect one of the elected representatives on the production committee to serve as a screening committee representative.

Functions: This committee shall screen out through joint discussion all suggestions that are designed to increase productive efficiency or reduce waste. Those that have been placed in effect at the production committee level shall be placed in the record, and decisions shall be reached concerning those suggestions which have not been disposed of at the production committee level.

It will also be the function of this committee to go over the facts and figures used in the calculation of the bonus for the previous month before it is announced, in order to establish the greatest degree of faith and confidence in the calculated results. The productive efficiency bonus will be announced on or before the 15th day of each month and will represent the bonus for the previous month.

Method of Bonus Calculation and Distribution

1. Assume that in the 12-month base period the payroll cost of making each dollar's worth of production value was 29.31 cents. This establishes a productivity norm or *ratio* against which to measure your performance each month:

For example

2. Assume that in this month the *value of production* comes to.......................... $1,053,444

3. If performance had been no better this month than the average for the base period, the payroll would have come to .... $ 308,764
    -This is your *allowed payroll* ($1,053,444 x 29.31%)

4. Say the adjusted actual payroll for this month, however, figured out to 250,946

5. This would mean an improvement over the norm of . 57,818
    -This is your *bonus pool*

6. Now set aside 25 percent of this as a *reserve* 14,455

7. Which leaves *for immediate distribution* the sum of . 43,363

8. Deduct the company's share (25 percent) 10,841

9. And the employees' share (75 percent) is 32,522

10. Eligible payroll for the period 250,500

11. This share for the employee is 12.98%
    of the eligible payroll.
    -This is your *bonus percentage* paid
    ($32,522 ÷ $250,500)

12. Suppose your own pay record for the month looked like this:

Name	Total Hours Worked	Including Overtime Hours	Hourly Rate	Total Pay
John Doe	190	30	$3.00	$615.00

Bonus %	Bonus $
12.98%	$79.83

IV:7
Joint UAW-Ford Summary of Terms of Tentative National Agreement, February 1982

The tentative new UAW-Ford national agreement includes the following features:

---A 24-month moratorium on outsourcing-related plant closings

---Outsourcing commitments aimed at maintaining job opportunities equivalent to those now encompassed by the total UAW national bargaining unit

---A pledge by Ford to manage non-volume related plant closings by the principle of attrition

---Pilot employment guarantee projects at selected facilities based on the "lifetime employment" concept

---A guaranteed income program for high seniority Ford workers which is a disincentive for the company to layoff workers

---A profit sharing plan

---A strengthened supplemental unemployment benefit (SUB) program with prompt resumption of payments to eligible laid off workers

---Equality of sacrifice provisions

---An economic reopener in the event of an unexpected major upturn in Ford sales

---New training programs

---An expanded UAW participation and voice in decision-making

---Improved seniority and early retirement provisions

---No paid personal holidays or bonus Sunday payment

---Vacation entitlements were preserved unchanged from 1979 agreement

---Personal absence allowance days were maintained unchanged

---COLA deferred in first three quarters will be restored later in agreement. There will be no annual improvement factor increases

---Life insurance increases

---Health, surgical, medical, drug, dental, vision, hearing and other benefit programs were maintained

---Duration to September 14, 1984

---Changes in wage rates and benefits for new hires

Plant Closings: There will be a moratorium for 24 months on plant closings that would have occurred as a result of outsourcing the product manufactured in the facility. The moratorium involves a commitment by the company not to close, beyond those for which announcements already have been made, any plant, parts distribution center or depot, tractor supply depot or other facilities constituting a UAW bargaining unit under the agreement. Closings would be permitted for volume-related reasons attributable to market conditions or internal company consolidations of operations within the units represented by the UAW. If such a volume-related permanent closing were contemplated, the company when possible, will provide the union with at least six months advance notice of the closing.

Outsourcing: The union won a commitment from the company that Ford will use every effort to maintain employment opportunities equivalent to those now encompassed by the total national bargaining unit. Ford agreed to a commitment to employ its best efforts to replace jobs which may be lost by outsourcing action.

The company also pledged to strive to manage indefinite workforce contractions, other than those related to volume considerations, by the principle of attrition rather than layoff. In addition, the company and the union have agreed to experiment at two locations with a pilot "employment guarantee" project, which will incorporate a "lifetime job security" concept which will apply to 80% of the workforce at each facility.

Ford also agreed to review major outsourcing decisions implemented during the 1979 agreement and to provide timely information to the union on any future major sourcing decisions.

The union also won a commitment that Ford will join with the UAW in supporting the principle that manufacturers who participate in the U.S. market should provide jobs, pay taxes and support the economy of the market in which they sell. Ford committed to support government acceptance of that principle, so that foreign producers will be encouraged to make their fair contribution to actions that will restore jobs to American autoworkers.

Preferential Placement Opportunities: New preferential placement opportunities will be provided to workers affected by plant closings, but who are not covered by other transfer agreements or who cannot move to any other unit through seniority rights. Under the new program, a seniority worker will have the right to apply within 30 days of layoff for preferential placement on available work, or to "bump" probationary workers if there is no work available. The work must be in jobs for which they are qualified or for which they could qualify in a reasonable period of time. The job must be either in another plant covered by the Agreement in the same labor market, or a plant covered by the Agreement in a different labor market as might be agreed to by the company and the union.

If a worker takes preferential placement, he or she will have the right for 30 days to return to layoff status. If a worker does this, however, or if a worker refuses an initial offer of work, his or her eligibility under the program will be sharply curtailed.

Duration: The new agreement, if ratified, would remain in effect until September 14, 1984.

Reopener: To protect UAW/Ford workers in the event of an unexpected upsurge in Ford's sales, the union negotiated a reopener clause. The UAW will be able to reopen the new contract and bargain on all economic matters any time on or after Jan. 1, 1983, if retail deliveries in the U.S. of new cars and trucks produced or imported by Ford in any consecutive six months exceed 1,925,000 units (roughly comparable to the average six-month rate during 1977-78). If the two sides cannot reach agreement on economics, then the provisions prohibiting or limiting the right to strike no longer will be in effect.

Paid Personal Holidays: There will be no paid personal holidays (PPH) during the agreement, except for the run-out of the current period (3/82).

Vacation: No changes. The existing vacation plan continues as it was in the old agreement.

Paid Absence Allowance: No changes. The five PAA days each year were maintained.

Bonus Sundays: In the past agreement workers received one day of extra holiday pay in December that will not be made under the new agreement.

Health Benefits: All health, surgical, medical, drug, dental, vision, hearing and other benefit programs in the past agreement are maintained for current workers. There are modifications phasing in benefits for new hires.

Health/Group Insurance: In the event of future layoffs, health and group insurance continues for those with 10 or more years of service for up to 24 months (currently coverage continues for up to 12 months).

Life Insurance: Life insurance will increase in November 1982. The increase is likely to be $6,000, but will be determined by inflation.

Equality of Sacrifice: The company has agreed that all economic adjustments made by hourly workers will be applied comparably to salaried personnel. In addition, the company will automatically restore to UAW-represented workers any specific wage and benefit items which may be restored to the salaried workforce during the term of the tentative agreement.

The company also noted that at times in some locations, the union has been concerned about supervisor/worker ratios which have often seemed out of line—workers get laid off, but supervisors stay on. As a result, the company agreed that the union may provide local management with data on excessive numbers of supervisors. The local management will then meet with the union to discuss the information provided. If the local union does not feel that local management has addressed the concerns adequately, and the claims are not settled, the matter may be referred to the National UAW-Ford Department which will take the matter up with the company's labor relations staff. If the matter remains unresolved, it may be referred to the Vice President and Director of the UAW-Ford Department and the Vice President of labor relations for resolution.

Ramification and Implementation: None of these changes will take effect until the tentative agreement is ratified by a majority of the UAW-Ford membership, and only then on the appropriate effective dates specified.

Supplemental Unemployment Benefits (SUB): SUB payments will resume promptly for workers who are currently laid off, but who are not receiving SUB due to assets having fallen below minimum levels recently.

Workers with 10 or more years of seniority will be eligibile to earn credit units for up to *104 weeks of SUB pay,* up from the previous 52-week maximum.

The overall strength of the SUB plan will be bolstered by increasing the company contribution to the fund by 3^c for every hour of compensation.

The resumption of payments will be financed by an advance credit of up to $70 million from the company to keep the fund in payment status and to pay benefits due. When a level of 70% of maximum funding is reached, the company will recover this credit advance at a rate of 5^c per hour of compensation.

Pensions: Current pension benefit levels have been maintained, and an increase due on August 1, 1982 will be paid as provided for under the previous agreement. The company, in its initial proposal, had wanted to eliminate pension increases due on February 1, 1982 and August 1, 1982.

There will be an improved special early retirement provision which will be helpful in plant closings and in facilitating reductions in the workforce through attrition. Workers will now be able to receive a special early retirement benefit of $15 per year of credited service for up to 30 years of service, rather than the previous maximum of 25 years. This is added to their regular retirement benefits for all years of credited service.

Laid off UAW members who are eligible for early retirement will now have five years from the date of layoff—instead of the current two years—to decide if they want to retire early and receive the early retirement supplement. Workers who choose early retirement with the supplement will lose all seniority. Workers who don't take early retirement within the time specified will lose their opportunity to receive the supplement, worth several hundreds of dollars monthly. This three-year extension gives a laid off UAW-Ford worker a great deal more flexibility in his or her retirement decisions.

Medicare Part B: The benefit pay to help people pay Medicare Part B premiums will be increased to $12.20 as of August 1982, $13.00 as of Aug. 1983 and $13.50 as of Aug. 1984. The payment will not be more than the actual Medicare premium.

Worker Counseling and Outplacement Assistance Programs: The company will provide counseling and outplacement assistance to workers who are affected by plant closings. The primary intent of the programs is that the company work aggressively in an effort to find suitable alternative for workers who will be displaced by plant closings. The union will have appropriate input into the development and execution of these programs.

Local Agreements: The union and the company agreed that local bargaining committees should be given the option of conducting local negotiations. Consequently, should either side wish to engage in bargaining, it must make its intentions known within five (5) days following the effective date of the new National Agreement. If approval is granted by the UAW National Ford Department and/or the Ford Vice President for labor relations, bargaining must commence within ten (10) days, and must be completed within sixty (60) days after approval is granted. However, if an agreement is not reached, the present agreement will remain in effect for the duration of the new National Agreement.

Profit Sharing

The new UAW-Ford agreement provides for the first time in UAW-Ford history, a profit-sharing program for eligible UAW members.

Eligibility

U.S. hourly workers with one-year seniority at the end of any plan year will be eligible to participate, except for those who quit or are discharged during the plan year.

Effective Date

The first profit-sharing plan year will begin Jan. 1, 1983, and eligible UAW members employed at Ford will share in the profits for that calendar year.

Formula

Those participating in the program will share in profits whenever before-taxes profits exceed 2.3% of total sales by U.S. Ford operations (excluding Ford Aerospace and Ford Motor Land Development Corp.).

The amount shared will be a percentage of the profits over that 2.3%, and the percentage to be shared will increase as profits measured against sales increase.

Distribution

The amount of money in the profit-sharing pool will be divided between hourly workers covered by the plan and salaried workers who do not receive bonuses. (In general, since hourly workers comprise about 70% of the total workforce, they will share in about 70% of the profit-sharing pool.)

Each eligible worker will receive a profit-sharing check at the end of the first quarter following the plan year. The amount distributed to each will be pro-rated on the proportion of each worker's yearly earnings compared to the total annual hourly payroll.

. . . . .

Wages—No UAW/Ford worker's paycheck will be reduced. Wages will increase substantially over the course of the agreement. If inflation averages 7.5 percent, for example, a Ford assembler now earning an hourly wage of $11.67 would receive $13.66 by June, 1983. A toolmaker (skilled trades) now earning $13.84 would receive $15.83 by June, 1983. Of course, a different inflation rate would result in different wage increases.

Base rates would remain unchanged during the agreement. There will be no annual improvement factor increases. Both the COLA principle and current 0.26 COLA formula are maintained.

COLA adjustments due in March, June and September, 1982, are deferred and restored in September, 1983, December, 1983, and March, 1984, respectively. Regular COLA adjustments will be made each quarter beginning in December, 1982. In the three quarters in which deferred COLA is recovered, there will be an increase that includes the regular COLA *PLUS* the deferred COLA. There is a two-cent diversion from each of the first three COLA adjustments which are deferred. The diversion means that the amount of the COLA increase generated, for example, in March, 1982, is reduced by two cents when it is restored in September, 1983. The first two diversions would have been required under the old agreement.

. . . . .

To protect UAW/Ford workers in the event of an unlikely massive surge in inflation, the total amount of the deferred COLA during the first three quarters will not exceed 60 cents. Thus, if high inflation generated 68 cents over that period (after the three 2^c diversions), 8 cents would be added to the hourly rate in September, 1982.

New Hires: A new hire will receive 85% of the hourly rate for his or her job and will receive 5% increases every six months until reaching the going rate. Rehires are not affected. Certain benefit programs will also be phased in for new hires.

Guaranteed Income Stream

Eligible UAW members employed at Ford Motor Co. will be eligible for a guaranteed income in the event of layoff, until they reach age 62 or until they retire—whichever is earlier. In addition to the income protection, the program provides a disincentive for the company to lay off workers and an incentive to help workers who are laid off to find employment.

Eligibility

To be eligible, an employee must
1. Have 15 or more years of seniority at the time of layoff.
2. Be working on or after the effective date of the agreement.
3. Be able and available for work, unless disabled, maintain registration with the state employment service, and accept employment arranged by the company or state agency.

Payments

The minimum Guaranteed Income Stream payment, for workers with 15 years of seniority, will be 50% of the employee's hourly rate as of the last day worked.

For each year of seniority over 15, the rate increases by one percentage point; i.e., a worker with 25 years of seniority would receive 50% + 10% for a total of 60%.

The maximum benefit will be either 75% of the employee's weekly wage, or 95% of the employee's weekly after-tax base pay, minus $12.50, whichever is less.

Health insurance and life insurance benefits will be provided for employees in the Guaranteed Income Stream program.

Upon retirement, an employee in the Guaranteed Income Stream will receive pension and other retirement benefits as if the employee had maintained employment until the date of retirement.

Other Provisions

Guaranteed Income Stream benefits will be reduced by other contractual or government benefit payments received, income replacement benefits, and/or 80% of earnings from other employment.

Falsification of information can be grounds for termination or suspension from the Guaranteed Income Stream program.

Disability benefits will be provided under the program.

Training and Retraining Program

The new UAW-Ford agreement addresses the problem of retraining both displaced and present workers by providing for the establishment of an Employee Development and Training Program.

Scope

This Program will be empowered to:

—Arrange for or provide "training, retraining, and development assistance for employees displaced by new technologies, new production techniques, and shifts in customer-produce preference." It also could undertake similar efforts for "employees displaced as a result of facility closings or discontinuances of operations."

—Provide present employees with a program so that training/educational courses can be made available to upgrade/sharpen present job skills, provide updating on the state-of-the-art technology for skilled and semi-skilled employees based on present and anticipated job requirements, and improve the job satisfaction and performance of all employees."

Governance

The Program will be under the jurisdiction of a new UAW-Ford National Development and Training Center that will

—Be governed by an equal number of representatives of the union and the company, and

—Initially employ an Executive Director and full-time staff of at least six persons.

Programs

The Center could "make available a wide range of educational, training, and retraining services" and, for example, could provide local on-site classroom training and outside consulting services, etc., when needs can't be met through existing internal and external resources.

Mutual Growth Forums

UAW members employed at the Ford Motor Co. will get new input into the management decision-making process through a framework of joint union-management bodies called Mutual Growth Forums, which will operate at both the local and national levels.

Scope

The Mutual Growth Forums will be empowered to undertake "advance discussion of certain business developments that are of material interest and significance to the union, the employees, and the company."

National Level

An equal number of union and company representatives will comprise the national Forum which will be empowered, among other things, to discuss the company's general operations and certain business developments, examine government relations matters, and take other actions. The Director of the UAW National Ford Dept. may address the company's board of directors twice yearly.

Local Level

At the plant level, it is suggested that the Forums meet at least quarterly to discuss such things as "the plant's general operation and certain business developments." The local Forums will get periodic financial and business presentations from management and the union.

Section V
Public Sector

V:1

Provisions of 1979-82 Agreement between State of New York and Civil Service Employees Association Establishing Continuity, Evaluation, Productivity and Quality of Working Life Committee

VI. Bylaws of the Continuity, Evaluation, Productivity and Quality of Working Life Committee

Article I. The Committee

Section One. The Committee shall be comprised of twenty-one (21) voting members to be appointed as follows:

A)   Three (3) impartial members shall be jointly appointed by and serve at the joint pleasure of the Director of the Office of Employee Relations (hereinafter "O.E.R.") and the President of the Civil Service Employees Association, Inc. (hereinafter "C.S.E.A."), and

B)   Nine (9) members shall be appointed by and serve at the pleasure of the Director of O.E.R., and

C)   Nine (9) members shall be appointed by and serve at the pleasure of the President of C.S.E.A.

Section Two. The Committee shall study and make recommendations to the Executive Committee concerning prospective mechanisms for the improvement of the work environment of State employees pursuant to its enabling provisions in the 1979-82 State of New York/CSEA collective bargaining agreements.

Section Three. The Committee shall meet at least annually for the purpose of integrating and evaluating the policy proposals of the subcommittees, preparing an agenda of topics to be analyzed by the subcommittees in the ensuing year, and making recommendations to the Executive Committee concerning policy and programs. Special meetings of the Committee may be called by the Chairperson upon ten working days notice to the members at a time, date and location mutually convenient to the members of the Committee.

Article II. The Chairperson and the Executive Committee

Section One. The Chairperson of the Committee shall be jointly appointed by and serve at the joint pleasure of the Director of O.E.R. and the President of C.S.E.A. from among the impartial members appointed pursuant to Article I, S1(A) of these Bylaws.

Section Two. There shall be an Executive Committee comprised of the President of C.S.E.A., the Director of O.E.R., and the Chairperson of the Committee.

Section Three. The Executive Committee shall approve or reject, upon recommendations from the Committee or sub-committees thereof or, upon its own initiative, any expenditures of monies appropriated to the "statewide major issues study fund" established pursuant to the 1979-82 State of New York/CSEA collective bargaining agreements.

Section Four. Upon authorization from the Executive Committee pursuant to Section Three, the Chairperson or his designees may authorize disbursements, hire employees and execute contracts to assist in the performance of Committee or sub-committee functions (as set forth in Articles I and III hereof, respectively). All employees of the Committee shall report directly to the Chairperson or his designees for purposes of attendance and leave.

Article III. Sub-committees

Section One. The Committee shall have three (3) standing sub-committees, as follows:

A) Continuity of Employment,
B) Performance Evaluation, and
C) Quality of Working Life and Productivity.

Section Two. The members of each standing sub-committee shall be appointed as follows:

A) The chairperson of the sub-committee shall be appointed jointly by the Director of O.E.R. and the President of C.S.E.A. from among those impartial Committee members appointed pursuant to Article I, S1(A) of these Bylaws,
B) Three (3) members of the sub-committee shall be appointed by the Director of O.E.R. from among those Committee members appointed pursuant to Article I, S1(B) of these Bylaws, and
C) Three (3) members of the sub-committee shall be appointed by the President of C.S.E.A. from among those Committee members appointed pursuant to Article I, S1(C) of these Bylaws.
D) No Committee members shall be appointed to more than one sub-committee.

Section Three. Each sub-committee shall be empowered to make recommendations concerning programs and the funding thereof directly to the Executive Committee.

Section Four. Each sub-committee shall submit, at least, an annual report to the Committee on or about March 1 concerning the results of studies undertaken by the sub-committee.

Section Five. All actions and recommendations to the Executive Committee, by the sub-committee, including any reports and recommendations concerning programs shall require a majority vote of the sub-committee taken at a meeting of the sub-committee. The chairperson of the sub-committee may vote only in the event of a tie among the other members.

Section Six. Each sub-committee shall meet at least quarterly and any meeting may be called by the respective chairperson upon ten working days notice to the members of the sub-committee at a time, date and location mutually convenient to the members. No meeting may be convened and no business transacted unless a majority of the entire membership of the sub-committee and an equal number of members appointed pursuant to Article I, S1(B) and members appointed pursuant to Article I, S1(C) of these Bylaws are present.

Article IV. Procedures

Section One. Except as otherwise expressly provided by these Bylaws, the meetings and business of the Committee and standing sub-committees shall be conducted, insofar as practicable, in accordance with Robert's *Rules of Order.*

V:2
Columbus/AFSCME
Quality of Working Life Agreement
July 26, 1976

Agreement among the city of Columbus, Ohio, Local #1632 of the American Federation of State, County, and Municipal Employees, and The Ohio State University Quality of Working Life Program of the Center for Human Resource Research to undertake a quality of working life demonstration effort in Columbus.

I. Background

Discussions with city administrators, city councilmen, and employee representatives in the city of Columbus, Ohio, have indicated an interest in efforts to improve both the quality of the work environment of municipal employees and the services provided by the city government. This mutual interest suggests the basis for a successful quality of work demonstration project in the city. This agreement outlines the steps which are involved in undertaking a quality of work effort and defines the nature of the participation of The Ohio State University Quality of Working Life Program (QWLP).

II. Funding

The QWLP, immediately upon the signing and ratification of this agreement, will forward a request to the U.S. Department of Health, Education, and Welfare to release funds allocated to the Columbus effort for the period of October 1, 1976, to September 30, 1977, and for the period of October 1, 1977, to September 30, 1978. The city of Columbus will contribute $25,000 a year for a 2-year period beginning October 1, 1976. Payments will be made quarterly beginning on January 1, 1977. Local #1632 will make $1,000 payments on October 1, 1977, and October 1, 1978. These funds will be used to cover QWLP questionnaires, supplies, seminars, educational services, etc. Should the U.S. Department of Health, Education, and Welfare not release the funds specified, this agreement is invalid.

III. Duration and Approvals

The agreed upon duration of this project is 24 months beginning on October 1, 1976, or, if agreement has not been reached by October 1 on the new labor contract, on the day following ratification of the new contract. Only 24 months of funding is being requested at this time. By the end of the project's 15th month, the city Quality of Working Life Committee will decide whether to continue the project for an additional

18-month or 2-year period. If so, the OSU QWLP will request additional funding and will continue to provide technical assistance for the additional period. Before the project can begin, ratification by the membership of Local #1632[1] and approval by the city council is required.[2]

---

1. The proposal will be put before the membership of Local #1632 at the next membership meeting, which will be held in September.

2. This proposal will be taken before city council for approval after it has been ratified by the membership of Local #1632.

IV. Scope

A. *Experimenting Groups.* This project will start with the establishment of one division level Quality of Working Life Committee in a division to be selected by the Public Service Quality of Working Life Committee and one working level committee in part of this division to be selected by the Division Quality of Working Life Committee. From there, the goal is to create additional experimenting groups (working level Quality of Working Life Committees) as rapidly as is feasible. The rate of spread will be determined by staff resources and the judgment of the City and Public Service Quality of Working Life Committees. The method will be the provision of technical assistance to city, department, division, and working level committees in structuring worker participation to improve the quality of the working environment and the quality of services provided to the public. The first experimenting groups will be selected and formed on the basis of existing knowledge of the operation and of the receptivity of workers, middle management, and first line supervision. Subsequent experimenting groups will be selected on the basis of questionnaire and productivity measurement results and other relevant factors.

B. *Questionnaire.* A questionnaire will be administered to all of the approximately 2,000 hourly and salaried employees in the Public Service Department including supervision and middle and top management. Some form of feedback, either written or oral, will be provided to all employees taking the questionnaire by Quality of Working Life Program staff. The results of the questionnaire will serve as a basis for selecting additional experimenting groups. Productivity information will also be gathered for all employees of the department.

V. Structure

A. *City Quality of Working Life Committee.* A City Quality of Working Life Committee will be formed consisting of the mayor and two or three management representatives appointed by him (including the director of the Public Service Department) and the president of Local #1632, the director of District 53, the president of the council, and one or two other union officials appointed by them. This committee will meet at least once each month to sanction and keep apprised of all quality of work life activities in the city. The mayor and the top officials of AFSCME District 53 and Local #1632 agree to give top priority to their personal attendance at these meetings. The city and AFSCME will each provide a part-time executive secretary to the committee who will be jointly responsible for preparing the agenda, developing staff proposals for the consideration of the committee, and doing the necessary staff work to assure that all committee decisions are implemented. They will report to the chairperson of the committee and will be assisted by such interns and clerical personnel as are considered necessary by the committee and assigned by the city.

B. *Public Service Quality of Working Life Committee.* A labor-management Public Services Quality of Working Life Committee will be formed and will meet at least once each month. Its composition, nature, and functions are as follows:

1. *Composition.* The director of the Public Service Department and the chief union official of that department will each sit on this committee. Its chairmanship will rotate every 6 months between management and labor. Management and the president of Local #1632 will each appoint four or five other management and union members.

2. *Nature.* This is a cooperative committee formed to create a cooperative relationship in addition to the adversary one. It can deal with matters on which there is mutual agreement but does not deal with grievances, collective bargaining, or other matters of a controversial nature. It is not intended to settle disputes. It is intended to remove the root causes for these disputes by improving the quality of the work environment for employees of the Public Service Department. Both the city and the union accept *on faith* that improved productivity and worker well-being will follow.

3. *Functions.* Its functions will be to plan a quality of working life program for the Public Service Department, to provide an umbrella to protect and preserve the program and assure the cooperation of all parties, to make such waivers of contractual and policy provisions as are necessary during the experimental period, to form such division-level and working-level committees as are indicated, and to monitor the progress of the committees in reorganizing work and in improving the working environment in the Public Service Department.

C. *Working-Level Quality of Working Life Committees.* These committees will be the heart of the Columbus Quality of Working Life project and will generally service groups of 30-50 employees. Shop stewards in the employee groups will automatically sit on these committees. Other employee representatives will be elected by a vote of the work group members and will serve staggered terms to assure continuity. The supervisor or head of the employee group will sit on the committee and will appoint the other management members. An internal election will be held by each committee each 6 months to assure that the chairmanship and secretaryship rotate between labor and management.

D. *Additional Department Quality of Working Life Committees.* The City Quality of Working Life Committee will, as circumstances indicate, establish additional departmental quality of working life committees.

VI. Technical Assistance

A. An Ohio State University QWLP staff member will sit with the City Quality of Working Life Committee, Public Service Quality of Working Life Committee, Divisional Quality of Working Life Committee, and working-level committees at their meeting and offer any possible assistance.

B. Educational and informational services will be available at the request of the committees. Such services include:

1. in house seminars led by nationally recognized experts in the field of work restructuring.
2. visits by committee members and others to organizations where successful experiments have taken place.
3. provision to the committee of reading material and research services by the Ohio State University Quality of Working Life Program.
4. training conferences for working-level committee members and others in communications, supervisory practices, and changing roles in quality of working life situations.

VII. Procedures

Phase I - Six Months.

The following steps will be taken under the guidance of the City and Public Service Quality of Working Life Committees.

A. *Questionnaire.* On a voluntary basis, all Public Service Department employees will fill out the questionnaire which appears as Appendix A to "The Quality of Work and Its Outcomes" (Ohio: The Academy for Contemporary Problems, 1975). Questionnaires will be completed during working hours in groups of approximately 20-25 employees. Data will be used in aggregate form broken down by organizational unit. Individual responses will be held strictly confidential.

B. *Formation of First Working-Level Committee.* As soon as the questionnaire has been administered, the Public Service Quality of

Working Life Committee will decide on the first unit to have a working-level committee and will take the necessary steps to establish this experimenting committee and any intervening committees which are necessary to assure an umbrella for the experiment. By the time the questionnaire report is made to the Public Service Quality of Working Life Committee, it will have some experience with one working-level committee and will be able to select the next units to have working-level committees and schedule their formation.

C. *Feedback*. Summaries of questionnaire results will be presented to employees in writing with a statement from the Public Service Quality of Working Life Committee informing them of the working-level committees that have already been formed and the Public Service Committee's plans for expanding and including more employees in the experiment. The results will be discussed orally with all employees who are in experimenting units covered by working-level committees as these committees are formed.

D. *Productivity Data*. Working with the various committees, the OSU QWLP staff will develop criteria for measuring productivity and/or the quality of services and make baseline measurements according to the criteria agreed to by the City Quality of Working Life Committee.

E. *Report to City Quality of Working Life Committee*. The OSU QWLP will furnish a report to the City Quality of Working Life Committee summarizing and commenting on the questionnaire results. Preparation of this report is estimated at 8 weeks from the time all questionnaires are complete.

Phase II - Two Months.

Quality of Work Plan. Upon receipt of the questionnaire report, the next steps will be in the hands of the City and Public Service Quality of Working Life Committees. Based on the information provided and on the educational seminars conducted during the first phase of the project, the Committee will develop, agree to, and implement whatever kind of quality of working life plan it deems appropriate.

Phase III - 16 Months.

While a number of work restructuring activities may already have begun during Phase I and II, Phase III will be the "implementation" phase. Educational activities and assistance will continue as requested by the Public Service Quality of Working Life Committee.

Phase IV - Remeasurement.

A remeasurement will occur 18 months from the date the questionnaires are initially administered. This will begin a regular program of keeping aware of employee attitudes toward working conditions. The remeasurement will also include some form of feedback mechanism. If it is mutually decided to continue the program beyond the 2 years which are now tentatively funded, remeasurements will continue at 18-month intervals.

VIII. Additional Provisions

A. All parties understand and believe tht a project of this type offers potentially significant benefits to all concerned. These benefits arise, in part, from the creation of a forum for the discussion of situations and solutions, which is free from the tensions inherent in the traditional labor-management relationship. Therefore, this forum will not be utilized for discussing or dealing with issues and questions which are properly in the province of existing, formal, collective bargaining institutions. All parties also agree to accept the working assumption that improvements in the working environment will benefit both services to the public and worker well-being and so do not have to be justified on an individual quid-pro-quo basis.

B. The following procedures are agreed to with regard to project training expenses:

1. Any lost time for activities of employees (management and non-management) in connection with the project (on or off of the job) will be borne by the city.
2. Travel, expenses, and fees of city employees (management and nonmanagement) representatives for offsite activities will be borne by the city.
3. Travel, expenses, fees, and lost time for AFSCME staff not from the local union will be borne by AFSCME.
4. The city will budget $22,000 per year cash for travel, expenses, and fees in connection with this training and $24,400 per year for lost time. The $22,000 will be included in the $25,000 payments mentioned in section II of this agreement.

IX. Dissemination of Experience and Results

A. *Experience Sharing.* Management and AFSCME people from the city of Columbus agree to participate in conferences and seminars as requested to share their experiences (when feasible within workload and time constraints) with other cities, states, etc.

B. *Publication.* Management and the union agree that, after each measurement process, the OSU QWLP can use the data gathered in published accounts of the experiment in order to assist other cities in their efforts to improve worker satisfaction and productivity.

X. Commitments

A. Management guarantees that:

1. No employee will be laid off or have his compensation reduced as a result of the QWLP.
2. It will "free up" city employees for the time necessary for committee meetings, training (both on and off the job), team building and communications. It accepts the possibility of an initial loss in productivity due to this lost time in hopes of an eventual increase due to these activities.
3. Management agrees to work with the union and employees in exploring and developing a means of sharing any productivity gains achieved through this project with the employees involved.
4. Management accepts the policy of utilizing productivity increases by expanding services to the public rather than reducing employment.

B. The union will make every effort to resolve any grievances filed on contract items set aside for trial periods to facilitate work activity outside the formal grievance procedure.

C. Management and union commit themselves to:

1. Keep adversary issues out of the quality of work project and continue the project and the cooperative relationship in the face of such issues—difficult though this may be.
2. A willingness to try new things—with the understanding that efforts which do not work to the satisfaction of both parties can be terminated without prejudicing the whole program.

The signatures on this agreement indicate a commitment to cooperate on a program, the purpose being to seek new approaches and, where indicated, implement these approaches in order that the employees of the city of Columbus can experience increased satisfaction and productivity. They also indicate a joint commitment to improving conditions of security, equity, individuation, and participation for municipal employees.

Signed by the following:

Tom Moody
Mayor, City of Columbus

Phil Chevallard
President, District 53

Warren Jennings
Director, District 53

Don Ronchi
The Ohio State University
Quality of Working Life Program

Robert C. Parkinson
Director, Public Service Department

Themistocles Cody
President, Local

V:3

Excerpt from Agreement between TVA and the Tennessee Valley Trades and Labor Council (revised through March 15, 1981) on Organization of Central and Local Cooperative Committees

Cooperative Committees

TVA and the Council agree to the following statement of organization of the central and local joint cooperative committees in accordance with, and for the purposes stated in Article X of this agreement.

A. Central Joint Cooperative Committee

1. The Central Joint Cooperative Committee is made up of the Executive Board of the Council and the following TVA representatives: Manager of Engineering Design and Construction, Manager of Power, Manager of Agricultural and Chemical Development, Manager of Construction, Manager of Power Operations, and Directors of Chemical Operations, Nuclear Power, Fossil and Hydro Power, Power System Operations, Power Construction, Property and Services, and the Director of Personnel.

2. A management representative on the central committee designated by the Manager of Management Services and the President of the Council serve as cochairmen on the central committee. A member of the Division of Personnel serves as secretary of the central committee.

3. The central committee develops the basic guidelines for an organized program of employee-management cooperation. It promotes the formation of local committees, determines the form or organization, and furnishes guidance for the conduct of the committees. It reviews the progress of the local committees, as reported by the secretary, and acts on any suggestions of TVA-wide significance which local committees refer to it. In addition, the central committee takes up such matters as are brought to it by its members, discusses major TVA programs and the general policies related to union-management cooperation, and sponsors suitable programs to provide information of general interest to employees concerning TVA activities.

4. The central committee meets at least once a year. This annual meeting shall be held in conjunction with an annual Valley-wide conference of the officers of local joint cooperative committees.

Other meetings of the central committee may be held upon call of the cochairmen.

5. All actions of the central committee are by unanimous concurrence.

B. Local Joint Cooperative Committees

1. Local joint cooperative committees are established by agreement between representatives of labor and management, and with the approval of the central committee, on a plant-, project-, or division-wide basis. Each local committee defines its scope as to plant, project, or division, providing for the inclusion of all employee groups represented by the Council.

2. Management and employees each designate members to serve on the local committee; the numbers need not be equal. All members shall be TVA employees. The employee representatives are designated by the labor organizations participating in the local committee and must be approved by the Council. The management members are designated by the top supervisor of the administrative unit served by the committee. The top supervisor serves as a member.

3. The local committee elects a chairman and a cochairman, one each from management and labor. The committee also elects a secretary.

4. The cochairmen and the secretary act as a steering committee which provides the leadership for planning and carrying on committee business and which handles matters between meetings.

5. The local committee schedules regular meetings. Special meetings are called by the steering committee. Committee members attend meetings without loss of time.

6. The committee receives suggestions made by either employees or supervisors. The committee evaluates each suggestion. Action is taken by unanimous concurrence. Suggestions relating to activities which extend in scope beyond the unit in which the committee operates may be referred to another committee or to the central committee.

Appendix B

Awards by the Federal Mediation and Conciliation Service under the Labor-Management Cooperation Act of 1978, Fiscal Year 1981

A. Joint Industry Committees

1. *City of San Francisco/Service Employees International Union (and others).* The present LMC working in the city's Housing Authority would expand to include at least four new city departments and relevant unions for the purpose of improving public service and employee relations. ($54,494)

2. *Houston Belt and Terminal Railway/United Tranportation Union and Brotherhood of Railway and Airline Clerks.* The Houston-based and FRA-financed labor-management committee would develop a training program so that railroad companies belonging to labor-management committees in Houston and Buffalo can implement the LMC concept in their own companies. ($88,142)

3. *Indiana University/Fraternal Order of Police and the Professional Fire Fighters Union.* This existing statewide LMC consisting of representatives of the Indiana Association of Cities and Towns and police and firefighters would be strengthened. ($57,247)

B. Regional and Community-Wide Joint Committees

1. *Chautauqua County Labor-Management Committee.* This newly created area LMC would create eight in-plant committees and attempt to reduce man-days lost to strikes by 50 percent. ($44,000)

2. *Chemung County Labor-Management Committee.* This upstate New York LMC would expand its activities and establish up to six new in-plant committees. ($40,750)

311

3. *Clinton County, Pennsylvania.* This existing LMC would be strengthened and enabled to create at least three new in-plant committees while reducing local workdays lost to labor disputes. ($79,753)

4. *Jamestown Labor-Management Committee.* The City of Jamestown would expand present LMC efforts and create at least four new in-plant committees. ($73,753)

5. *Michigan Quality of Work Life Council.* The Council would be enabled to establish up to six new area LMCs throughout the state of Michigan over an 18-month period and promote the LMC concept through training sessions and conferences. ($150,000)

6. *Northeast Labor-Management Center.* This Boston-based LMC would establish five in-plant committees in five different major industries in the state of Massachusetts as pilot demonstration projects for those industries. ($98,275)

7. *Philadelphia Area Labor-Management Committee.* This newly established LMC would hire permanent staff and develop what may become the nation's largest local area LMC whose goals include the creation of both in-plant and industry committees within the Philadelphia area. ($150,000)

8. *Siouxland Labor-Management Committee.* This Sioux City, Iowa area LMC would expand its operations and create at least three new in-plant committees. ($76,000)

C. In-Plant Labor-Management Committees

1. *Diamond International Corporation/United Paperworkers International Union* (Palmer, Massachusetts). Labor-management committees would be set up in three sites (Natchez, Mississippi, Red Bluff, California, and Plattsburgh, New York) to oversee a new and innovative employee incentive program. ($37,494)

2. *Rath Packing Company/United Food and Commercial Workers Union* (Waterloo, Iowa). This worker-owned plant would expand the efforts of its labor-management committee in establishing Action Research Teams to improve productivity and reduce grievances. ($24,400)

3. *Rome Cable Company/International Association of Machinists and Aerospace Workers* (Rome, New York). An in-plant labor-management committee designed to increase plant productivity and improve the quality of work life would be established. ($26,010)

Appendix C

Directory of Major Organizations Assisting Labor-Management Cooperative Programs

U.S. Government Agencies

Federal Mediation and Conciliation Service
Kenneth Moffett, Director (202) 655-4000
2100 K St., N.W.
Washington, DC 20427

Labor-Management Services Administration
Office of Labor-Management Relations Services
John Stepp, Director (202) 523-6487
U.S. Department of Labor
Washington, DC 20210

Occupational Health and Safety Administration
Office of Policy Analysis
Frank Frodyma, Director (202) 523-8021
U.S. Department of Labor
Washington, DC 20210

National Organizations

American Productivity Center
Pete Moffett, President (713) 961-7740
123 North Post Oak Lane
Houston, TX 77024

American Quality of Work Life Center
Ted Mills, Chairman (202) 338-2933
3301 New Mexico Ave., N.W.
Washington, DC 20016

Association for Workplace Democracy
John Simmons, Coordinator (202) 265-7727
1747 Connecticut Ave., N.W.
Washington, DC 20009

Center for Productive Public Management
Marc Holzer, Director (212) 489-5030
City University of New York
445 West 59th St.
New York, NY 10019

Center for Quality of Working Life
Louis E. Davis, Chairman (213) 825-1095
University of California
405 Hilgard Ave.
Los Angeles, CA 90024

Harvard Project on Technology, Work, and Character
Michael Maccoby, President (202) 462-3003
1710 Connecticut Ave., N.W.
Washington, DC 20009

Management and Behavioral Science Center
Charles Dwyer, Director (215) 243-5736
Wharton School of Finance and Commerce
University of Pennsylvania
Philadelphia, PA 19104

National Association of Area Labor-Management Committees
John J. Popular, President (703) 777-8700
Box 118
Fairfax, VA 22030

National Center for Employee Ownership
Corey Rosen, President (703) 931-2757
4836 South 28th St.
Arlington, VA 22206

National Council for Alternative Work Patterns, Inc.
Gail Rosenberg, President (202) 466-4467
1925 K St., N.W.
Washington, DC 20006

National Council on Alcoholism, Inc.
Labor-Management Services Dept.
William Dunkin, Director (212) 986-4433
733 Third Ave., Suite 1405
New York, NY 10017

New Systems of Work and Participation Program
William H. Whyte, Director (607) 256-4530
Cornell University
Ithaca, NY 14850

Profit Sharing Research Foundation
Bert L. Metzger, President (312) 869-8787
1718 Sherman Ave.
Evanston, IL 60201

Quality of Work Program
Stanley E. Seashore, Director (313) 763-4064
Institute for Social Research
University of Michigan
Ann Arbor, MI 48106

Work in America Institute, Inc.
Jerome M. Rosow, President (914) 472-9600
700 White Plains Road
Scarsdale, NY 10583

Regional and State Organizations

Maryland Center for Productivity and Quality of Working Life
Tom Tuttle, Director (301) 454-5451
University of Maryland
College Park, MD 20742

Michigan Quality of Work Life Council
Basil Whiting, Director (313) 362-1611
755 West Big Beaver
Troy, MI 48084

Northeast Labor-Management Center
Michael J. Brower, Executive Director (617) 489-4002
30 Church St., Suite 301
Boston, MA 02108

Ohio Quality of Working Life Program
Don Ronchi, Director (614) 422-3390
Center for Human Resources Research
The Ohio State University
Columbus, OH 43201

Productivity Institute
Thomas P. Fullmer, Director (602) 965-7626
College of Business Administration
Arizona State University
Tempe, AZ 85281

Quality of Working Life Program
Milton Derber, Professor (217) 333-0981
Institute of Labor and Industrial Relations
University of Illinois
Champaign, IL 61820

Texas Center for Productivity and Quality of Working Life
Barry Macy, Director (806) 742-2011
College of Business Administration
Texas Tech University
Lubbock, TX 79401

Utah Center for Productivity and Quality of Working Life
Gary Hanson, Director (801) 752-4100
Utah State University
Logan, UT 84321

DATE DUE

DHUB	APR 30 1986	
	DHUB	APR 1 6 REC'D
	DHUB	DEC 1 5 REC'D

GAYLORD · PRINTED IN U.S.A